Cesar's Rules

CESAR MILLAN

with *Melissa Jo Peltier*

Cesar's Rules

Your Way to Train
a Well-Behaved Dog

THREE RIVERS PRESS · NEW YORK

The techniques presented in this book are for informational purposes only. As each individual situation is unique, you should use proper discretion, in consultation with a professional dog expert, before utilizing the information contained in this book. The author and publisher expressly disclaim responsibility for any adverse effects that may result from the use or application of the information contained in this book.

Published in the United States by Three Rivers Press, an imprint of the Crown Publishing Group, a division of Random House, Inc., New York.

www.crownpublishing.com

Three Rivers Press and the Tugboat design are registered trademarks of Random House, Inc.

Originally published in hardcover by Crown Archetype, an imprint of the Crown Publishing Group, a division of Random House, Inc., New York, in 2010.

Library of Congress Cataloging-in-Publication Data
Millan, Cesar.
Cesar's rules : your way to train a well-behaved dog / Cesar Millan with Melissa Jo Peltier.—1st ed.
p. cm.
Includes bibliographical references and index.
1. Dogs—Training. 2. Dogs—Psychology. 3. Dog owners—Psychology. I. Peltier, Melissa Jo. II. Title.
SF431.M628   2010
636.7'0835—dc22   2010024379

ISBN 978-0-307-71687-3
eISBN 978-0-307-71688-0

Illustrations by Victoria Parr; see page 293 for photograph credits

Printed in the United States of America

10 9 8 7 6 5 4

First Paperback Edition

I dedicate this book to my sons, Andre and Calvin, because I want them to learn that many different people from varying experiences can come together for the common good. As a father, I want to train my kids to know that they can have a meeting of the minds with people who might come from different belief systems than they do. I want them to always keep their minds open to new ideas and knowledge, because only with an open mind can we change the world for the better. I don't want to leave my boys great material wealth. I want to bequeath them a wealth of knowledge so they become men of integrity with the power to transform their world.

CONTENTS

Contents

ACKNOWLEDGMENTS

First and foremost, I want to thank all the people—the trainers, the behaviorists, the academics, and all the other experts—who generously contributed their expertise and knowledge to this book, including Bob Bailey, Michael Broffman, Bonnie Brown-Cali, Patrick Burns, Dr. Alice Clearman, Martin Deeley, Barbara De Groodt, Dr. Ian Dunbar, Kelly Gorman Dunbar, Mark Harden, Katenna Jones, Karen Rosa, Joel Silverman, Jerome Stewart, and Kirk Turner, among others.

It has always been my dream to bring together people who might not always agree with one another and work with them to find a balanced approach. The fact that we've accomplished that with this book proves that most dog people really want to do what is best for dogs and the planet at large. That has a lot of meaning for other people in the world, especially children. I hope all the experts listed above feel proud and happy that we all found a way to become calm and submissive with one another so together, we can honor what dogs have to teach us: that it's not about a breed, or a race, or a type of training, or a school of thought—it's ultimately about what's best for the pack. When a pack of dogs needs one another to better their environment, they find a common ground. They find a way to survive by coming together, not pulling apart. Together, all the experts in this book are going to lead by example, and that's going to create an amazing ripple effect in the world.

My friend Martin Deeley, executive director of the International Association of Canine Professionals, was instrumental in helping me pull together such an illustrious collection of professionals. Thank you, Martin, for reaching out and believing in me long before anyone else in the professional training world ever did. I also want to thank the board of directors of the American Humane Association for sitting down with me to discuss where our many similarities and shared goals might overcome our differences.

It's also important for me to acknowledge the fans of many of the experts who appear in this book, because people like Dr. Ian Dunbar have their own fans and supporters who might not agree with me. My goal is for them to understand that this is for the greater good. This is not about enhancing one person's career but about improving the lives of all dogs and owners, broadening the perspective of humans, and showing people that there are many different ways to achieve balance. I'm very grateful that these amazing, experienced, educated people all shared their wisdom with us. This is not about making me more successful; it's about me contributing what I can to be part of a greater pack. And I'm very grateful and I'm honored to be a part of the illustrious pack that's represented within these pages. As always, my co-author and I want to thank our literary agent, Scott Miller, of Trident Media Group; and Julia Pastore, Shaye Areheart, Tina Constable, Maya Mavjee, Kira Walton, Domenica Aliota, and Tara Gilbride at Random House.

Melissa Jo Peltier wishes to thank: my partners at MPH, Jim Milio and Mark Hufnail, as well as everyone else at MPH and CMI who gave 150 percent to make this book possible—artist Victoria Parr, researchers Crystal Reel, Shanna Sletten, Lindsay Taub, and Jackie Younce, and especially Ben Stagg, who went above and beyond to meet this new and daunting challenge.

All of the diverse trainers represented in this book gave up many hours on the phone, via e-mails, and in person to help us make this as comprehensive a guide as possible, especially Bob Bailey, Ian Dunbar, Kirk Turner, and, of course, Martin Deeley. Their breadth of knowledge and willingness to candidly discuss their differing opinions on dog training was an enlightening and a once-in-a-lifetime education for me. Thanks also to Dr. Alice Clearman for her wise perspective and assistance.

As always, my heart belongs to my husband, John Gray, whose support makes possible everything I do.

INTRODUCTION

People don't usually seek me out when their dog won't sit on command.

They beg me for help when their dog is destroying their life.

In the opening of my show, *Dog Whisperer with Cesar Millan* on the National Geographic Channel, I always say, "I rehabilitate dogs; I train people."

Yet, still, the press refers to me as "dog trainer" Cesar Millan. And owners constantly ask me for my favorite training tips.

The first part of this book recounts my early experiences in the world of dog training and relates how I came to do what I do today. I grew up in a Third World country, a place where you can't always run down to the local supermarket or shopping mall to get what you need. In rural Mexico, we learn to adapt and to work with what we have. For me, it turned out to be a way of living that really promoted my personal creativity. From a very early age, I knew I wanted to work with dogs, and I knew I had a gift for it. I didn't have any formal training, or access to scientific studies, but I did have my passion for dogs—and the advantage of growing up around packs of them. I spent years side by side with them, working with them, and, most of all, observing them. I'm proud of how I was able to use my own ingenuity to become successful at rehabilitating so many hard-to-reach and "last chance" dogs.

Since I began my TV show in 2004, I've had the opportunity to work with hundreds of different dog owners, and through these experiences, I've learned that in the vast majority of cases, it's the people who usually need the most training in the human-dog relationship. The *Dog Whisperer* show has given me a working classroom in which to hone my abilities to communicate with and reach out to people, and to help them to see that everything they do—often, things they themselves are unaware of—influences the way their dogs behave. It's not easy to look in the mirror and admit, "I am the problem." But I hope that with kindness and love I have helped many of the owners who have appeared on our show to do just that. So many people who have been on our show come back years later to relate how the experience totally transformed both their dogs and their own lives.

When I finally gave in to requests that I write a training book, however, I decided that my own experience and special ability were not enough to give readers a comprehensive view of all the options for dog training that exist out there. So I reached out to some of the most experienced and acclaimed dog trainers, educators, and animal behavior professionals in the world. I am so grateful that so many of them agreed to participate. Some of the professionals in this book have openly disagreed with me in the past, and yet here they are, pooling their knowledge and experience with mine on these very pages. That is a beautiful thing, and it tells you a lot about their strong commitment to bettering the lives of dogs and dog owners. These open-minded leaders in their fields have helped me make this volume perhaps the very first place where you'll find such a wide range of training theories and methods all fairly represented between the covers of the same book.

One of the things I love most about America is that it is a place of many options. I am grateful for all these choices. I want my readers to know that there are so many possibilities available, they are sure to find something that works for them and their dogs.

MEET THE TRAINERS

An impressive array of trainers and other experts graciously shared their vast knowledge and experiences with us for this book. Here's a guide to their varied and amazing backgrounds:

Robert E. Bailey, even as a small child, had an interest in science, and especially in animals. His mother had to contend with live rattlesnakes in the refrigerator and rocket fuel in her kitchen. Studying fishes, reptiles, and birds at UCLA in 1958 was Bob's first exposure to behavior analysis and ethology. After a stint in a biochemistry lab and another in the field as a fish and game biologist, he became the first director of training for the U.S. Navy Marine Mammal Program. Joining Animal Behavior Enterprises (with Marian and Keller Breland) in 1965, Bob became research director and then general manager. Over the years, Bob has trained more than 120 species of animals and thousands of individuals, including many in a free environment using long-range control and guidance systems. Bob is also an inventor, designer, writer, teacher, diver, photographer, and video editor.

http://www.behavior1.com/page8.html

Bonnie Brown-Cali (IACP, APDT) has professionally trained dogs since 1990 and is the owner of Dog Dynamics. Bonnie was a master trainer for AppleGate School for Dogs Inc. and American Detector Dogs. She is an evaluator for the American Kennel Club and a certified field representative for Paws With a Cause, an organization that trains service dogs for the disabled. She has worked as a canine field handler for the University of Reno, the Desert Research Institute, and Working Dogs for Conservation and as a trainer for the Contra Costa County Sheriff's Office, the California Rescue Dogs Association, and the California Office of Emergency Services. She has conducted national workshops on training and deploying service dogs, dog behavior and obedience, reliable retrieving training, and the ethical use of training equipment.

Bonnie teaches weekly community group obedience classes and offers private instruction as well.

http://www.dogdynamics.org/about.html

Patrick Burns, who has had terriers for more than forty-five years, is a passionate defender of working dogs in general, and working terriers in particular. He is a monthly columnist for *Dogs Today* in the United Kingdom and has also written for *Dog World, True Grit,* and *Just Terriers* and appeared on ABC's *Nightline* to talk about the need to protect pedigree dogs from both inbreeding and exaggerated and contrived standards. Patrick is the author of the how-to book *American Working Terriers,* and his Web site and its associated blog (Terrierman's Daily Dose) are widely read and pull few punches. Most weekends Patrick can be found hunting in the fields and forests of Virginia and Maryland. He has worked with teckels (working dachshunds), Patterdale terriers, border terriers, fell terriers, Jack Russell terriers, and dogs "of pedigree unknown" and says he is "less interested in the paint and pedigree on a dog than the engine inside and the performance in the field."

http://www.terrierman.com/

* * *

Martin Deeley (IACP, CDT) is an internationally recognized companion dog and gundog trainer, writer, and commentator. In the field he specializes in spaniel and retriever training and is renowned throughout Europe and America as an authority on training both dogs and their owners. In 2007 Martin was voted U.K. Gundog Trainer of the Year by the readers of the leading magazine *Countryman's Weekly*. Martin is also the only journalist ever granted a personal interview with Her Majesty the Queen of England (herself a talented hunting dog trainer and handler). Martin considers this 1993 interview the greatest honor of his life because it reflected the confidence and trust that Her Majesty had in his integrity to fairly and honestly portray her, her love of dogs, and the effect they have had in her life. This rare and unique interview was published worldwide.

Over the years Martin has trained and guided many to succeed in the world of dogs as the Florida Dog Trainer (www.floridadogtrainer .com). The International School for Dog Trainers was established in response to demand for his expertise in providing training for both experienced and prospective dog trainers. Martin is also the executive director, past president, and co-founder of the International Association of Canine Professionals (www.canineprofessionals.com), a certification organization established to maintain the highest standards of professional and business practice among dog trainers. His best-selling book *Working Gundogs* has recently been reprinted.

http://www.martindeeley.com/

Barbara De Groodt is the owner of From the Heart Animal Behavior Counseling and Dog Training in Monterey County, California. The motto of From the Heart is "Respect your pet: train without the pain!" All programs at From the Heart are behavior-based rather than based on the older compulsion training methods.

Barbara was one of the founders of the Association of Pet Dog

Trainers (APDT) (under the guidance of Dr. Ian Dunbar); she is also a professional member of the International Association of Canine Professionals (IACP) and several behavior-based organizations. In 2005 she was given the Devoted Animal Friend of the Year Award. She has lectured around the world to veterinary groups, law enforcement agencies, trainers, and pet owners. Each semester she is a regular speaker at Western Career College, where she addresses the Animal Health Department. Barbara works closely with shelters and rescues in her area, giving discounts for all shelter/rescue dogs for classes and providing a good deal of pro bono services. Having worked for rescues in both the Katrina aftermath and the 2010 Nashville floodings, she understands the special bond between dogs and their owners.

http://www.fromtheheart.info/about.html

Dr. Ian Dunbar is a veterinarian, animal behaviorist, and writer. He received his veterinary degree and a special honors degree in physiology and biochemistry from the Royal Veterinary College (London University) and a doctorate in animal behavior from the psychology department of the University of California–Berkeley, where he spent ten years researching olfactory communication, the development of hierarchical social behavior, and aggression in domestic dogs.

Ian is a member of the Royal College of Veterinary Surgeons, the American Veterinary Society of Animal Behavior, the California Veterinary Medical Association, the Sierra Veterinary Medical Association, and the Association of Pet Dog Trainers (which he founded). Ian joined the Society for Veterinary Ethology (SVE, now the International Society for Applied Ethology) over thirty-five years ago, at which time he was the only member specializing in dog and cat behavior problems. Later he was involved in the establishment of the American SVE (now the American Veterinary Society of Animal Behavior). He also founded SIRIUS® Puppy Training, the first training program for young puppies at a crucial stage of development. There are very few educated trainers who have not been strongly influenced by Ian Dunbar's dog-friendly, fun-and-games dog training from the dog's point of view.

http://www.siriuspup.com/about_founder.html

Fate cast **Mark Harden,** a professional animal trainer for motion pictures and television since 1978, in the role of "Jack of All Trades— Master of None." "I wanted to specialize," he says, "but I decided the ability to put a multitude of animals on film is itself a specialty." Since embracing that notion, he can proudly boast the creation of many principal characters, including the Golden Seal (*The Golden Seal,* 1983), Virgil the chimp (*Project X,* 1987), Dodger the capuchin monkey (*Monkey Trouble,* 1994), Paulie the parrot (*Paulie,* 1998), Snowbell the cat (*Stuart Little,* 1999; *Stuart Little 2,* 2002), Butch the dog (*Cats and Dogs,* 2001), Ben the Gambian rat (*Willard,* 2003), and Midnight the Egyptian Mau (*Catwoman,* 2004).

To see a more comprehensive listing of Mark's credits, please visit the Internet Movie Database (www.imdb.com).

http://www.boonesanimals.com/pages/3102/Mark_Harden.htm

Katenna Jones has been a lover of animals all her life. She was the first animal behaviorist for the Rhode Island Society for the Prevention of Cruelty to Animals (SPCA), as well as a special agent helping with cruelty investigations, conducting state vicious-dog hearings and playing an active role in animal legislation.

Katenna now works for the American Humane Association in the Human-Animal Bond Division as a humane educator and animal behaviorist. Her job is to handle all animal behavior- and training-related information and also to help create new humane education programs and materials.

http://sites.google.com/site/katenna/howitallbegan

Joel Silverman turned a childhood dream into a thirty-year career, from training killer whales at Sea World, dolphins at Knott's Berry Farm and Magic Mountain, and birds, dogs, and cats at Universal Studios to training animals to star in live shows, Hollywood films, and television programs and commercials. As a host of the popular television series *Good Dog U* on Animal Planet and the syndicated show *Dog Training with Joel Silverman,* Joel has problem-solved behavior issues with a wide variety of dog breeds and owners.

Appearing on national programs such as *Live with Regis and Kathie Lee* and CNN, MSNBC, and FOX news programs, as well as hundreds of local morning news programs, Joel has offered advice on pet care and training based on his lifetime commitment to the welfare of animals and their special place in our lives. Joel does dog training seminars across the nation to promote his book *What Color Is Your Dog?* He resides in Rancho Santa Margarita, California, and offers dog training classes as well as private sessions.

http://www.companionsforlife.net/Meet_Joel.html

Jerome M. Stewart has been involved in the sport of herding since 1986, when he acquired his first Shetland sheepdog. He has been teaching all-breed herding classes since 1988 and currently teaches three classes a week in Southern California. In addition, Jerry offers clinics each year throughout the United States and has given numerous lectures on the sport of herding. He organizes and puts on demonstrations so that the general public can see herding dogs in action.

His students have finished over twenty herding championships, and several have become licensed herding judges. Jerry is an AKC (American Kennel Club) and AHBA (American Herding Breed Association) judge, licensed to judge all breeds in the trial and test classes. His articles have been published in many herding magazines, including *Pet Trader, The Herdsman,* and *Wag-N-Tale.* Jerry and his dogs have also been the subject of many new stories, including being featured on CNN and in the *L.A. Times.*

http://home1.gte.net/jerstew/biography.html

Kirk Turner, a professional dog behaviorist, is the head trainer for the Pine Street Foundation, which researches dogs' scent capabilities in the detection of cancer. He has trained multiple dogs to detect breast, lung, ovarian, and pancreatic cancers using breath samples for clinical trials performed in 2003 and again in 2009. Kirk got his start in dog training at the Pro Train Academy, a professional dog trainer school, in Venice, California, in 1989. From there, he moved to Eztrain, another professional dog training company, and also the San Francisco SPCA, a local shelter for abandoned dogs. He worked with the worst problem dogs to make them more adoptable and rescued many dogs from euthanasia. Kirk reached a career training record in personally training over four thousand dogs to be good canine citizens and provide comfort for their owners. Since 2003, Kirk has organized and presented many seminars and published articles in scholarly journals and is currently writing three books and creating four training videos.

http://www.kirkturner.net/

THOSE MAGICAL AMERICAN DOGS

My Evolution from Training Dogs to Training People

Cesar favorite Rin Tin Tin

The television set was an old black-and-white Zenith made of plastic that was supposed to look like wood. When you walked into our Mazatlán apartment, you could hear it before you could see it as you walked down a narrow hallway into the living room with a floor of large black-and-white tiles and a couch against one wall. My mother loved to watch her *telenovelas*—the daily soap operas that were so popular in Mexico. My sister loved the program *Maya,* which was about an elephant. But me? I had only two favorites: *Lassie* and *Rin Tin Tin.*

I still remember the way the *Rin Tin Tin* television show opened. Over a distant shot of a low-lying fort set in a cradle of mountains somewhere in the American West, there came the sound of a bugle playing reveille. At the sound of the call, American cavalry officers in Civil War–era uniforms rushed from their posts inside Fort Apache to fall into formation. Then there was a cut—the one I always waited for—to a shot of a magnificent German shepherd dog, sitting stoically on a rooftop, his ears pointed high, on alert to the bugle call. When Rusty, a little boy, joined the formation line, Rin Tin Tin barked, leapt off the rooftop, and got into the line of soldiers, just as if he were a soldier himself. By the end of the opening credits, I was filled with excitement and anticipation, wondering what incredible adventure Rusty and Rin Tin Tin would face this week.

Then there was *Lassie*. None of the dogs on my grandfather's farm looked anything like Lassie, with her downy cream-and-white-colored coat and her elegant, pointy nose. Our dogs had raggedy coats and muddy faces, but Lassie was always meticulously groomed. Every week Lassie's boy owner, Timmy, would get into some sort of trouble, but Lassie would never fail to save her master and help Timmy's parents teach him a life lesson, all within the span of one thirty-minute show.

By the time I saw *Lassie* and *Rin Tin Tin* on television, I was nine or ten years old and already entranced with dogs. From as early as I can remember, I was fascinated by, drawn to, and in love with the packs of working dogs that lived with us on my grandfather's farm in Sinaloa. They weren't pretty like Lassie or obedient like Rin Tin Tin, but sometimes I felt more a part of them than I did my human family. I never tired of just watching them—the way they interacted and communicated with one another; the way the mothers so effortlessly but firmly raised the pups; and the way they managed to solve disputes with each other quickly and cleanly, usually without even fighting, then move on to the next thing without bitterness or regret. Perhaps in some way I envied the clear and simple rules of their lives compared with the complexity of the human interactions in my own close but sometimes troubled family. All I knew then, however, was that dogs fascinated me, took me out of myself, and made me want to spend every spare minute learning everything I could about them.

Then Lassie and Rin Tin Tin came into my life through television, and I began to wonder if there wasn't something about dogs I was missing. You see, at first I was totally fooled by these professional performing dogs. As a father, I used to watch my son Calvin watching kung fu movies on television when he was younger, and I could see by the look in his eyes that he believed the guys were actually fighting each other. He didn't realize that the fight was choreographed by a stuntman behind the scenes. Well, I was the same way in my beliefs about Lassie and Rin Tin Tin. As primitive as television may have been back then, it did a great job convincing a naive little Mexican boy that there were amazing magical dogs in America that were born being able to communicate with humans, march in the army, and always manage to save the day. Before I even knew that there was a trainer behind the scenes, signaling to Rin Tin Tin to jump off the roof, I got it into my head that somehow, someday, I just had to get to America to meet these amazing dogs that could talk to people, leap over fences, and get mischievous little boys like me out of the trouble we were always getting into!

I think I believed Lassie and Rin Tin Tin did the things they did all on their own because the dogs on our farms seemed to do everything we wanted of them without being told or coerced by us to do it. They would naturally follow my grandfather out into the field and help him corral the cows. They would naturally accompany my mother or sister along the road, as guides and escorts. We didn't reward them with food every time they followed us across the river or when they barked to alert us of a predator in the area. We did ultimately reward them—but always at the end of the workday, with our leftover meat or tortillas. So I already knew dogs that seemed to be able to communicate with people. To my mind, Lassie and Rin Tin Tin were just a cut above that.

By the time I realized that Rin Tin Tin and Lassie were specially trained dogs, I was a few years older and living with my family in the city of Mazatlán, always wishing for the weekends when I could go back to my grandfather's farm and be with nature and the animals again. Instead of being disillusioned by the discovery that humans were manipulating those dogs' behaviors, I was even more excited. You mean, there are people who can *make* their dogs do these things? How? What are their secrets? It became even clearer in my mind that I would have to get to America as soon as possible to learn from the Americans about creating these amazing behaviors in dogs.

One weekend when I went back to my grandfather's farm I decided to see if I could teach some of the dogs there how to do specific behaviors. First, I tried to teach the dogs to jump on command. I started with my leg. I'd stick it out in front of me and hold a ball right on the other side. When they'd go over my leg to get it, I'd make the sound "Hup!" Gradually I raised my leg higher and higher until they were jumping right over it. Within the span of a day or two, I could make the dogs jump over my back when I bent down and said, "Hup!"

These dogs were already conditioned to respond to what humans needed from them—not in a "trained" way, but as part of doing their job. And it was a job they wanted to do, because it challenged them and fulfilled their need for a purpose in life. Doing their job was also the way they survived from day to day. We didn't use leashes for our dogs on the farm. I couldn't imagine a dog on a leash. Other than every once in a while when my grandfather would get the old rope from the barn to do something like get a donkey out of a ditch, I didn't know what a leash was until I moved to the city and saw rich people walking their dogs on leashes.

Because of their lifestyle, my grandfather's dogs naturally wanted to follow me, and they naturally wanted to please me. When the dogs were in a playful state, I caught the energy of that moment and used it to create something new. And they didn't ask for anything in return except, "What are we going to do with our time?" I learned that I could teach them how to crawl on the ground just by encouraging them verbally and letting them imitate me crawling. Dogs are great at copying behavior—that's one of the many ways in which they learn from one another when they are pups. And dogs' brains crave new experiences. If a dog finds what you're doing interesting, and he is interested in you, and it's a challenge for him, he naturally wants to be a part of it. The learning experience, the figuring it out, becomes such a thrill to a dog when it's fun.

Every weekend at the farm I'd try to teach the dogs a new behavior. I wasn't using food rewards to get this behavior—that strategy wasn't yet in my mental tool kit. But the dogs wanted to be with me and wanted to do what I wanted. When you have a dog that is eager to do things for you, he doesn't need food rewards. And to make him eager to do things for you, you have to motivate him with something he wants. What I was offering these dogs was a challenge, plus the entertainment value of it all. It was fun for me, and it was fun for them— an overall positive experience for all of us. By the end of a few weeks I could get them to jump over me, crawl under me, and jump up and give me five. The dogs were happy to be doing it. And with verbal encouragement and just my general enthusiasm, I let them know very clearly how happy I was that they were doing it for me. The outcome was a deeper bond between us.

To me, that was the whole point. Ultimately, you want your dog to do things for you just because you love him. And he loves, respects, and trusts you.

THE SEARCH FOR A TEACHER

My quick and easy experiences training the farm dogs to do simple behaviors encouraged me to learn more about training, any way I could.
It was obvious that it might be a very long time before I'd be able to go
to America to meet the magical dogs and their trainers.

When I was a teenager, I learned of a man in Mazatlán who was
the only person I'd ever heard of who called himself a professional
"dog trainer." He was from Mexico City, and he would train dogs to
do tricks for performances. That was the first time I saw, from behind
the scenes, how a dog can fake getting shot. The guy would fire off a
gun, and the dog would fall down. I was fascinated by the hand signals and other cues the man used to get the dog to do the behaviors.
For the first time, I also saw someone using verbal commands ("sit,"
"stay," "come"). On the farm, it hadn't occurred to me to use human
words (in my case Spanish words) to get a dog to do something. It was
interesting to see a dog responding to human language as if he were a
person who actually understood what the words meant.

I was intrigued by how this man accomplished all this and asked
him if I could volunteer to clean his kennels and help him, sort of like
an apprentice. It was the first opportunity I'd had to learn from someone I thought was a real professional.

Meeting this man and seeing him work behind the scenes was my
first experience of being totally disillusioned by a dog trainer. Unlike the dogs on the farm, this man's dogs did not seem particularly
excited about doing the things their trainer wanted them to do. The
man was very forceful. As I watched him pry open one dog's mouth
and tape in the item he wanted the dog to carry, I became extremely
uncomfortable. I left that situation very quickly because even though
I had no formal training, I knew in my gut that there had to be a better way.

FROM BAD TO WORSE

I was a pretty trusting kid, I was naturally honest, and I tended to be-lieve what people said to me. I didn't understand then that there are people who are in the animal business not because they love animals. Sometimes they are just in it for the money. My next two experiences in trying to educate myself as a dog trainer taught me that lesson the hard way.

The next man I met who said he was a trainer claimed that he had trained animals—including dogs—in America, the land of the magical dogs. He worked in the city where I was born, Culiacán, so I went to see if I could learn from him. But when I arrived, I found that the real way he made his money was as an illegal exotic animal broker. This was pretty shocking to me, but this man swore up and down that he could teach me how to work with dogs. So I tentatively waited around in order to be this man's student. In the meantime, I volunteered by cleaning the dogs' kennels, feeding them, and gener-ally looking after them.

One thing that probably should have tipped me off right away that this guy was not someone I should be around or learning from was that he had a lot of out-of-control and aggressive dogs. I remem-ber wondering, *How could he be a very good trainer if his dogs are like this?* I used to take his dogs out and walk them, and he seemed amazed that I could do it. Here comes this kid who can easily walk these dogs that were aggressive with him and biting him. To me, it was easy. It was just common sense. If a dog shows teeth to me and growls at me, I don't become afraid and I don't get angry or blame the dog. I try to understand why the dog is growling and gain the dog's trust. Then I walk with him. I spent time with these dogs, mostly walking them for hours. By the time the walk was over, the dogs and I understood one another. There was trust and there was respect, something they did

not have for their owner. Forget about training—this was the beginning of what I would later call "dog psychology." Of course, I didn't
know it yet.

It wasn't long before I learned why this man's dogs were out of
control and aggressive. I saw him give the dogs some kind of injection
that made them really go crazy. I don't know what he gave them, but
I knew right away that this was not dog training, and I left in a hurry.
This experience was traumatic for me at the time, but today I think it
was important that I got to see the worst of the worst right up front,
so that I would always know the difference.

I was still determined to find someone in Mexico who could help
show me the way to train dogs. I kept hearing about other dog trainers, but they were always far away—in Guadalajara, in Mexico City.
And I was just a teenager. When I was fifteen, I met another man who
offered to take me to Mexico City to meet two brothers who were
amazing dog trainers—the champions of the champions—but it
would cost me one million pesos. Today that would be about $10,000.
You can imagine how overwhelming a sum that would have been for
a fifteen-year-old working-class Mexican kid. But I had been saving
money from my job as a kennel boy at a vet's office and some other
odd jobs for a very long time. I planned to go to Mexico City during
my school vacation to learn from the "best of the best."

The man who took my money drove me to Mexico City—which
was over five hundred miles from my home in Mazatlán—and
dropped me at the place where he said the brothers did their dog
training. I went to the address, but there was nobody there. I'd been
conned. Not only that, I was stranded and had to find a place to live
while I figured out how I could get back home. Fortunately, a very
kind woman took me in. She happened to have a German shepherd
that was out of control. So I said, "Señora, while I'm here, can I just do
something with your dog so I can pay you back for your hospitality?"
And that's what I did. The dog was obviously frustrated from pent-up

energy because he lived in the city and the owners never walked him. One thing I knew from the farm was that dogs really like to walk. So I just started walking him at first. I would tire him out until he was calm and relaxed. And then I tried a little training on my own. The woman and her family lived in front of a park, so I would go there with the dog and ask him to wait, ask him to stay, ask him to come—just basic stuff. Mostly I captured the behavior that he was already doing. I had no idea that capturing a behavior an animal is already doing is one of the core tenets of operant conditioning–based animal training. I had no idea what that was, or what those words meant. It just felt very natural to me to encourage a dog to do more of what he was already doing right. So I ended up taking a class in animal training after all, except that this German shepherd ended up being my teacher.

Eventually I got a ride back to Mazatlán. I never told my parents what had happened to me—that I'd been tricked out of my money.

THE PROMISED LAND

Despite all my setbacks in Mexico, my dream of making it to America and becoming a real dog trainer was still at the forefront of my mind. In fact, my dreams had become even bigger. I wanted to become the best dog trainer in the world.

In my first book, *Cesar's Way,* I tell the story of how I crossed the border into America, got a job as a groomer in San Diego, and finally made it to Los Angeles. It didn't work out the way I'd fantasized—which was that I'd walk into Hollywood; ask, "Where is Lassie? Where is Rin Tin Tin?"; and get apprenticed to one of the big-time movie trainers to work with him on his next movie. But I was practical—I knew I had to start somewhere. So I took a job as a kennel boy at a very big, successful, and busy dog training facility. Most of my work involved cleaning kennels and feeding, grooming, and walking dogs.

We were very busy: with people dropping off dogs every day, there were thirty to fifty dogs at any one time waiting to be "trained." It wasn't unusual for me to work fourteen- to sixteen-hour days.

People brought their dogs to this facility to be trained in what was called Basic Obedience, which was "sit, down, stay, come, heel." Basic Obedience was divided into three courses. The most common course was on-leash obedience; after going through this course, the dog would be ready, the facility promised, in two weeks. This was in the early '90s, and the course cost $2,500. Then there was off-leash ground obedience, which was the same thing except now the dog was dragging the leash on the ground. Learning off-leash ground obedience was supposed to take three to four weeks, and the course ran about $3,500. For the hefty sum of $5,000, the final course was off-leash obedience: the dog stayed at the facility for two months, after which we would return the dog to the owner able to perform basic obedience completely off-leash—or at least, capable of performing off-leash with our people, in the little yard of our headquarters, where we would give the owner a demonstration to show off what we'd accomplished. The facility offered sessions for the owner afterward for an additional cost. And owners could get a pretrained dog as well—if they could afford the $15,000 price tag.

The methods used at this facility back then were what most people today would consider very harsh. There were no food rewards, and there was no positive reinforcement. It was all about choke chains and prong collars. If the first didn't work, we moved to the second, and finally to the e-collar if all else failed. That was the protocol. Now that I've worked with hundreds of dogs myself, I believe that these tools have their places in some specific situations, but almost never in simple obedience training. To my mind, the whole training methodology being used at this facility was flawed because it was based on a ticking clock . . . and a ticking clock that just wasn't realistic. I have come to believe that patience is the most important quality anyone who works with animals can possess. When we work with animals, we have to be prepared to first gain the animal's trust, then wait for as long as it takes to develop communication with the animal and earn its respect.

This isn't to say that the trainers at this facility were unkind to the animals—I'm sure most of them didn't intend to be. A lot of accusations of "animal abuse" are thrown around today when people don't agree with one method or another, and I've been at the center of some of those accusations myself. I like to remind these critics that most people who go into animal-related fields do truly care about animals and that very few people who train or work with animals make a lot of money at it. They do it for the love of the work itself and their love of animals. And the jobs are hard to come by.

When I first arrived at the dog training facility, I had no opinion one way or the other about the methods being used there. But after a little while I came to see that those methods worked only to the extent that they created short-term changes in outward behavior; they had no effect on a dog's state of mind. Because the dogs would do the behavior just long enough to get the trainer off their back, I doubt very much that the "lessons" they learned stuck with them. In addition, many of the dogs had no motivation to learn the behavior because not only did they have no real relationship with the trainer, but the process of learning wasn't pleasant or fun for them.

The man who ran this facility may well have been a good dog trainer, but I never saw him train a dog personally. Most of what he did for the company was sales. He was the best salesman in the world. He would bring in a dog that he had purchased in Germany and that had been through advanced training for a number of years, give a demonstration with that dog, and then say, "This is what your dog will be able to do when it leaves here."

The key problem was that he didn't tell owners *how* their dog was going to be able to learn these things, but most people back then didn't know enough to ask that question. I don't remember people being concerned about how their dogs were going to be trained; no one asked questions like: "What method do you use?" "Do you use positive rewards?" "Are your trainers certified?" I don't think for a minute that these owners asked no questions because they didn't care. I'm certain they cared a great deal about their dogs, as most dog owners do. I truly think they just didn't have the right information to know what questions to ask.

I did a lot of observing during my time as a kennel boy at this place, and that's when something in my mind clicked. I began asking the question, "Is obedience training really what this dog needs right now?" Many of the dogs were fearful and insecure, and the process of training made them worse. They might have left the facility being able to respond to commands, but they still had the behavior problem they'd come in with. Observing these dogs, I began to think about the idea of dog *rehabilitation* as opposed to dog *training*. I also noticed that the owners were never encouraged to be a part of the process. They would drop off their dogs at the place expecting them to be fixed, like a car or an appliance. No one considered the possibility that the owners' own behavior was contributing to the dog's problem behavior.

The issue was that the owners didn't know what to look for. What the dogs needed was behavior modification; obedience training did not help them, especially the nervous ones, the fearful ones, and the extremely aggressive ones. Facing a behavior issue with their dog, owners were told, "You've got to *train* that dog." Nobody told them, "You have to *rehabilitate* that dog." Nobody told them, "You need to fulfill the needs of that dog." The word for all of that—for everything that had to do with behavior—was *training*, the assumption being that a *trained* dog was going to be okay. I could see from the dogs that came through the facility day after day that this absolutely wasn't the case.

Cesar's Rules FOR CHOOSING A DOG TRAINER

1. First, ask yourself what you want your dog to learn. Is your dog like one of the extreme cases on my show *Dog Whisperer*? Then learning "sit," "stay," "come," and "heel" is not necessarily the first lesson your dog needs. Some dog trainers don't do rehabilitation, some don't do obedience work, and some do both. Choose the right tool for the job you need done.

2. Think about your own philosophy and ethics. For example, some people are opposed to choke chains. I am not opposed to them and find them helpful in some cases, when used correctly. But I will not use a choke chain or any other tool an owner objects to, because if the owner feels badly about the tool, I guarantee you that the dog will have a bad experience with the tool. And there could be other reasons why I might not be the right trainer for you. You have a world of options when it comes to dog trainers, as I hope this book will show you. Make sure that the trainer you choose agrees with and supports your own values, because you are the one who is going to live with your dog and work with him every day.

3. Check out a trainer's certification.[1] There are many gifted dog professionals out there who aren't certified (I used to be one of them!), and the truth is that there are no hard-and-fast rules that necessarily mean a certified trainer is an expert. But having certification ensures that the person you hire has had to pass some minimum requirements, put in some hands-on hours with dogs, and do some studying. Certification also makes a trainer accountable to some basic standards and guidelines, which you can research.

(continues)

4. Get referrals. This may sound obvious, but even if you find a trainer in a phone book, ask if you can talk to a couple of his or her previous clients. They can give you an idea of the trainer's methods, "bedside manner," reliability, and willingness to follow through.

5. Make sure the trainer includes you as part of the training process. There's nothing wrong with a trainer who asks you to drop off your dog in order to work with him. I do that myself from time to time, because often an owner is the cause of the dog's bad habits and he needs to be away from his owner in order to learn new ones. But I make it clear to my clients that I don't "fix" broken dogs. I work closely with the owners on identifying their own issues and behaviors so that they are able to change as much as their dog changes. If you've watched my show, you already know that more often than not it's the owner who needs the most "training."

TRAINING AT THE CAR WASH

I knew I wanted to become a different kind of dog "trainer," but I didn't have a handle on exactly what to do or how to do it yet. I left the professional facility anyway and went to work for a businessman who had been impressed with the way I handled his dog. He hired me to wash his fleet of limos and also threw me extra work training his friends' dogs on the side. Because they were his friends, he asked me not to charge them very much, so I would bring the dogs to my job with me and work with them during my breaks. While I was working, I wanted to keep the dogs occupied and give them something challenging to do. So I taught them how to help me wash the limos.

There was a German shepherd named Howie whose owner wanted

me to teach him obedience. I didn't want to use the methods I'd left behind at the facility, and I remembered how easy it had been to train my grandfather's dogs back home, especially when they wanted to be a part of what I was doing. So I figured out a way to teach Howie how to carry the bucket of water and bring it to me as I washed all thirteen cars.

Most dogs naturally love to chase prey, and many naturally retrieve. With Howie, I started by throwing the bucket instead of the ball, so he'd go and retrieve the bucket. He would naturally bite the inside of the bucket to get a hold of it and carry it to me sideways. I realized that wouldn't work if I wanted the bucket to hold any water, so I put a tennis ball on the bucket handle. Howie was immediately attracted to the tennis ball, and that's how he learned to grab the handle and carry the bucket to me upright. We worked on that for a long time. Eventually, Howie learned how to raise his head and walk very proud and tall carrying the bucket. That's when I started putting just a little bit of water in it. But before I put the water in it, I would tell him with my energy and body language to stay where he was, to build up his eagerness to get the bucket. As soon as I saw that intensity in his posture—that he really wanted to get the bucket—I'd let him go. This was new: the bucket was not being thrown, it was in one place, and he was expected to bring it from that place to me. I eventually took the tennis ball off the bucket handle and replaced it with layers of thick tape, to make the handle easier for Howie to hold in his mouth.

Finally, I'd give a name to the activity: "Go get the bucket." Howie learned to get the bucket from wherever it was and bring it to me wherever I was. Later on, I was able to teach this routine to other clients' dogs.

Now that I had a bucket assistant, I needed someone to carry the hose. I chose Sike, a rottweiler whose owner wanted me to teach him obedience. The hose was much easier to teach. Using a sort of early combination of dog psychology and dog training, I began the exercise

Howie carries the bucket by the handle.

by making sure the dog was relaxed around the water coming out of the hose. Once I accomplished that—simply through gradual exposure to the hose and the water stream—I had to train Sike not to puncture the hose when he pulled it. I learned that lesson the hard way: my boss got mad at me the first time Sike bit through a hose, and he made me buy him a new one. Teaching a retriever to be gentle with a water hose is easy—they're bred to have very soft mouths for carrying ducks intact back to hunters—but teaching a German shepherd or a rottweiler not to sink his teeth into something is a bit trickier. My solution was to put a thick roll of tape around the part of the hose I wanted the dog to target—up near the nozzle, where the surface was harder—which made the hose easier for the dogs to hold.

It took me about two weeks to teach each new behavior, but when I was done, people would come by the garage to see me washing the car with a German shepherd carrying the water bucket for me and a

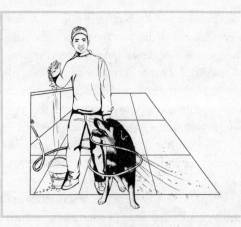

Sike helps Cesar with the hose.

rottweiler rinsing the wheels with a hose. After we finished each car, I'd reward the dogs with food, but I wasn't rewarding them constantly. The tasks were complex enough to hold their attention, so it wasn't as though they would lose interest in the middle of the process and drop the bucket or the hose. The task was challenging for them, and it was fun for them to be involved in what I was doing. In my mind, I was saying, *Okay, if I finish this car, I get paid, and if I get paid, I can give you food.* So I was getting as much out of the process as the dogs were. They knew that if we finished a car, they got fed. And with the dogs' help, I washed thirteen cars that much quicker.

EARLY PROTECTION TRAINING

Back then I lived in the crime-ridden "hood" of Inglewood, California. There were a lot of break-ins and a lot of gang activity. Just wanting to be able to walk safely on the streets and in the parks, people started to be interested in getting dogs for protection. I quickly learned that protection dog training was big business in our area. Aside from my work at the professional facility and the tricks and obedience work I did on my breaks washing limos, doing protection work with dogs was my first professional experience as a dog "trainer." I had already begun to experiment with my theory of pack-power–related training, and my ability to get packs of dogs to work reliably in tandem was getting me some attention—especially when I was out in the park with a pack of perfectly behaved rotties following me off-leash. And it was that growing reputation that drew my first celebrity client, Jada Pinkett.

Jada has been a friend ever since our first meeting, and she and I have been through a lot together. She has since married actor Will Smith and has a beautiful family with him, but at the time I met her, she was just a young actress starting out. Living alone in Los Angeles, she felt she needed protection dogs. She did not have a lot of experience with or knowledge of powerful dogs, but she had a very open mind and was willing to learn. Jada is a tiny woman, and she would have to handle all her dogs alone, so it was imperative that I

A pack walk with Jada

teach her to go beyond issuing commands to sit, stay, come, and even to attack—she needed to achieve the pack-leader position among her dogs. We did much more than advanced protection work with her and the pack. We took them on hikes in the mountains, to the beach, and through the tough neighborhoods of South L.A. We practiced with "bad guy" dummies in the trees and in the bushes, and Jada learned how to start and stop a protection activity. I wanted her to know beyond the shadow of a doubt that she could be in control of all the rotties at all times, in any situation. She learned more than simply which commands to use or how to choose a leash or style of "dog training." It was really all about teaching her how to feel confident as the leader of her dogs. We achieved this through weeks and weeks of hands-on practice but also through the body language she expressed, the thoughts she focused on, and the energy she projected when she was with her dogs.

Sharing this experience with Jada was an "aha!" moment for me. It really clicked for me, working with her, how important the owner is when it comes to dog training. I knew then that this would be my new challenge and my mission—training people to understand how to communicate with their dogs.

TRAINING VS. BALANCE

Around this time in my development I stopped thinking of myself as a dog "trainer" and also let go of thinking about what I do with dogs as "training." I was realizing that I would need to train owners and rehabilitate, fulfill, or balance their dogs.

I always like to say that, as immigrants, we Latinos are not taking away the jobs of Americans. We fill in where there are empty spaces. When I came to this country, there were no professionals focused on helping dog owners to understand their dogs. Nor were there any who focused on fulfilling the basic needs of the dogs themselves. It was all about getting dogs to do what people want, using our language or our own means of teaching them. So I took it upon myself to fill that empty space.

Since that time when I changed my focus, I've personally re-defined the word *training* to mean answering to commands ("sit," "stay," "come," "heel"), doing tricks, or doing some behavior that is not necessarily natural to the dog. Or the behavior may be natural to the dog, but we want to control it in a way that is more based on human needs than the dog's needs. I believe that dog *training* is something cre-ated by humans, but that dog *psychology*—what I try to get my clients to practice first and foremost—is created by Mother Nature.

When any mother animal raises her babies to survive in the world, she isn't thinking consciously about what it will take to teach them how to find food or how to spot a danger or how to follow the rules of behavior for being that particular animal. The babies learn from her what it takes to be a successful animal in that particular environment without a lot of extra effort on her part, much less bribes or punish-ment. Surviving, fitting in, and functioning in the world around them is their most fundamental motivation. I believe it's important to un-derstand a dog's natural inclination to fit into his environment first before thinking about commands, special behaviors, or tricks.

Professional animal handler Mark Harden has been training ani-mals for film and television for over thirty years. He's trained every-thing from the wolves in *Never Cry Wolf* to the spiders in *Arachnophobia* to the parrots in the *Pirates of the Caribbean* movies to the cats and dogs in—what else?—*Cats and Dogs.* Mark trains a lot of movie dogs, but he also keeps dogs at home as family pets. And he differentiates between training and good behavior in much the same way that I do, although we use different words to describe our ideas.

"I say there's *raising* and then there's *training*," Mark told me. "Those are the two things that I do, and I link it to my kids. For example, I *raise* them to behave in public. In a restaurant, they know how to behave. I don't give them a treat for behaving in the restaurant. If they misbehave in the restaurant, there will be consequences, but I expect them to behave. So that's part of how I raise them. Now, if they go and get an A-plus in math analysis, well, that might be a trick. I might be willing to reward them for that, to give them an incentive for it, because I don't see an obvious incentive for a child to get an A-plus in math analysis. I mean, my motto with people on set is: 'Treats are for tricks.' I 'pay' for tricks, but I raise animals to behave like I would my children. I would train tricks, and I would raise them with manners."

OTHER DEFINITIONS

There are other experienced and educated professionals who don't necessarily agree with how I define dog training and separate it from dog rehabilitation or balance. They would say, "Bottom line, Cesar is a dog *trainer.*" I respect the views of many of these pros and want to share with you a few of their thoughts about what dog "training" is, to help you get a taste of the range of opinions and ideas out there. As you read, think about how each definition might apply to your relationship with your dog.

Ian Dunbar is a pioneer in off-leash puppy training, prevention, and reward-based dog training; he is also a veterinarian, emeritus college professor, author, television star, and lecturer from whom we'll hear much more later in this book. "If I were to define training," Ian says, "I would say it comprises altering the frequency of behaviors, or putting the reliable presence or absence of specific behaviors on cue. Whenever you're reinforcing a behavior in a dog, you're training him. Whenever you're punishing a dog for the wrong behavior, you're training him. I mean, that's the very definition of training."

Like Ian Dunbar, Bob Bailey is a man who truly knows animal

training. Along with his late wife, Marian Breland Bailey, he was among the very first to use Skinnerian operant conditioning—that is, the science of using consequences to change and shape animal behaviors. In fact, Marian Breland invented the "clicker," which is among the most important tools in positive animal training today. In his sixty years in the trenches, Bob has worked with everything from marine mammals to ravens to snakes to chickens, training them for stage shows, commercials, movies, television, corporate demonstrations, and top-secret military work. Although Bob told my co-author that he likes to call himself a *behavior technician* and not a trainer, he also uses a much broader definition of the word *training* than I do.

"I believe that the purposeful changing of behavior is, more or less, defined as 'training,'" he says. "We may call it 'instruction,' or 'teaching,' or whatever, but in the greater scheme of things, behavior is behavior, whether it be sitting, lying down, or even thinking. After a long time of observing animals in the wild and training animals to do things to put bread on my table, I know that animals respond very well to very subtle environmental stimuli. For instance, if I'm working a dog, or any animal, a slight change in the environment, including a change in my demeanor and activity, can tell the animal that now is the time to 'chill out.' Such 'chill-out' behavior by the dog may appear casual, not as obvious or dramatic as jumping on a table and grabbing some flowers out of a vase, but that behavior is under stimulus control just as much as flower-grabbing. I think most of the trainers I have known, especially the very good ones, adhere to the view that training—learning—goes on all the time, not just when we want it to."

My friend Martin Deeley and I agree on many things, but the specific definition of *dog training* is not exactly one of them. Martin is an internationally known professional pet dog trainer, gundog trainer, and executive director of the International Association of Canine Professional Dog Trainers (IACP-CDT). "Training happens every moment of every day of a dog's life, with everything you do," says Martin. "Every interaction between you and a dog is training." Martin would define all the different things I do when I rehabilitate dogs as every bit as much "training" as what he does when he teaches a pack of retrievers to hunt down and retrieve a fallen duck in the woods.

"In training," he says, "I share information—information from my body, my hands, the tools I use, and the situations I'm in with the dogs. I am always looking for the best way to communicate the information. Now, some information is translated and interpreted by the dog well and quickly, and some information may not be. We change our ways of communicating information to achieve the results we seek. Information is knowledge acquired through experience or study. In training, a dog is gaining information in both ways. Do not think of information as just written or verbal. Think of it as versatile and totally understandable communication. But the aim of that communication is to change and create behaviors, which, to me, is how I define 'training.'"

I agree with Ian, Bob, and Martin that we are teaching our dogs all the time—every minute—how they should react to us and act around us. To me, that concept involves leadership more than training, but this is a semantic difference. However different we four dog professionals may be in our definitions and approaches, we all have the same goal in mind, which is to help you communicate well and live happily with your dog.

I always begin by fulfilling the dog's needs first, making sure the dog is what I refer to as *balanced.* Let me be clear: *balanced* is not a scientific term, but to me it's incredibly descriptive of what it means for any animal—including the human animal—to be comfortable in its environment and in its own skin. Let's look into the relationship between balance and behavior in the next chapter.

2

THE BASICS OF BALANCE

The Foundation of Training

Mathew Imaging

Rollerblading at the Emmys

Back in the 1920s, L.A.'s majestic Shrine Auditorium was the largest indoor theater in the world, and today its looming Moorish architecture makes it just as impressive a structure. On September 19, 2006, its gleaming yellow Persian domes cast long shadows on the red carpet for the fifty-eighth Creative Arts Emmy Awards celebration. The September afternoon was hot, and I was a little uncomfortable in my black shirt, tailored tux, and fancy dress shoes, but it didn't matter. I couldn't have been more excited. It was the second season of my show *Dog Whisperer,* and my team and I had been nominated for the first time, in the category of "outstanding reality show."

"Cesar! Right here!" one of the paparazzi shouted. That's what they do to get you to turn to look at them as they try to snap your picture.

"Daddy! Daddy! Look over here!" another one cried out. Standing next to me on the red carpet, wearing his best formal collar, my faithful pit bull Daddy instinctively looked up at the sound of his name. The photographers clicked away, and pretty soon all the attention was on him. Daddy being Daddy, he just took it all in with serene interest. Daddy was always up for new adventures, and nothing—not even shouting paparazzi and flashing lights—ever really fazed him.

Our turn on the red carpet came and went in an instant, and we joined the throngs of glittering guests pressing through the arched doorways of the auditorium. I might have looked just like all the other men in their standard penguin suits and bow ties, but waiting backstage for me were some special accessories for my outfit.

I had brought along my Rollerblades.

About an hour after the ceremony began, I peered out from the wings at the vast, packed theater—an old-fashioned opera house just like the one that Andrew Lloyd Webber's Phantom might have haunted, filled with plush red-velvet seats and ornate details and gold trim. Strangely, I wasn't nervous at all. I was calm and focused when the words I was waiting for boomed out over the giant sound system:

"Ladies and gentlemen, the Dog Whisperer, Cesar Millan!"

The smooth voice of the female announcer was timed perfectly to coincide with the upbeat music cue of "Who Let the Dogs Out?" That's when I Rollerbladed across the 194-foot stage at the Shrine Auditorium, with six happy pit bulls trotting beside me.

The audience gasped and applauded wildly. They burst into spontaneous laughter when Pepito, one of the pits, became hypnotized by our image in the giant video monitors that flanked the stage so that

even those in the nosebleed seats could see the reactions on the winners' faces when they came up to accept their statues. After my assistants had removed all the dogs except Daddy from the stage so I could
do the actual presentation, I threw the envelope containing the names
of the winners to Daddy and had him bring it to me at the podium.
The audience roared again when Daddy, now off-leash, sauntered
over to greet, sniff, and check out a very nervous Jimmy Romano, the
winner in the "best stuntman" category. As we left the stage to make
room for the next award presentation, I felt elated by how smoothly
the whole production had gone, especially considering we'd only had
one rehearsal earlier in the day.

When I was asked to present an award for the ceremony, I leapt at
the chance to do something totally different. I wanted to show people
that pit bulls are pack-oriented and that they can be wonderful and
obedient dogs. The pits had come through with flying colors, and I
was thrilled at how well we'd succeeded.

I wonder if the show director would have been so enthusiastic if I'd
told him ahead of time that only one of those pit bulls was what most
people would call "trained."

I call them well behaved, and I call them balanced. But not one of
those dogs had had any formal preparation to be on a stage, under
bright lights, with loud music blaring, in front of 6,500 people.

So how did I create such a polite, open, obedient pack of pit bulls
without what I would call "formal training"?

OBEDIENCE: WHAT'S YOUR DEFINITION?

In the opening of my show, I always say, "I rehabilitate dogs. I train
people."

There's a reason for that claim. Usually, humans need much more help understanding their dogs than dogs need in understanding their humans. Dogs are hardwired to understand us. It's in their genes to know how to read our facial expressions, body language, and changes of mood and energy. Dogs are the only animals besides primates that understand that when we raise an arm to point at a distant object, they are supposed to look in the direction we are pointing. Other animals can learn this, but it's not natural for them. Their instinct is to just stare at our outstretched arm![1]

Humans, on the other hand, are constantly misreading dogs' attempts at communication. Many people interpret any wagging tail as a signal of friendship, but an experienced observer of canines would notice that when a dog's body language is tense, her teeth are slightly bared, and her tail is swishing slowly side to side, it means the exact opposite of "friendship." You may think your dog is trying to punish you when she destroys your favorite shoes while you're at work, but in fact she's just frustrated and bored out of her mind. And if you reach out to "comfort" a nervous dog by petting her, you will only make her even more nervous. A dog in distress needs for you to stand strong and show leadership, not melt into sympathy because you're feeling sorry for her. These are only a handful of the many ways in which humans misjudge what dogs are trying to say to them—and ironically, it's these crossed wires of communication that are the reason I have a career today.

When my clients say they want an obedient dog, most of the time the situation has gone way beyond a dog that won't sit on command. It's about a dog that's ruining someone's life—or a dog whose own life is on the line if the owner can't get its behavior under control. Even in less extreme cases, however, people's definition of an obedient dog varies greatly, just as people are vastly different in what they want from their relationships with their dogs. Our relationships with our dogs are very personal, reflecting our individuality and the choices we've made for our own happiness. For example, I would never put up with some of the things many other dog owners think are just fine—such as jumping on anyone who walks in the door, barking excessively when someone comes up the driveway, or monopolizing the owner's bed at night. In my experience, these behaviors can escalate into worse problems if left unchecked and can send your dog confusing messages about who sets the agenda in the household. In addition, you are not doing your dog any favors by letting him live without limits—dogs, like most creatures, thrive on structure.

But ultimately it's your life, and your dog. Plenty of people—and plenty of dogs—live blissfully happy lives doing it their own way, and more power to them. I've handled cases in which the owner didn't want to follow my prescription and decided, "I just love my dog so much, I'm willing to live with the problem." Okay, that's fair. Owners like these looked at their options and then chose to stay with the status quo. I don't believe in judging other people or the way they raise their dogs—unless, of course, a person, society, or the dog itself is harmed in the process. I believe my job is to show people their options. It's up to them to decide what to do with those options.

For most of my clients, a dog that rolls over, plays dead, or "speaks" on cue is not at all what they're looking for in a canine companion. Most people don't want a guard dog, a protection dog, or the winner of the next Frisbee Dog Olympics. In truth, many dog owners only dream of a warm, loving, comfortable companion with whom to share their lives. In their minds, it's fine if the dog does his own thing at times, even having the run of the house, the yard, and the furniture, but they still want him to stay within a certain range of acceptable behaviors. Other dog owners are much more finicky. They absolutely do not want the dog on their $2,000 couch, ever, period, end of story. They don't want their dog to dig up their precious rose bed. They want their dog to be able to get right into his crate on cue, ready to travel with them anywhere. The bottom line is that, with the exception of a dog that's a danger or nuisance to others, what we want from a dog is a very personal thing.

We decided to do an informal survey in our Cesar's Way e-newsletter, asking readers about the most important behaviors they want or expect from their pet canines. Four thousand readers responded by rating a list of ideal behaviors as "very important" to "not important." Beginning on the next page is a list of the questions we asked, with the results. As you read the list, take the survey yourself and think about these questions: What are your expectations for your life with your dog? How do you define an "obedient dog"?

As you can see, the same basic answers come up again and again. If you use Hollywood trainer Mark Harden's definition, what people really want from their pet dog seems to be more *manners* than training.

When I worked at the dog training facility as a kennel boy, I remember that the big issue for everyone who came to the company was a dog that didn't "come when called." "My dog doesn't come when called" was absolutely the biggest complaint we heard, and our informal survey shows that it is still right up there at the top of our readers' wish list of behaviors they really want their dogs to exhibit. To get your dog to come when you call him, you've got to give him a reason to want to come to you. This begins with your bond, and it also involves understanding your dog's motivation. We'll go into the details of this in Chapter 7.

My point is this: when it comes down to it, most people's expectations for a well-behaved dog aren't really that outrageous. The top items on the list are not much to ask for, and I'm happy to tell you that these things are not that hard to achieve, once you've established a proper leadership role and a bonded connection of trust with your dog. It's my goal in this book to help you understand not only these basic foundations of creating a fulfilled and balanced dog, but also the wide range of options you have that will help you achieve all your other obedience goals as well. You don't have to go to formal

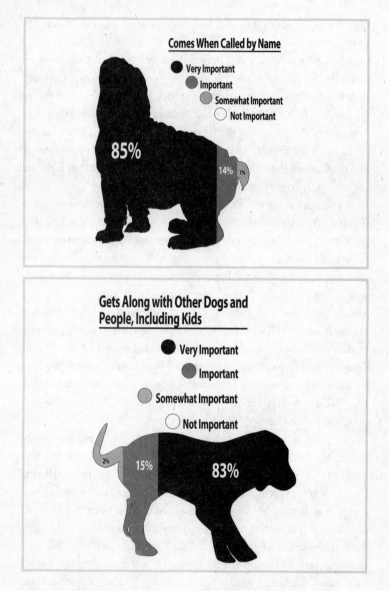

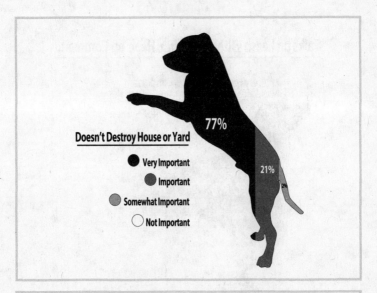

Doesn't Destroy House or Yard

- ● Very Important
- ● Important
- ● Somewhat Important
- ○ Not Important

77%

21%

Allows You to Come and Go Without Separation Anxiety

- ● Very Important
- ● Important
- ● Somewhat Important
- ○ Not Important

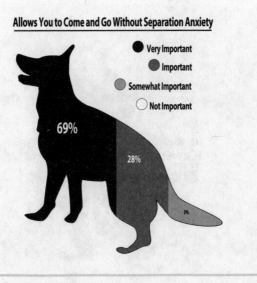

69%

28%

3%

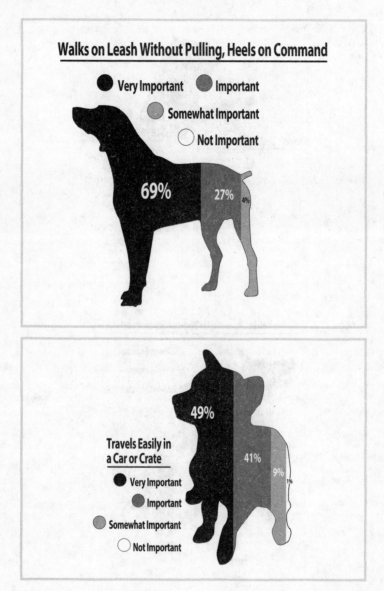

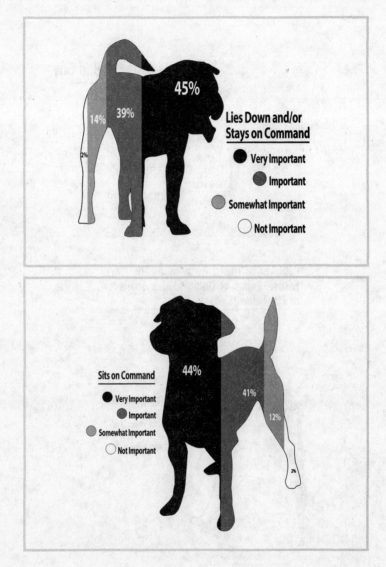

Lies Down and/or
Stays on Command

45%
39%
14%
2%

● Very Important
● Important
● Somewhat Important
○ Not Important

Sits on Command

● Very Important
● Important
● Somewhat Important
○ Not Important

44%
41%
12%
2%

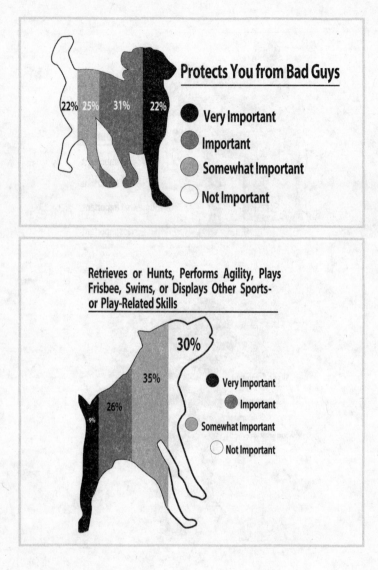

Protects You from Bad Guys

22% 25% 31% 22%

● Very Important

● Important

● Somewhat Important

○ Not Important

Retrieves or Hunts, Performs Agility, Plays Frisbee, Swims, or Displays Other Sports- or Play-Related Skills

30%

35%

26%

9%

● Very Important

● Important

● Somewhat Important

○ Not Important

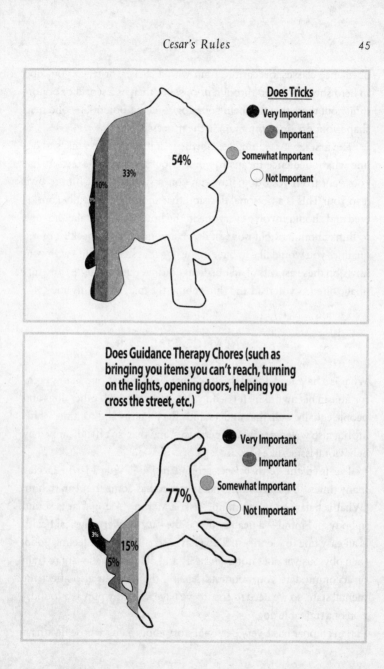

obedience classes, or learn to train with a clicker, or teach your dog to herd sheep or jump through hoops. But there is a world of opportunity out there that will help your dog reach his potential—and help shape your dream companion in the process.

The first key to gaining the obedient dog of your dreams is to define what obedience means to you. If you don't know exactly what you want from your dog, how can you possibly expect him to give it to you? This is a personal decision that should be carefully considered and should involve everyone in the household. So take the time to think about it. Right now, sit down and make up a checklist of the qualities you would like to have in the dog that shares its life with you. Envision these aspects of an obedient dog and refer to this list and this image often as you read and think about the material in this book.

BALANCE FIRST

What is a balanced dog? I think of a balanced dog as one that is comfortable in his own skin. It is a dog that gets along with other dogs and people equally well, that understands the patterns and routines of his life but also welcomes new experiences, and that isn't handicapped by behavioral issues like fear, anxiety, or obsession.

I've used the term *balance* around my colleague Martin Deeley many times, so I asked him what the word has come to mean to him. "What is balanced in my mind?" asked Martin. "A dog that is sound in body and mind—a healthy dog is the easy answer. Physical health is an easy one to identify. If a dog has any pain or is not feeling good, then obviously it does not train easily and may not even want to train or accommodate your requests. Health, though, can also affect the mental state, so we need to ensure we have a healthy pup as a foundation of a trainable dog."

Ian Dunbar has a very personal story about a dog whose health affected his ability to be trained. "I have a rottie-and-redbone-coonhound mix, Claude. He's getting pretty old now. And he blew out his cruciate. And so he had to have a TPLO [tibial plateau leveling osteotomy] operation. A tremendous operation. You go in and the dog walks out two days later. Within three days, his entire personality changed," Ian recalls. "He became a totally happy, silly dog. We realized we've been living with a dog for five years who was in extreme pain. And that's why he was slow to sit and slow to come and slow to lie down. After this operation, we had a totally different dog on our hands. So there may be very good reasons why the dog doesn't want to come or sit."

Then there's the mental/psychological side of balance. "What am I looking for in a mentally stable dog, or a 'balanced' mind?" Martin Deeley ponders. "Like in ourselves, stability in dogs comes from rules, structure, and stability in life. We know what is going to happen, we know what to expect, and we are confident in how it all occurs. Even new situations, new people, new dogs, and other animals are approached with confidence and acceptance."

If your dog is to achieve balance, he must be fulfilled as an animal first, then as a dog, then as whatever breed he happens to be, and then as your specific, individual dog with a particular name. You can read more in-depth explanations and instructions about how to create balance in your dog in some of my earlier books. Here I provide what I consider the basics for creating a balanced dog:

Cesar's Rules FOR A BALANCED DOG

1. When you bring a dog into your life, don't just think of what you want from him. Think first of what you need to give this dog to make him happy under your roof. Start by thinking of your dog as an animal, then as a dog, then as a breed, then

(continues)

as a name, and fulfill your dog's needs in that order. In my experience, once you've fulfilled these needs of your dog, he will automatically want to fulfill your needs in return.

2. Of course you want a dog to love, but love is not the first or only thing dogs need to be happy. Just as with most humans, love alone is not enough. Follow my three-part formula—(1) exercise, (2) discipline (rules, boundaries, and limitations—this includes training!), and (3) affection—in that order.

3. *Exercise:* Exercise means at least one—and preferably two—long walks every day of forty-five minutes or longer (thirty minutes minimum!), depending on your dog's breed, size, energy level, and age. Letting your dog run free in your backyard doesn't cut it. By *exercise* I mean a structured walk with you by his side. This fulfills your dog's need to work for food and water, in concert with his pack. It's also the single most powerful tool you have at your disposal for creating a deep, meaningful bond with your dog—and on top of that, it's free!

4. *Discipline:* Your dog's mother began teaching him rules, boundaries, and limitations from the second he took his first breath. Rules aren't something your dog resents—they are something he craves. Your job, as a dog owner, is to be clear and simple about these rules—and to always remain consistent about them! It's important for any balanced dog to know the parameters of his world and where he stands in his pack.

5. *Affection:* Affection doesn't necessarily mean petting, and it doesn't necessarily mean treats. First and foremost, it means the bond of trust and respect between human and dog. A person with no arms can have a bond of affection with her dog, even if she's unable to pet him. The beautiful thing about dogs is that when you show them honor and respect, they return the same to you a thousandfold. Dogs are perhaps the most generous and fair beings on the planet. Beyond

that, being affectionate with your dog in any form—sharing games, toys, adventures, treats, and, of course, massage and petting—is incredibly good and even therapeutic for you as well as your dog.

BALANCE ACCOMPLISHES MIRACLES

So, back to the original question: How did I get six pit bulls to perform onstage at the Emmys in front of thousands of people without formal training?

I believe that balance accomplishes miracles. I had made sure that the six pits I brought with me to the Shrine Auditorium that day—Daddy, Pepito, Spot, Pattern, Sam, and Dotty—were balanced, but in fact not all of them had begun life as a well-behaved pup. Sam was afraid of people and children when he first came to me, and Pattern had been dog-aggressive when I met him. Both dogs belonged to my friend Barry Josephson, a Hollywood film and television producer. Spot came to me from Much Love Animal Rescue because he was dog-aggressive. These dogs had lived with me and my pack for weeks and months, and because of the work I did with them, by the time we all went to the Emmys together I totally trusted all three of them to behave well in any completely new and challenging situation. I believe almost all dogs have the ability to change their negative behavior—under the right circumstances and in the hands of the right humans. But most important on Emmy night, all of the pits totally trusted me in return.

The changes I produced in these three troubled pits didn't come instantly or without consistent hard work over a period of time. Despite the quick turnarounds you see on *Dog Whisperer*, no change in behavior becomes permanent without regular practice and repetition. Even

the happy families with dogs that are cured at the end of each episode have to follow through with their own behavioral changes, every
single day, or their "transformed" dog won't remain transformed. At
the Dog Psychology Center, my staff and I had worked hard to fulfill
the lives and basic needs of all six Emmy pits on a daily basis, providing them with vigorous exercise; a set routine; clear boundaries and
limitations (discipline); plenty of challenges, such as obstacle courses,
ball-playing time, swimming, and other games; outings to new places
like the beach and the mountains . . . and of course, healthy food and
affection. In my experience, even dogs that have come from horrific
pasts filled with abuse and neglect can and do come back to balance
eagerly and willingly, whereas a human with the same kind of "baggage" might be forever haunted by bad memories. Dogs don't hang
on to resentments, so they can change and adapt much more readily
than humans. But it's up to the humans to do the work to make those
changes stick. That's why, to me, it's the owners who are the hard part
of the dog rehabilitation equation, not the dogs.

The six pits that came to the stage with me that day lived with me
daily and knew what I expected of them as well as exactly what they
could expect from me. Just as dogs living with each other in a pack
have a very basic set of rules of behavior, I too want very basic things
from the pack that lives with me.

My rules and conversations with the dogs in my pack are simple
and clear: my aim is to define for them the rules of life that are essential for their survival in a particular environment. And the basis of that
communication is always the same—trust and respect, from human
to dog, and from dog to human. It has to work both ways.

Christine Lochmann and Tina Madden, two of my assistants from
the Dog Psychology Center, came along with me for the afternoon rehearsal. When I went back home to change into my tux, they were
responsible for preparing the dogs for the evening's performance.

"All six pit bulls were what Cesar calls 'balanced,' or well behaved,

CESAR'S SIMPLE RULES
OF GOOD PACK BEHAVIOR

1. I'm the pack leader. Trust, respect, and follow me.
2. You don't have to figure out what to do when I'm around. Just wait for me to tell you what to do (including the many times I'll release you to "just relax and have fun!").
3. We always interact politely with other dogs and humans. We always avoid situations where there might be conflicts.
4. No fighting with each other.
5. I'm the one who starts and stops all play activity that we do together.

---

but only Daddy had any formal training. None of them were really trained in the 'sit,' 'stay,' 'come,' 'heel' kind of way," Tina recalls. "They weren't performing dogs. This would be their first time on a stage, with bright lights, in front of an audience of hundreds of people. It

Backstage at the Emmys

was [our] job to keep them relaxed and happy backstage so they'd be in the right state of mind to go onstage."

How do you prepare six pit bulls for their first command performance? First of all, we made sure that they had all their physical needs met—elimination, water, and exercise, though I asked Tina and Christine not to feed the dogs that day. Fasting until after the event would make them more motivated, and if I had to use food to inspire their performance, a hearty appetite would make them more likely to pay attention. Their dinner afterward would then become a celebration and a really big reward. In the morning we took a long run with them—longer than usual. And of course, we bathed and groomed them so they would be looking their very best for the cameras.

"At nighttime, after the rehearsal, Christine and I went downstairs and walked the dogs again," says Tina. "We were in makeup and dresses and were walking around in heels outside the Shrine Auditorium, with this pack of pit bulls in tow. After a good long walk, we went backstage and waited. Cesar would be in the audience, and we wouldn't be able to see him until, like, fifteen minutes before the actual presenting."

Whenever you bring your dog into a new and possibly intimidating situation, it's important that the dog understand as much as possible where he is and what is happening to him. We made sure not to just take the dogs from the van, stick them in a room, and then bring them onstage. We walked them from backstage to the room a couple times to get them familiar with the route. We also played a little bit of ball to keep their minds challenged and to get their energy up into what I call "a happy hype."

A balanced dog, in my book, is one that doesn't get carried away in a chaotic situation—as long as her pack leader or owner stays calm. Tina and Christine were great pack leaders backstage. They kept the greenroom tranquil, prevented overexcited humans from overstimulating the dogs, and let the dogs know at all times that they were safe and in good hands.

"The dogs weren't overexcited at all—they were relaxed and happy, thrilled to be in a new environment, and interested in everything that was going on around them," says Tina. "I must have had at least ten people come up and say, 'These dogs are so well behaved.' Somebody even wanted to adopt Spot after meeting him."

Finally, it came time for me to present the award for best stunt. Tina and Christine brought the dogs upstairs, and I met them backstage with my Rollerblades on. It was a very narrow area, and we were climbing over cables and squeezing past stagehands who were running by, doing their thing all around us.

When you bring a dog into an unfamiliar situation, introducing something he is already familiar with can ease the transition. Definitely, my trusty Rollerblades were something the six pit bulls were familiar with. The minute they saw them, they understood, "Okay, this is something fun. We're going into migration mode!" Since I had Rollerbladed with them through the busy, loud, distraction-filled streets of South Central so many times before, they were well prepared to Rollerblade calmly past most any other chaotic and noisy situation we might encounter. They also knew that when I stop, they stop—whether to cross the street or to let other people or dogs pass by. Seeing the Rollerblades, the pack collectively gave me a look like, "Okay, we get what you want us to do next!" And Rollerblading is something they absolutely love, so their energy was up, excited, and positive.

The energy around us before we went onstage, however, was tense and frenetic, and we couldn't totally prepare them for that. That atmosphere could have created an anxious response in them if that was all they were paying attention to. But because of my relationship with the pack, they took all their emotional cues from me. Since I felt safe and calm and made it clear that all the commotion hadn't changed my state of being, they were able to mirror my energy as they went through the same experience. This is the payoff of a strong leadership bond with your dogs. When the dog's reaction is, "Oh, this is new for me," he looks at you. If he sees that you're still calm and communicating clearly what it is you want from him, he thinks, "Okay, fine, I guess we're going to do the same thing we've been doing when a bus passes by, when somebody blows a car horn, or when somebody opens an umbrella."

The Emmys show presented new, unexpected, and potentially unsettling experiences, but the dogs had shared at least a thousand similar experiences with me before and everything had been okay—and even fun. So the Emmys became their new experience number one thousand and one. It was just another great adventure for all of us to share.

It was a long day for everyone. While I got to go home in the limo, Tina and Christine drove the pack of tired but contented pit bulls back to the Dog Psychology Center in their large rented van. "I remember as we were driving through the really rough neighborhoods in South Central Los Angeles," Christine says, "Tina just looks at me and starts smiling. She goes, 'Do you think we're safe here with six pit bulls in the back of the car?' We had a blast. It was a magical night."

I recounted this wonderful experience of ours for a reason: I want to make clear to you the amazing things you can accomplish with your dog through balance and a strong leadership relationship alone.

Cesar's Rules FOR BRINGING A DOG INTO A STRANGE NEW SITUATION

1. Don't throw any dog into a new situation without some prior preparation! Find creative ways to "rehearse" well in advance of the main event. Make sure your own demeanor is

calm and steady. The more times you've shown leadership in different environments, the more your dog will trust you even when she's unsure.

2. If it's a situation where you can prepare the dog in the actual environment itself, even better! Let the dog associate the new place with relaxation, fun, affection, and treats.

3. Bring along something familiar to your dog, something that represents calmness, comfort, or joy. For example, for the pit bulls the Rollerblades were a symbol of their very favorite activity.

4. Fulfill your dog's basic needs—on a regular basis of course, but especially on the special day. Extra exercise is always helpful—a tired dog with no pent-up energy is more likely to be relaxed rather than stressed in a new situation.

5. Finally, check your own energy. Are you yourself unsure in the new situation? Are you nervous or distracted? If you are, how can you expect your dog to stay calm? Deal with your own fear, or anxiety, or frustration, before you bring your dog into the picture.

TRAINED DOESN'T NECESSARILY MEAN BALANCED

At the Emmys, I was able to get amazing performances out of the pit bulls because they were balanced and we had a solid bond and clear, consistent communication between us. The dogs knew exactly what I wanted from them, and I knew what they wanted and needed from me. Isn't it amazing what is possible to achieve with six fulfilled dogs using just balance alone? Another person might bring six "trained" dogs up on the same stage. Those dogs might be able to sit, stay, roll

over, and jump through hoops. But what if there is an accident backstage, or someone on the crew panics? If the dogs are trained and not
balanced, you can still run into trouble.

The truth is that, as human beings living in an often stressful, competitive world, we all have known members of our own species who
are trained—or highly educated or credentialed—but definitely not
balanced. I believe the world is in a fight-or-flight avoidance state because we have very intelligent people ruling the world, but not necessarily the people with the best common sense or the people who
genuinely have the good of the rest of their human "pack" at heart. We
need more of those people in positions of power in order to return
our own world to balance.

The same thing applies to dogs. On *Dog Whisperer* and in some
private cases I've taken on, I've worked with dogs that are among the
most highly trained animals in America, yet because their needs as
animal-dog were not being fulfilled, they were unbalanced and therefore unreliable in one way or another. Some of them were frustrated

Cesar works with trained explosive-detection dogs
in Miami.

and aggressive, some were obsessed in some way, and others had developed fears and phobias.

VERY SPECIAL AGENT GAVIN

L. A. Bykowsky is a twenty-five-year veteran of the Bureau of Alcohol, Tobacco, Firearms and Explosives (ATF). In 2002 a new responsibility was added to her official duties—canine handler. A special dog was chosen for her—a gentle, calm, well-behaved yellow Labrador retriever named Gavin.

Together, L. A. and Gavin went through the ATF's Explosive Detection Canine Training Program. Gavin graduated with the ability to detect the scents of up to nineteen thousand different explosives. His protocol after being asked to search was to sit down whenever he detected a target scent. Gavin's new skill put him on the front lines of the war against terror.

Immediately after graduating, L. A. and Gavin embarked on their

L. A. Bykowsky and Gavin the ATF dog

new career adventure together. "I've actually spent more time with Gavin in the past five years than I have with my husband," L. A. told me. They worked several Super Bowls and NASCAR events before being sent on a mission in Iraq.

"In Iraq he never once shut down," L. A. said. "When loud noises went off, he quivered and shook, but then, so did I." Clearly, Gavin was stressed out by the experience, but he stuck to his training protocols and continued to work. However, immediately after he returned to the home he shared with L. A. and her husband, Cliff Abram, in coastal Pompano Beach, Florida, he faced the additional trauma of two back-to-back hurricanes. The trauma of the wind, rain, thunder, and lightning, followed by a Fourth of July celebration with exploding fireworks, finally pushed his frayed nerves over the edge. "He ran from room to room to room," Cliff remembers, "and couldn't stop shaking. He wouldn't even eat. After that, you couldn't pick him up and bring him into the house."

Once Gavin snapped, any noise at all—answering machines, phones, alarms, fire alarms—would turn him into a quivering lump of Jell-O. Suffering from what L. A. concedes was a canine form of post-traumatic stress disorder, Gavin was forced to retire from his five-year career of decorated service to his country.

"What I really want for Gavin is to be able to enjoy his retirement and to not be afraid all the time," L. A. told me when I went to visit her and Cliff in Florida.

Gavin was a highly *trained* dog, but his training hadn't prevented him from developing a very serious behavior issue, an issue that threatened not just his own well-being but that of his family as well. My sense from the moment I first met him was that this was a dog that hadn't been allowed to be himself—meaning, just an animal-dog first—for a very long time.

"The work he has been doing is not instinctual. It's not instinctual to sniff out explosives. It's instinctual to sniff out a duck. The explosives stuff is created by humans, for humans," I explained to the couple. "He has been Gavin, Labrador, ATF. Not animal, dog, breed, name."

Cliff nodded thoughtfully as I spoke. "When they finished the ATF course, they told us, 'He's not a pet anymore, he's a tool.' In all that time, you forget he's a dog."

It was my goal to help Gavin recover the essential "dog" in himself. I asked L. A. and Cliff if I could bring Gavin back to South Los Angeles with me.

At the Dog Psychology Center, Gavin was welcomed by the pack in our traditional quiet way—no touch, no talk, no eye contact. The pack approached him and sniffed him and instantly accepted him as one of them. When you watch dogs greet other dogs, you will see that much of their communicating is done in silence. The nose comes first, then the eyes, then the ears. They talk to one another through scent, then eye contact, then body language, and finally touch. Human training, on the other hand, is almost always ears first. That was the style of training used by the ATF to turn Gavin into a heroic working dog. On his first few days living with the pack, I'd rely mostly on the other dogs to help him relax into our routine. As I've seen hundreds of times, a pack of dogs can do more rehab in a few hours than I can do alone in a few days.

By the beginning of his second week with us, Gavin had relaxed visibly, and he and I had started to get to know and trust one another. We did fun, silly things like go on hikes, play catch, go for runs along the beach—things that would help Gavin remember the pure joy of just being a dog! Truth be told, I was already falling in love with the guy.

The *Dog Whisperer* crew went on the road to San Diego, and I decided to take Gavin along with us so that I could observe how he reacted in new situations. He did amazingly well. I even let him play the role of a calm-submissive dog in order to help some out-of-control dogs for the show. He and Daddy had already hit it off when we met Gavin in Florida, and they made a great team of *Dog Whisperer* canine assistants. I could see what a sweet, gentle soul Gavin possessed. He was calm and confident all day, and I didn't see any signs of the fearfulness that had brought him to rehab in the first place. I was beginning to think this might be a slam-dunk case.

I was wrong. When we returned to our hotel that evening, I brought Gavin with me into the elevator, and when the floor alerts started to beep, he descended into a fearful state again, lowering his head and putting his tail between his legs. He didn't run or try to hide, but he just sat down, in the same position he was trained to assume whenever he found explosives. Somehow his trained response had become his default response to stress. I knew I was going to have to figure out a new strategy to help him break through this fear.

Over the next thirty days or so, I continued to use the pack and playtime to build a trusting bond with Gavin, while gradually introducing new experiences and sounds to him. L. A. had told me that carrots were Gavin's favorite treat, so I'd toss a carrot to him at the same time as I'd expose him to a loud but unthreatening noise, like heavy footsteps or the crumpling of a paper bag. I increased the intensity of the sound very slowly as Gavin showed me that he wasn't going to shut down near it. In the early phases of the therapy, sometimes he would sit down, freeze, or avoid the noise. My response was to ignore him for a moment. Gradually, he stopped fleeing and instead came and stood by me. That was a big change, because he had been running away from L. A. and Cliff when he was nervous. "If you come stand by me, buddy, I can influence you with my calm energy," I whispered to him. It was gratifying to me that he was looking to me as a cue for how to behave.

The next level of challenge was to encourage Gavin to walk toward a loud sound, then to reward him when he reached it. I took advantage of his ATF training and hid treats in and around a boom box, commanding him to "search" for his rewards. The combination of his ingrained training and his love of treats worked to overcome his aversion to the speakers and the sounds coming out of them. Soon I was making feeding time itself a loud experience for him. I'd shake the food up and down in a metal bowl and call him over to the sound, then feed him. Associating mealtime with a loud noise also helped to quell his anxiety.

To make sure Gavin wasn't overexposed too soon, I didn't let any of these exercises go on for longer than five minutes. We'd do five minutes of stress exposure, then run and play in the pool for fun. Gavin caught on quickly that he'd get his favorite reward—playtime or pool time—after every completed exercise, so even the challenges became something he'd look forward to.

As the weeks passed, I continued to bring Gavin onto the set for a variety of different *Dog Whisperer* stories. I found him so appealing that I wanted to be around him all the time. I even brought him to my home, where he and I practiced tricks in the garage while my son Calvin, then eight, practiced on his earsplitting new drum set. Gavin never even flinched at Calvin's drumming—which was more than could be said for our neighbors!

Another feature of Gavin's rehabilitation was regular acupuncture treatment. Acupuncture stimulates endorphins—the brain's natural painkillers—and other feel-good neurotransmitters.[2] I've found acupuncture to be incredibly beneficial in my own life as a way to deal with stress and anxiety, and animals, it seems to me, respond to this ancient Chinese art even more readily than humans do. It's been especially helpful in cases of extreme fear, depression, or anxiety.

Play continued to be a major part of Gavin's return to serenity. On day forty-eight of his rehab, a couple of old friends from Gavin's ATF training school days, Todd the handler and ATF agent Corey, Todd's black Lab, came by the Dog Psychology Center to visit. Corey and Gavin remembered each other right away and went into a boisterous

Labrador celebration dance. Their reunion turned into an impromptu giant pool party for all the dogs at the center; taking center stage, Corey and Gavin would fly off the platform into the water and send tidal waves of splashes onto every human and animal in the vicinity. I had seen the playful side of Gavin many times before, but never anything as carefree and unbridled as he was with Corey that day. Once again, another dog had succeeded in moving Gavin's rehab forward, right when I was worried that it was beginning to stall. Corey and Todd's visit became another milestone in Gavin's forward progress.

I believe in relying on Mother Nature first and foremost when working with dogs—but there's no reason not to take advantage of modern technology when it can help! On day fifty, I finally introduced Gavin to the high-tech virtual-reality trailer that I had invented to take him to the next stage of his rehabilitation. I retrofitted an old Airstream with a video projector, surround sound, and a lighting grid, and I even set up jungle plants and a sprinkler system to simulate a rainstorm. With the help of three members of my *Dog Whisperer*

Gavin's pool party

"pack"—Murray Sumner, Todd Henderson, and Kevin Lublin—I designed three virtual-reality scenarios based specifically on the things that Gavin feared the most: a thunderstorm, a fireworks display, and a combat scenario.

Dogs can focus well on only one thing at a time, which is why I often use a treadmill to distract an anxious dog's mind and focus his physical energy. Most dogs come to love walking on the treadmill—some even become addicted to it! I started Gavin at a slow speed, two miles per hour, and tried him out with just a little rain and thunder. Focusing on the treadmill, he was doing just fine, so I added more rain and some light flashes to represent lightning. While we raised the volume and intensity of the storm, I commanded Gavin to search for treats in the plants that lined the trailer, and when he found them, I asked him to "speak." He remained happy, calm, and motivated throughout. Despite our success, however, I made sure the first session lasted only a few minutes. As a reward, we raced outside for a splash in the pool.

I was very proud of the whole concept of the virtual-reality trailer, and I hope to use it as a blueprint for other extremely fearful dogs. It's important to note, however, that I didn't rush Gavin right into facing the worst of his fears. We were almost two months into daily, intensive rehabilitation before I introduced him to this strategy. Before that, I focused on restoring his peace of mind by just letting him be a dog.

Over the next few days I exposed Gavin to both the fireworks and the combat scenarios in the trailer, rewarding him when he succeeded and finishing every short session with a vigorous play period. For his final challenge in the trailer, I had Tina Madden fire off a starter pistol. The first two times, Gavin tried to bolt off the treadmill. I slowed the treadmill speed while calmly redirecting him to keep going as if nothing had happened. The third time, he kept his eyes on me for reassurance but kept right on walking. That session got him the most joyful praise from me and the biggest reward and play break of them all. We were both so happy at his success.

Once I was certain that Gavin had mastered the virtual-reality trailer scenarios, I took him to the setting of his real final exam—an actual firing range. To give him an advantage, I brought along Chipper, a ridgeback/boxer mix, who was unfazed by any noise or commotion. I knew Chipper's calmness would rub off on Gavin. While the proprietor of the firing range shot his rifle, Gavin, Chipper, and I ran back and forth behind him. After he passed the first few minutes with flying colors, I ran Gavin over to a kiddie pool I had brought with me, so he could get a little of his favorite reward, the favorite thing of all Labradors—water. After a few more laps around the firing range, I was convinced that my good little soldier Gavin was ready to graduate from my boot camp.

Seventy days after Gavin arrived at the center, L. A. and Cliff arrived to bring him home. It took him a moment to figure out who they were, but once his scent memory kicked in, he was all over them, jumping with joy. I proudly showed Gavin's owners the virtual-reality trailer I'd made just for them. But what really knocked them out was seeing Gavin splashing ecstatically in the pool with his new friends from the pack. "We'd never seen him like this," L. A. said. I like to say that I don't favor one dog over another at the Dog Psychology Center, but Gavin had such an amazingly special way about him, it brought me to tears to say good-bye to him. I was content, however, because the transformation from Gavin the ATF agent to Gavin the happy-go-lucky Labrador was complete.

For Gavin, his training had actually worked against him when he came under the stress of battle, hurricanes, and fireworks, because he didn't know how to just be a dog. Even a dog as highly skilled as Gavin must have his animal-dog-breed–related needs fulfilled before he can be expected to perform his human-imposed duties.

VIPER THE CELL-PHONE DOG

Viper the cell-phone dog is another example of a well-trained dog that was severely unbalanced. Viper's behavior issues—extreme fear and lack of confidence—were preventing him not only from performing the functions he'd been trained for but also from having the close, loving bond that his owners very much wanted with him.

Most people don't know that cell phones are considered the number one most dangerous contraband to be found inside of maximum-security prisons. With a cell phone, an inmate can arrange a crime, put out hits on witnesses, arrange gang violence, and orchestrate drug trafficking both inside and outside prison walls. In 1995, decorated former Fullerton, California, police officer Harlen Lambert founded All-States K-9 Detection Agency, which in 2007 became the first facility in the nation dedicated to training dogs to detect the specific odor of cell phones. Harlen came out of retirement to oversee this incredibly specialized scent training. "That's my giveback to society," he says.

Viper and Harlen Lambert

Harlen's dogs are so highly trained that they can seek out and find the individual components of a cell phone, such as the battery and SIM-card, if an inmate has disassembled and hidden the parts of the phone in various locations. Inmates also try to foil the dogs by putting their cell phones inside food containers, the idea being to disguise the scent of the components with other strong smells, but the ASK-9 canines are not easily fooled. These tenacious dogs are trained to find cell phones inside mattresses, freezers, books, peanut butter, and garlic, and even underwater in a toilet tank.

Harlen has trained hundreds of dogs over the course of more than thirty years, but one dog has earned a very special place in his heart: Viper, a three-year-old Belgian malinois. "He's the smartest dog I have," says Harlen. "He can find a cell phone in a field of approximately one hundred yards. He will not stop until he finds the phone." The only rewards Viper seeks are a play toy and the joy and approval of his handler, Harlen.

The problem is that, for all his smarts, Viper is afraid of people and afraid of loud and sudden noises. Prisons are noisy, unpredictable environments. Viper can't use his stellar skills unless he's in totally controlled conditions. To demonstrate Viper's problem to my *Dog Whisperer* crew, Harlen had us wait outside a one-way glass window while Viper quickly and accurately found the phones hidden in a mock-up room. Alone with Harlen, his tail was up, and he was energetic, happy, and playful. Then one of the cameramen and segment producer Todd Henderson entered the room, and Viper became a completely different dog. His body posture shrank, his tail went behind his legs, and he completely shut down.

"We learned after we got him that he had spent the first eight months of his life in a crate," Harlen told me, shaking his head in disbelief that such a beautiful animal would be confined in such conditions. "So his skittishness isn't just a habit; it goes really deep."

Harlen is a tough, burly ex-cop, but the more we talked about

Viper, the more emotion I could see welling up in his eyes. "I hate to see him unhappy. If I ever have to pull on him or force him in any way, it upsets me more than I think it does him. He's so gentle. All he wants to do is please. This dog will never be for sale. Viper will never leave me."

I asked Harlen if Viper had ever had a chance just to be a dog. Harlen said he'd take Viper to a dog park, but he would always be by himself. "He needs to have a pack of dogs," I thought to myself. "He is so stressed out, completely rock-bottom. Viper really needs a vacation!"

After Harlen and his wife, Sharron, gave me permission to bring Viper back to the Santa Clarita Dog Psychology Center in California, I wanted to make sure I spent time with him before leading him out of the facility. But even after I'd sat quietly with him for several minutes while he calmed down and got used to my presence, he still froze up when I tried to gently lead him with a leash out from under the mock-up prison bunk on which I was sitting. So I did what I have done for many years when I get stuck on a case. I called in a Dog Whisperer with more wisdom than me.

Daddy.

Even at fifteen years of age, struggling with stiff bones and arthritis, Daddy performed like the total pro that he always was. As soon as Daddy arrived, Viper stuck his head out from under the bunk to sniff him, and a silent communication went on between them. It took only four and a half minutes for Daddy to lead a very willing Viper out of the room. Daddy became the link of trust between Viper and me. Once again, Daddy had my back.

"I don't believe what I just saw," said Sharron when she witnessed how instantly and enthusiastically Viper responded to Daddy. "It almost made me cry," said Harlen.

Viper was rock-bottom when I took him. Any dog that spends the first eight months of his life—the most important months developmentally—in a crate is going to have a lot to overcome in life. Viper had no self-esteem or confidence whatsoever. I needed to remove him from his environment and start fresh in a new place.

The first thing I did was bring him into the *Dog Whisperer* mobile home, where he was greeted by the pack. The presence of a group of laid-back, friendly, balanced dogs had an immediately relaxing effect on him. By the time we arrived back at the ranch, it was still daylight. I wanted him to just be able to express the dog inside him, so I let him run with the rest of the pack in the wide field I call the sheepherding area. By the time it was getting dark, his nose kicked in, and he finally came right to me, without a leash or any other type of coercion.

During the first week with me Viper became a member of the pack. Through the dogs in the pack—Viper's new family—I gradually earned his trust. He loved going on long runs through the hills and on hikes in the mountains.

While living with Harlen, Viper had become fearful of every tool there was—from a choke chain to an e-collar to a simple leash. Any of those items—and even just the presence of a stranger—would cause Viper to shut down immediately. Because a human was connected to all of these tools that Harlen had tried to use, and since we live in a world in which dogs must be controlled on-leash, I needed to transform these tools into a healthy experience for Viper. I had to wipe the slate clean and reintroduce him to them as if it were the first time he'd seen them.

I started with the basics: I needed him to be familiar with a simple leash so that I could take him off the property and give him the exposure to new scenarios that would be a major part of his rehab. Viper is a natural ball player, so once he became engaged in playing with the ball, it was easy for me to put the leash on his neck. Soon the leash had a positive association—ball time! In dog training, most people put the leash all the way at the base of the neck. If you've watched my show, you know that I like to place the leash all the way on the top, so it gives the dog less of an opportunity to control the situation by pulling. From that point on, Viper realized that if the leash was all the way on the top, he had to move forward. After that, he just relaxed because that's what he'd wanted to do from the beginning. It was just that nobody had known how to help him get over this fearful obstacle.

The following week, right in the middle of Viper's rehab, I had to fly to New York for some business meetings, book signings, and television interviews. I needed Junior and Angel for the television appearances, but I decided to take Viper with us as well. The trust he and I were building together was still fresh, and I didn't want a setback. And for a dog that was afraid of people and commotion, New York City would be an amazing challenge. But I'd already seen such progress in Viper that I wanted to raise the stakes in his rehabilitation. Angel and Junior already knew how to be comfortable in places like New York, so Viper would be able to follow their calm example. When I was busy with appearances, producer Todd Henderson kept the dogs busy. As close as I was getting to him, I also didn't want Viper to get so attached to me that he would see me as the only human who could help him.

Dog Whisperer *producer Todd Henderson with Viper in New York City*

Todd is a long-distance runner, so every day in New York City he took Viper and Junior running with him in Central Park. "One day I decided to march straight on down to Times Square, to actually walk the thirty-some blocks into the heart of midtown Manhattan, with all of the lights, all of the people. To have Viper continue to walk with me right into the heart of the beast and not be afraid—that was really exciting. That was the highlight of my trip."

I was still in New York on day sixteen of Viper's rehab, and I decided to use a tool I rarely use—a flexi-leash—to give him a little less structure. Because Viper had a tendency to get a bit clingy with the few humans he trusted, I wanted him to be able to resolve some of his anxiety issues on his own, rather than constantly relying on me to provide the solutions for him. He did amazingly well—through Central Park, all the way to the Museum of Natural History. There were joggers and bikers passing by us, Rollerbladers, strollers, and Viper's biggest fear, skateboarders, but he just kept moving forward. With every new adventure, I could see his confidence growing.

Once we were back in L.A., I continued to take Viper to new places—Venice Beach, Hollywood Boulevard, a photo session with lots of lights and commotion. I even brought him along on a few *Dog Whisperer* episodes.

Creating Good Vibrations

As Viper grew stronger and more confident, I decided to try to replay a scenario that had been very traumatic for Viper the first time I'd witnessed it.

When Harlen Lambert brought Viper out of his kennel that first time I met him, all the yanking and resistance was a very traumatic experience for both of them. Harlen was pulling and tugging, and Viper was pulling and tugging in the other direction, and eventually Viper just shut down. Harlen became distressed at having upset Viper, so the energy between them was tense and negative. The leash and the collar worked against the relationship and had damaged the trust between them.

Although Viper had already become accustomed to a leash, I didn't want to undo the work I had done with him by allowing him to associate the leash with the only reason he comes out of his kennel. I decided to use a vibrational e-collar to give guidance to Viper from a distance and enable him to believe he was making his own decisions and was not connected to a human with a leash.

It's important to note that an e-collar of any type is a short-term, not long-term, solution to a behavior problem. If you have to use it long-term, you're doing it wrong. Never use an e-collar in standard obedience training or to add a new behavior. And whenever you introduce any new tool, make sure your dog is comfortable just being around the tool before you use it to try to change his behavior. Viper had already been upset by the e-collar that Harlen used, so I took my time to create a positive association for him with just wearing the collar on a casual basis. Once he was comfortable having it put around his neck, I had him wear it as a matter of course for weeks before I ever pressed the button. He did all the activities that he was already familiar with, both with and without the e-collar, so he would get used to having the weight of it sometimes and not having the weight other times.

About twenty-eight days into his rehab, I determined that Viper was comfortable wearing the new tool. We had already done the hard work together to build a solid platform of trust. Only then did I set out to redo the scenario in which I invited him to come out of his kennel and join the *Dog Whisperer* crew—a pack of humans that now represented family and good times to him. In the past, when Viper was nervous, shy, or unsure in a situation, he wouldn't just go into flight state—he would turn his back to the wall or find a place to hide and completely shut down. Viper's reaction was in fact worse than a full-out flight reaction, because at least when an animal is fleeing it's taking a positive action, in forward motion. Viper's freezing up was the opposite of the behavior of a balanced dog, which, even if cautious, is always curious.

The reason I chose this tool for this particular situation was to separate Viper's experience of me—or any human—from his experience of a correction (such as the pulling of a leash) that told him not to run away from humans. It also allowed him to have the feeling of choice—that is, the freedom to come out of the kennel and the freedom to be with people. It's important to take note of when I did and didn't use the vibration. If I'd used the vibration when he started to run away, then he would have related the vibration to the person or object he was running away from. This was not what I wanted. Instead, I used the vibration when he stopped moving away and went into freeze mode, or when he got to the wall or fence or whatever place he was trying to hide in. That encouraged him to go away from the hiding situation and back toward the human or thing where he didn't have the vibration. The vibration became a simple communication— a yes or no, a way of saying "Getting colder" or "Getting warmer."

Because of Viper's severe lack of trust in people in the past, it was important to create a "circle of trust" for him among the crew members, who stood quietly and ignored Viper and let him figure out the vibration on his own. As Viper moved away from the vibration, gradually he realized that people were not trying to grab him or make him do anything. He was able to choose on his own to move away from the wall or hiding place where he felt the sensation and toward the humans who were not putting pressure on him to perform. We let Viper take his time and come to his own conclusions, which became, "It's a warm, comfortable place within the circle of humans, and not as comfortable a place when I run and hide away on my own."

When, nine minutes later, Viper finally came to me and joined us inside the *Dog Whisperer* circle, I rewarded him with praise and petting. Junior came to him and licked his face, giving his own form of reward and also saying, "You can relax, it's okay out here." This is one more good example of why I always use dogs to help other dogs. They can get the message of trust across much faster than we humans can. As you can see, the e-collar wasn't even the most important tool I used in this exercise with Viper. The most effective tools were the warm, patient, calm-assertive energies of the crew members and the support of Viper's canine friend Junior.

On day thirty-seven, I decided to give Viper his toughest challenge yet. I brought him to a busy skateboard park in Santa Clarita, one that my boys like to frequent. My goal was to desensitize him to the skateboard noises—not by telling him how to do it, but by letting him figure out that nothing bad would happen to him when he was around strange sounds. Once again, I used the flexi-leash to give him some room to solve his own problems and to keep him from using me as a crutch or a way to hide from the things he feared.

First I walked him all around the park. Whenever you are working with a dog, always introduce him to his environment before you introduce him to the challenge.

Viper, Cesar, and Calvin at the skate park

I wanted to free Viper from his fears by immersing him in the sounds and movements he used to be so afraid of. But once again, it's important to note that I didn't just start working with him and throw him into the skateboard park from day one. This was more than a month later, after we'd been through the chaos of New York, the hustle and bustle of Hollywood, and regular nightly practice at my home with a single skateboard, thanks to the participation of my son Calvin. This was more like a final exam for Viper.

As we got closer to the park, the noises got louder. Viper didn't shut down the way he used to, but I could see he was alert and nervous. To help him out, I brought him his human pack—my sons Calvin and Andre. He definitely relaxed in their presence. Whenever you are exposing a dog to something new, it's helpful to bring in people, dogs, or things that signify relaxation to him. Next, all four of us sat beside the skateboard rink and just watched the action for about five minutes.

I was proud of Viper—he was alert but not too anxious. After a few minutes, I brought him back out to the quiet green surrounding the park so he could have a break; then we returned to the concrete skateboarding rink once again. By the third time around the park, Viper was walking in front of me, relaxed, confident, tail high, despite the fact that the skateboard action was still going on all around us. It was a very successful day—a day when confidence and trust overpowered irrational fear.

On day fifty-five, we brought Viper home to Harlen and Sharron Lambert. Viper had come up from rock-bottom. He was still a slightly hesitant, cautious dog, but he had a new confidence and a much more measured way of responding to things that made him anxious. I brought the pack along with him in the van, for moral support.

When I arrived at Harlen's place and opened the tailgate, Viper immediately leapt out and tore around the corner of the ASK-9 office building, with his pack chasing after him. To a certain extent, he reverted to the flight state he had been in before when he was on the ASK-9 grounds. I called the pack back to me, and Viper followed them to us.

At first, Viper gravitated to producer Todd and location manager and dog handler Mercer from my crew, because they had represented safety to him for the past two months. Harlen was very upset. He felt that Viper didn't recognize him or care about him anymore. I told Harlen that Viper was used to being a certain way in his old environment and that we should give him time to adjust to the new situation. It was important that we all stay calm and put no pressure on him. When Viper turned away and went toward the places where he used to hide before he came to rehab, I used the vibration collar to remind him that the safest place was back with us. I instructed Todd and Mercer to ignore him. In this way, I was passing Harlen an invisible leash.

Twelve minutes after we arrived, Viper recognized Harlen—jumping on him, licking him, celebrating their bond of affection. Harlen was incredibly emotional. "I could feel the tears forming. 'Cause that's my boy. His whole demeanor has changed."

So how did Viper change from a totally fearful guy at rock-bottom into a cautious but affectionate and balanced dog? I believe Viper's insecurity had arisen from his stunted puppyhood experience, but unfortunately Harlen had tried to repair him using dog training instead of dog psychology. Anyone who knows how to train dogs to find cell phones is an exceptional dog handler, but what Harlen didn't know was how to rehabilitate a dog that was as far gone as Viper was. My rehabilitation wasn't based on tools, even though it was helpful to use them now and then along the way. It was based on the very foundation of the human-dog relationship—the foundation of trust.

The beautiful thing about Viper's rehab was the help that came from everybody in my *Dog Whisperer* family—from the producers to the crew to my kids to my trusty pack of dogs at the Dog Psychology Center. When I followed up with Harlen and Sharron three months

Viper and Harlen Lambert

later, Viper was doing much better. He was going everywhere with Harlen, including outings around town and trips to the busy grocery store, and he had become much warmer toward strangers too. Harlen told me that Viper even slept near his bed now.

The most remarkable change was that Viper had become much more balanced in his trained task. Before his rehab at the center, Viper would become nervous if anyone but Harlen was in the room with him. When the *Dog Whisperer* crew came back to tape him for a follow-up shoot, Viper was able to locate all eight hidden cell phones while the whole crew was right there in the room with him.

When a dog is at rock-bottom like Viper was and is able to come back and live a full and happy life, it makes me feel like there is hope in the world for all of us.

Cesar's Rules FOR HELPING A FEARFUL DOG REGAIN BALANCE

1. Take the time to build the dog's trust. When you first meet him, use no touch, no talk, and no eye contact. I often sit sideways with a dog, ignoring him, until he eventually gets curious and comes to me. You can't ever clock the process of building trust, especially with a fearful dog. It takes as long as it takes.

2. Don't feel sorry for the dog or pet him when he acts fearful. This only nurtures his fears. Instead, stay calm and assertive. Your own demeanor will tell the dog that he is in a secure situation. Once again, you may have to go through this process many times before you can influence a fearful dog with your own energy, but eventually you will.

3. A dog that is too fearful needs to learn the fun of being a dog before he needs formal "training." Use a backyard pool, a favorite toy, a game, his best doggie friends, or food rewards to distract the dog and help him enjoy himself, even around the thing that makes him fearful.

4. Don't invade the dog's space too soon. Let the dog come to you and offer himself for affection before you reach down into his personal space. To avoid intimidating him, pet the dog under his chin and face instead of on top of his head.

5. Gradually expose the dog to the things he fears. Start very small, in three- to five-minute intervals, then reward after the exposure with whatever it is that the dog loves best, be that food, the pool, or a Frisbee session. Reward every tiny success. Make sure your energy is calm and centered at all times. Work up to longer sessions and more difficult

(continues)

challenges once the dog has mastered the shorter lessons. To make the exposure more pleasant, pair it with something the dog likes, such as treats or a favorite toy.

6. If the dog can be around other dogs that are well behaved and balanced, nothing in the world beats the power of the pack. Another dog can influence a fearful dog much faster than we humans can.

In the next chapter, we discuss how you can prepare your dog for all types of learning so that he becomes the obedient companion of your dreams—while retaining the natural balance and "dog-ness" that Mother Nature intended him to have.

3

REWARDS, PUNISHMENT, AND EVERYTHING IN BETWEEN

Is There a "Right" Way to Train a Dog?

Cesar works with Paul Diaz and Junior.

I always work from my instincts—the gift I believe gives me my understanding of dogs in the first place—but I've also been able to add a lot of new tools to my tool kit. Dogs are my teachers, but in the past few years, in my travels around the world since I started my TV show in 2004, I've met some interesting human teachers as well, some of them the top names in their field. Among these animal and dog experts—veterinarians, trainers, academics who study animal behavior or learning theory—some have disagreed strongly with me, many have challenged me, but all have influenced my growth, as a man and as a dog professional. Some of them have generously contributed their experience and wisdom to this book, and I hope my own insights and experiences have helped a few of them as well.

THEORIES OF DOG TRAINING

There are dozens of theories and ideas about how to train dogs. One saying in the field is that if you ask any two trainers to agree on one thing, the only thing they'll find they have in common is the belief that a third trainer is doing it all wrong. In doing my research for this book, however, I haven't found this to be entirely true. Though there is plenty of disagreement and occasionally even ugly infighting, many of the best trainers are open to sharing information and ideas with one another. It's clear that these trainers are in it for the dogs, not their own egos. I would never criticize another professional because I like to remain open to what that person might have to teach me. And I like to think the best of people, because when I do I find that they often rise to meet my expectations.

Most trainers agree that dog training methods can be broken down in a few general ways. The first division is between techniques based on learning theories and techniques based on natural dog behavior. I am a very new student of learning theories, so my techniques are all pretty much based on hands-on experience and the dog behavior I've observed throughout my lifetime. Then there are the different "schools" of dog training, which some people break down simplistically into "traditional" (punishment-based), "positive" (rewards-based), and "balanced" (incorporating elements from both schools).

The truth is that things aren't quite so simple. A look at the history of dog training will show that techniques and styles of training haven't always evolved in a straight line.

SOME LANDMARKS IN THE
HISTORY OF DOG TRAINING

THE STONE AGE (CIRCA 8000 B.C.) Dogs live side by side with humans, helping in hunting and drafting and providing warmth. They begin to genetically evolve the ability to read human cues as they become domesticated. At the same time, human interdependence with dogs may be changing the course of human evolution. "For instance, a hunting dog that could smell prey reduced the need for humans to have an acute sense of smell for that purpose. Human groups that learned to train and work with dogs had a selective advantage against human groups that did not do so. So just as humans have exerted selective pressures in dog evolution, it seems highly likely that dogs have caused selective pressures in human evolution."[1]

CIRCA 3500–3000 B.C. Drawings of dogs with collars appear on the walls of pre-dynastic Egypt.

CIRCA 2600–2100 B.C. In the Egyptian Old Kingdom, murals, collars, and stelae let archaeologists in on the names of favorite dogs, such as Brave One, Reliable, Good Herdsman, North-Wind, Antelope, and even Useless. Other names come from the color of dogs, such as Blacky, while still other dogs are given numbers for names, such as "the Fifth."

CIRCA 350 B.C. Alexander the Great raises Peritas—either a mastiff or a greyhound-type dog—from puppyhood and takes him along as a companion on all his campaigns. When the king is ambushed by Persia's Darius III, Peritas allegedly leaps up and bites the lip of a charging elephant, saving Alexander's life and empire. Legend has it that Alexander was so devastated when Peritas died that he went on to erect numerous monuments to Peritas's bravery, even naming a city after him.[2]

CIRCA 127–116 B.C. Marcus Varro, a Roman farmer, records tips on training and raising puppies for herding. This and other written evidence indicate that even the Romans understood the value of early training.

55 B.C. Roman armies conquer Europe accompanied by their "Drovers' Dogs," probably ancestors of the modern mastiff and rottweiler. These dogs perform guarding and herding duties for the military and their camp followers.

CIRCA A.D. 700 Ancient Chinese dog breeders and trainers enjoy great status and respect, owing to the advances they have made in the miniaturization of dogs and development of the early toy breeds. Chinese toys, originally bred merely to be companions and foot-warmers, are kept inside the palaces, and their ownership is restricted to members of the royal family.

THE 1500S From royalty on down through the classes, the popularity of dogs as companions, not just hunters and herders, begins to take off across Europe. Dogs perform functions as varied as going into battle with full suits of armor to walking on a primitive treadmill to turn a spit for cooking.

THE 1700S Truffle hunters learn to give their dogs bread as reinforcement when they locate truffles. This technique turns out to be cheaper than using pigs, which cannot be stopped from eating all the truffles they locate.

1788 The first training facility for Seeing Eye dogs is established at the Quinze-Vingts hospital for the blind in Paris, France.

1865 British general W. N. Hutchinson publishes *Dog Breaking: The Most Expeditious, Certain and Easy Method, Whether Great Excellence or Only Mediocrity Be Required,* dealing primarily with the training of hunting dogs such as pointers and setters. Despite the title, the author advocates an early form of positive training: "[The] brutal usage of a fine high couraged dog [by] Men who had a strong arm and a hard heart to punish—but no temper and no head to instruct [has] made my blood boil." Hutchinson adds, "It is hard to imagine what it would be impossible to teach a dog, did the attainment of the required accomplishment sufficiently recompense the instructor's trouble."[3]

1868 Sir Dudley Majorbanks, First Baron Tweedmouth of Scotland, sets out to create the "ultimate hunting dog"—a companion and retriever. He begins a breeding line that will produce America's best-loved dog—the golden retriever.

1882 S. P. Hammond, a writer for *Forest and Stream* magazine, advocates in his columns and in a book entitled *Practical Training* that dogs be praised and rewarded with meat when they do something right.

1880s Montague Stevens, a famous bear hunter and friend of Theodore Roosevelt and the sculptor Frederic Remington, trains his New Mexico bear dogs by rewarding them with pieces of bread instead of beating and kicking them, as others of this era are generally doing.

1899 The first canine school for police dogs is started in Ghent, Belgium, using Belgian shepherds, which have recently been established as a breed.

1901 The Germans begin Schutzhund work, a competition devoted to obedience, protection, tracking, and attack work.

1903 Ivan Pavlov publishes the results of his experiments with dogs and digestion, noting that animals can be trained to have a physical, eating-related response to various nonfood stimuli. Pavlov calls this learning process "conditioning." In 1904 he will be awarded the Nobel Prize for his research.

1907 Police begin patrolling New York City and South Orange, New Jersey, with Belgian shepherds and Irish wolfhounds.

1910 In Germany, Colonel Konrad Most publishes *Dog Training: A Manual* and thus by default becomes the father of "traditional" dog training. Relying heavily on leash corrections and punishment, Most's methods will still be used in many police and military training settings one hundred years later. Ironically, Most's theories are based on the same operant conditioning principles that will later create clicker training.

1911 Edward Thorndike writes a book discussing his "law of effect" theory of learning based on stimulus and response. Thorndike shows that "practice makes perfect" and that animals, if reinforced with positive rewards, can learn quickly. His studies on rewards and consequences will influence Harvard's B. F. Skinner in his development of behaviorism.[4]

1915 Baltimore police begin using Airedales from England to patrol the streets. The use of Airedales will be suspended in 1917 after the dogs prove unhelpful in making arrests. The police will fail to notice, however, that no robberies occur where the dogs are on patrol.

• Englishman Edwin Richardson wants to revive the Greek and Roman generals' practice of using dogs in wartime. Apparently a very spiritual man—Richardson describes the "soul" of a dog and its "sixth sense" when someone it loves is dying—he has trained dogs, mostly collies, Airedales, and retrievers, for the military during World War I. His methods incorporate games and some other forms of positive re-inforcement, and the dogs prove to be quick studies. Many dogs are used during the war for communication and for guard duty.

1917 The Germans begin to use dogs to guide soldiers who have been blinded in mustard gas attacks. The French soon follow suit.

1918 U.S. Army corporal Lee Duncan finds an abandoned war dog station in Lorraine, France, with five puppies in a kennel. Duncan takes one of the pups and names him Rin Tin Tin after the finger dolls that French children give to the soldiers. The dog travels to California, proves easily trainable, and is soon employed making movies so suc-cessful that the Warner Brothers studio is saved from bankruptcy. The dog will die in 1932 in the arms of his neighbor Jean Harlow and will be buried in Paris. His descendants will work in the movies through-out the 1950s, inspiring many people to try to train their own dogs to do simple tricks.

1925 One of the very first German-trained guide dogs for the blind is given to Helen Keller.

1929 Dorothy Harrison Eustis establishes the American Seeing Eye Foundation to train guide dogs for the blind.

1930 About four hundred dogs are employed as actors in Holly-wood, the majority of them mongrel terriers, which have proven to be small enough for indoor scenes, rugged enough for outdoor scenes, and exceedingly smart.

1933 The American Kennel Club obedience competitions are de-signed by Helen Whitehouse Walker, who wants to prove that her standard poodles are more than just pretty faces.

1938 Harvard's B. F. Skinner publishes *The Behavior of Organisms,* based on his research into operant conditioning as a scientifically based learning model for animals and humans. His special focus is on teaching pigeons and rats.

1940 The Motion Picture Association of America (under the Hays Office Production Code) gives the American Humane Association the legal right to oversee the treatment of animals in films, motivated by public outrage over the 1939 movie *Jesse James,* in which a horse is ridden off a cliff to its death.

1942 The U.S. military says it needs 125,000 dogs for the war and asks people to donate their large breeds. The military manages to train only 19,000 dogs between 1942 and 1945. The Germans reportedly have 200,000 dogs in service.

1943 Marian Breland and her husband, Keller Breland, form a company called Animal Behavior Enterprises (ABE) to teach animals for shows. The Brelands have been students of B. F. Skinner and have begun teaching animals to perform tricks for shows and for commercial clients, such as the dog-food maker General Mills. They will pioneer the use of a "clicker" to teach animals at a distance and to improve timing for affirmations and delayed rewards. The Brelands will also be the first people in the world to train dolphins and birds using Skinner's principles of applied operant conditioning.

• The movie *Lassie Comes Home* is filmed. It features a purebred male collie playing the female starring role. The dogs are trained by Rudd Weatherwax and his son Robert, soon to become Hollywood's first "celebrity" trainers.

1946 William R. Koehler becomes the chief animal trainer for Walt Disney Studios, where he will remain for more than twenty-one years.

A former U.S. Army K-9 Corps instructor, Koehler has published a top-selling series of training guides, developed effective programs to train receptive dogs, and devised ways to correct problem animals that would have otherwise been destroyed. He will popularize the use of choke chains, throw chains, long lines, and light lines. Though Koehler's correction-based methods would later be frequently criticized as unnecessarily harsh and forceful, his methods would become the mainstay of dog training from the 1950s to the 1970s.

1947 The Brelands begin using chickens as training models because they are cheap, they are readily available, and "you can't choke a chicken" (or you'll just teach it to run away).

1953 Austrian scientist Konrad Lorenz publishes *Man Meets Dog* and *King Solomon's Ring*, books that popularize animal behaviorism.

1954 Blanche Saunders, author of *The Complete Book of Dog Obedience*, travels the country to spread the gospel of pet obedience training. She believes that food should not be used as a primary reinforcer (or "bribe," as she calls it) and advocates praise and head pats as better ways to communicate a job well done.

1956 Baltimore reestablishes its police dog program, which remains the oldest police K-9 program in the country to the present day.

LATE 1950S TO 1960S Frank Inn, an assistant to Rudd Weatherwax in training the original Lassie, goes out on his own and adopts a shelter mutt named Higgins. While wheelchair-bound from an injury, Inn must train Higgins using only his voice, treats, and positive reinforcement. Higgins will soon be cast as the world-famous Benji.

1960S Marian and Keller Breland are hired by the U.S. Navy and meet Bob Bailey, the Navy's first director of training for its Marine

Mammal Program. They will begin a partnership with him, and after Keller Breland dies in 1965, Marian and Bob Bailey will be married in 1976.

1962 William Koehler publishes *The Koehler Method of Dog Training*, which will become a staple of AKC obedience competitors and the most popular dog training book in history. Koehler's techniques include the liberal use of praise for good behavior and the important concept of "proofing" a dog—making training effective by ensuring that it takes place in all sorts of different places and under different conditions. He and his son, Dick Koehler, will use their methods to save many last-chance dogs from being euthanized. Despite Koehler's controversial reputation among modern-day trainers, some of his techniques remain the core of many effective dog training systems still in use.[5]

1965 Dr. John Paul Scott and Dr. John Fuller publish *Genetics and the Social Behavior of the Dog*, which some still consider the definitive study of dog behavior. Among many other things, the book identifies the critical periods in the social and learning development of puppies.

1966 The U.S. Supreme Court dissolves the Motion Picture Association's Hays Office Production Code on First Amendment grounds. A side effect will be the American Humane Association's loss of the legal right to monitor animal action on movie sets.

1970S The U.S. Customs Service begins to use dogs to detect drugs; dogs will soon also be employed to sniff out explosives and fire-starting chemicals.

1975 American veterinarian (and hunting dog breeder) Leon F. Whitney publishes *Dog Psychology: The Basis of Dog Training*. It integrates research from Scott and Fuller and other data to posit that understanding how dogs see the world is integral to their successful training. (Whitney will later die a controversial figure for his involvement in the modern eugenics movement.)

1978 Barbara Woodhouse publishes *No Bad Dogs,* one of the first wildly popular books on basic dog training. It relies heavily on the walk and the proper use of a choke chain. Woodhouse says that most "bad dogs" have inexperienced owners who are not training their dogs properly by being consistent, firm, and clear. This book and her British television show will make her the first international celebrity dog trainer.

• The Monks of New Skete, elite breeders and trainers of German shepherd dogs in Cambridge, New York, publish *How to Be Your Dog's Best Friend: A Training Manual for Dog Owners,* which sells more than 500,000 copies. They advocate the philosophy that "understanding is the key to communication and compassion with your dog, whether it is a new puppy or an old companion," and employ a method that combines "traditional" training with positive reinforcement techniques. In later years, the compassionate monks will be dismissed as too harsh by some critics.

1980 The intentional explosion of a horse on the set of the movie *Heaven's Gate* enrages a group of crew members and actors. They successfully demand that the Screen Actors Guild include in their contracts with producers a provision to protect animal actors and to reinstate the American Humane Association's legal right to oversee the treatment of animals on movie sets.

1980s Veterinarian and animal behaviorist Ian Dunbar is dismayed to discover that most trainers won't work with puppies until they are six months old, long after their most teachable development period has passed. He pioneers off-leash training for puppies and begins writing books and giving seminars on the advantages of off-leash, reward-based training, not just for pros but for the average pet owner as well.

1984 The U.S. Department of Agriculture begins to use beagles to patrol airports for contraband food and other perishable items.

1985 Dolphin trainer Karen Pryor publishes *Don't Shoot the Dog! The New Art of Teaching and Training*, which focuses on timing, positive reinforcements, and shaping behavior. Building on her successful work with marine mammals, she reintroduces the concept of distance training—through whistles and clickers—as an advancement of the Brelands' (see 1943 and 1960s) earlier efforts.

1987 Phoenix-based trainer and behaviorist Gary Wilkes combines Pavlovian conditioning and operant conditioning with a deep knowledge of instinctive dog behavior, gleaned from years working in shelters with tens of thousands of dogs. The result is Click and Treat Training—the first fusion of reinforcement and punishment in the context of instinctive dog behavior designed for pet owners.

1990 Veterinarian Bruce Fogle publishes *The Dog's Mind: Understanding Your Dog's Behavior*, which stresses understanding a dog's biology and psychology in order to communicate well with him.

1992 Gary Wilkes and Karen Pryor team up to teach behavior analysts and dog trainers what will soon be dubbed "clicker training" by an anonymous trainer on the Internet. Rather than a revision of former methods, clicker training includes extensive use of targeting for practical dog applications, such as heeling, directed movements, and object identification/scent detection. This original "clicker training" method also included some aversive control.

2001 Within hours of the September 11 attack at New York's World Trade Center, specially trained rescue dogs are on the scene, including German shepherds, Labs, and even a few little dachshunds. Tragically, they make no live finds.

2000S AND BEYOND A slew of cable television shows feature various dog training and rehabilitation methods. The notion that there are "new" and "old" dog training methods obscures the fact that *all* dog training methods involve some form of operant conditioning, which is in fact pretty old stuff (as old as dogs).[6]

In researching this book, my co-author and I are grateful to have had help from several different trainers from divergent backgrounds. Surprisingly, we didn't find as many working professionals who were religiously loyal to one camp or another as we did people who told us they preferred not to be categorized. Instead, they liked to draw from the best and most effective elements of every method available, as well as create original solutions of their own.

Kirk Turner, a professional dog behaviorist who is now a trainer for the Pine Street Foundation cancer-sniffing dogs project, has evolved his own method of working over the span of a twenty-year career. "Because I have the background in pretty much all the different kinds of training, I can make stuff up as I go along. I feel that each dog is different. On my business card, it says that I have a *balanced approach*. I don't like to use the word *only*. And I don't like to use the word *never*. And I don't like to use the word *always*."

Barbara De Groodt owns From the Heart Animal Behavior

Counseling and Dog Training in Salinas, California, and considers
herself a positive behavior-based trainer. "All these methods have
a place. Positive has just gotten to the place where everybody says,
'Oh, if you're a positive trainer, you're a cookie pusher.' No, it doesn't
mean that; it can be praise, playing ball, going for a walk. Any life
reward can be used by a positive trainer."

Bonnie Brown-Cali has trained dogs since 1989. She volunteered
for CARDA (California Rescue Dogs Association), sheriffs' depart-
ments, and the Office of Emergency Service in California training and
deploying dogs in urban and wilderness searches for missing persons
as well as for human remains. She is an independent contractor for
Paws With a Cause, training dogs for people with disabilities, and for
Working Dogs for Conservation, which trains dogs to look for exotic
or endangered species. She does all of this plus her "bread and butter"
job as an obedience trainer.

With such a wide spectrum of experience, Bonnie is a member
of both the IACP—which advocates balanced methods that include
leash corrections—and the APDT, which supports positive, rewards-
based training methods. "I like to be a member of various organizations to keep my mind open. But my philosophy always stays the
same: bring out the best in a dog by using the training techniques that
are appropriate to the dog's temperament and the ultimate training
goals." She prefers clickers and other reward-based operant conditioning methods to train her service dogs, but she warns against relying on this method for an antisocial dog.

WHAT ARE CESAR'S METHODS?

My co-author tells me that on occasion someone will say to her, "I
don't approve of Cesar's training methods." When she tells the person that what I'm doing isn't dog training but dog rehabilitation, he

or she often grudgingly admits to having watched only one or two episodes of the show or a one-minute clip on YouTube and typically has not read any of my books or seen my videos. When my co-author asks, "What do you think his methods are?" the answer invariably is something like, "Oh, all the choke chains and the e-collars and the alpha rolls."

Well, any regular viewer of *Dog Whisperer* knows that these tools don't fairly represent what such a critic would call "my methods." Curious about this, our producers did a show-by-show breakdown, watching hundreds of hours of television and counting when a particular technique was used in any given episode. At the time the breakdown was done, we'd filmed 140 shows, covering over 317 separate cases of problem dog behavior.

Here are the results:

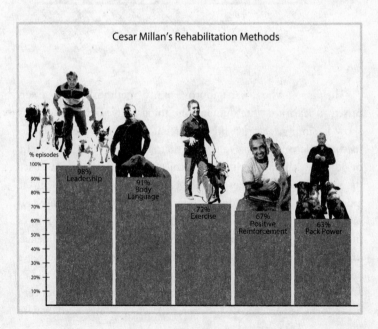

Cesar Millan's Rehabilitation Methods

% episodes

98% Leadership

91% Body Language

72% Exercise

67% Positive Reinforcement

63% Pack Power

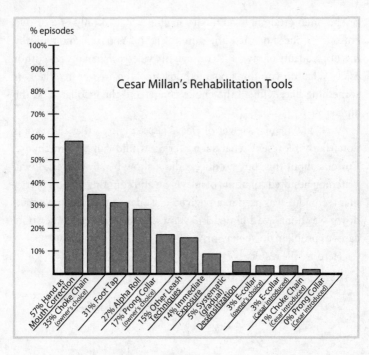

% episodes

Cesar Millan's Rehabilitation Tools

- 57% Hand as Mouth Correction
- 35% Choke Chain (owner's choice)
- 31% Foot Tap
- 27% Alpha Roll
- 17% Prong Collar (owner's choice)
- 15% Other Leash Techniques
- 14% Immediate Exposure
- 5% Systematic (gradual) Desensitization
- 3% E-collar (owner's choice)
- 3% E-collar (Cesar introduced)
- 1% Choke Chain (Cesar introduced)
- 0% Prong Collar (Cesar introduced)

The person who doesn't approve of my "methods" might be surprised to learn that the number one thing I advocate nearly every show is simply *leadership* (in 98 percent of the episodes), which I teach as the calm-assertive energy that any leader, teacher, parent, or other positive authority figure projects to her followers. I've used the word *dominance* to describe the energy of leadership, but in the animal world *dominance* doesn't mean "brutality," and *assertive* certainly doesn't mean "aggressive." I believe that good leadership never involves bullying or intimidating; instead, it depends on confidence, knowing what you want, and sending clear, consistent messages about what you want.

The number two method I advocate, according to the producers' breakdown, is *body language* (91 percent), which is a primary way in which leadership is projected in most animal species. My third top "method" is *exercise*—walk your dog properly at least twice a day (72 percent). And what is the fourth most common "method" I've used on *Dog Whisperer* episodes?

This one may shock a few people. I used *positive reinforcement* in one form or another 67 percent of the time in the first 140 shows. As Barbara De Groodt reminds us, positive reinforcement doesn't have to mean cookies. It can mean anything that a dog likes and that becomes a motivator or reward for the dog.

Personally, I don't think I have a specific "method" or "system" that I apply in order to change or improve a dog's behavior. For me, there is no magic formula. I believe in trusting my instincts and in treating each dog as an individual. Most important, I base my philosophy on this core principle—in order for a dog to be your best friend, you must first be his. If you want an obedient and well-behaved dog, you must fulfill that dog's needs before asking him to fulfill your own.

Cesar's Rules FOR BASIC FULFILLMENT

1. Let your dog be a dog. Think of him as an animal, a dog, a breed, and a name, in that order, and fulfill his needs accordingly.
2. Fulfill your dog using my three-part formula: give him exercise, discipline (rules, boundaries, and limitations), and then affection—in that order.
3. Know what your particular dog needs. A very high-energy Jack Russell terrier has different needs from a low-energy English bulldog or a medium-energy German shepherd. I classify dogs as low-energy, medium-energy, high-energy, and very high-energy, and I've observed that most problems

(continues)

between owners and dogs can be traced to a human picking
a dog that does not match her energy level.

4. Project clear and consistent leadership using energy that is
   calm-assertive—which is another way of saying "relaxed
   and confident."

5. Base your relationship with your dog on two core principles:
   trust and respect. You must have both, and they have to go
   both ways: you trust and respect your dog, and your dog
   trusts and respects you.

6. Always remember that your dog is a mirror of your own emotional state. If you are tense, anxious, or stressed, your dog
   is likely to reflect those emotions right back at you.

One of the things I learned from my grandfather is to always work
with Mother Nature and never against her. The truth is that all behavior modification—and by definition all training techniques—orig-
inated in one way or another with how animals learn to survive in
nature.

OPERANT CONDITIONING: REWARD AND PUNISHMENT

"An animal is an animal is an animal," says Bob Bailey. You'll recognize Bob's name from the short history of dog training presented
earlier because he is truly one of the pioneers. A very youthful seventy-
something gentleman, Bob still jets all over the world teaching both
individuals and governments the most effective ways to work with
animals, and he has trained everything from slugs to raccoons to killer
whales. Because of his more than sixty years of hands-on experience
with animals, as well as his extensive scientific background and train-

ing, my co-author approached Bob for an interview for this book. Though he did not know me personally and had heard decidedly mixed reviews about my show and my work, he graciously agreed to play the role of neutral teacher and historian when it came to explaining some of the history and science of operant conditioning. Bob Bailey is a genuine class act as well as a man who is truly passionate about and committed to the subject of his life's work—animals.

"When I say an animal is an animal, now, that doesn't mean that I don't recognize evolutionary situations. Yes, a slug is really very different from a killer whale. But nature has been working on these animals for two billion years. And it really hasn't treated the slug any differently than it treated the killer whale. It's totally neutral on this. And the evolutionary process has been the same on all of them, and reinforcement, by and large, generally works the same for all of them, as does punishment. Animals tend to avoid things that are punishing and to go towards things that are not punishing or that they find favorable."

When I first came to the United States, or even when I started working with dogs, I had no idea what the term *operant conditioning* meant. To my inexperienced ears, it sounded like something that had to be very complicated and intimidating, something you had to have a PhD to understand. Imagine my surprise when I learned that, when you boil it down, operant conditioning—a term coined by psychologist B. F. Skinner in the mid-1930s—is the science of learning from consequences. This is something animals themselves have been doing without our help since the dawn of time! Animals will do things that produce good consequences, and they will stop doing things that produce bad consequences. Many of you will recognize the "Skinner Box" from your high school or college basic biology courses. B. F. Skinner invented a laboratory-based mechanical-training machine that rewarded animals with food when they pressed levers or pecked at a lighted key. This was how Skinner used the scientific method to analyze and quantify exactly the way a rewards-based training system works.

Operant conditioning is such a key principle of animal behavior that it is a mainstay of human psychology as well. I asked my friend Dr. Alice Clearman Fusco, a psychologist and college professor, to break the concept down for me the way she would for one of her first-year students. "In a nutshell, with operant conditioning the dog is 'operating' in the world—he's doing something—and there is a consequence," Alice explained. "On the other hand, there is classical conditioning, which occurs when the dog isn't doing anything and an event occurs in his environment that causes him to make a connection between things."

We've all heard about "Pavlov's dog." What Pavlov did was ring a bell and put meat powder in a dog's mouth. The dog soon associated the bell with food. Very soon the dog would salivate when he heard the bell—not normal behavior. That's classical conditioning at work. Many of the dogs on my show who have developed what seem to be irrational fears or phobias have actually been classically conditioned to have that fear. For instance, the ATF agent Gavin had been classically conditioned to his fear of loud noises. Gavin wasn't thinking about the past, and he certainly wasn't rationalizing; he just knew that a loud noise was a really bad, dangerous experience and his safest response was to shut down. I would describe Gavin as having a canine form of post-traumatic stress disorder that first began when he was around fireworks and thunder on the Fourth of July. Humans can develop the same condition in a similar way. "Most of the research I've seen on PTSD regarding conditioning has mentioned classical conditioning as a current theory," says Dr. Clearman.[7]

In operant conditioning, while an animal is doing something—engaging in a behavior—something good or bad happens. This gives the lesson that the behavior is desired or not desired. I have spent my life watching dogs interact with one another and with their environments. Operant conditioning is the way nature's own classroom works. If a dog pokes his nose at a porcupine, he is operantly conditioned (punished) by the quills. If he turns over a trash can and finds a half-eaten cheeseburger, he is operantly conditioned (rewarded) by the food.

Many people don't realize how easy it is to unintentionally use operant conditioning in their daily lives—and to end up with a dog doing the exact opposite of what they want it to do. "I always tell my clients, whether you intentionally or unintentionally do it, you are always reinforcing particular behaviors," says Barbara De Groodt. "Even if it's behavior you don't like, it's probably because you have unintentionally reinforced it. The classic example is the dog running to the door barking and the owner running behind it yelling, 'Shut up, shut up, shut up!' The dog sees it as the whole pack running to the door barking and thinks, 'Oh, this is great!'"

With operant conditioning, there is positive and negative punishment and positive and negative reinforcement. Punishment reduces behaviors and reinforcement increases them.

Note that the terms *positive* and *negative* are only about adding or subtracting. They have nothing to do with something being nice or not nice.

"I'm not a positive-*only* trainer," Kirk Turner told me. Kirk uses the "clicker method" in training and obedience classes. The clicker method, which will be covered in depth later in the chapter, is often touted as being a positive-only training method. "I believe in relationships, and relationships are not always positive," he said. "You can try." Kirk likes to let the consequences come from the environment so they are not associated with a human and seem natural. "I've been with wild animals in Africa and they certainly provide consequences, and those aren't so pretty sometimes."

Kirk's training philosophy tends to lean toward reward versus punishment whenever possible, which is one reason he finds the clicker to be a useful tool. His metaphor of a relationship comes into play here. "Relationships with humans and dogs are emotionally based," he told me. "When I'm using operant conditioning I remove all my emotions except for when the dog offers the behavior that I'm looking for." So Kirk has turned the "consequence" by which the dog learns into a reward by not reacting to the dog. "When the behavior has happened and I can mark that thought then I will use that emotional attachment to let the dog know that's what I'm looking for. It's part of the reward."

Here's a table that those who study animal behavior often refer to as the "quadrant" of +P/–P or +R/–R.

	Punishment	Reinforcement
Positive	ADDING something not desired or wanted. Quills are "added" to the dog's nose when he sniffs too closely at a porcupine.	ADDING something desired or wanted. Treats, massage, praise, play, throwing a ball for a dog to chase—all of this is positive reinforcement.
Negative	SUBTRACTING something desired or wanted. If a dog is food-aggressive, claiming the food as yours is negative punishment.	SUBTRACTING something not desired or wanted. The dog comes to you and you pull the quills out—taking the pain away.[8]

It's important to know these definitions when we are talking about reinforcement and punishment. Sometimes I am criticized for using punishment when I rehabilitate a dog, but in nature, punishment is a part of everyday life. That is one of the reasons I tend to use the term *correction*—because I learned that in America people get very upset at just hearing the word *punishment* and assign all sorts of horrible meanings to it. Of course, as Bob Bailey reminds my co-author, using the word *correction* is just a pretty synonym for the scientific concept of *punishment*.

"The scientific definition of punishment, by the way," says Ian Dunbar, veterinarian, animal behaviorist, and a science-based dog trainer from whom we will hear a lot more later in this book, "is that it decreases the immediately preceding behavior such that it is less likely to occur in the future. That's it, period. It says nothing about punishments being scary or painful. However, by definition punishment must be effective in reducing unwanted behavior; otherwise, it's not punishment. Let's put it this way. Behavior is changed by consequences. Consequences are good or bad. From the dog's point of view, either things get better or things get worse. You can teach the dog to do a lot by encouraging him to get it right and by rewarding him for getting it right. Setting him up so he can't fail, luring him and rewarding him for getting it right. But you will not get reliability unless you punish the dog when he gets it wrong. Now, this is the biggest thing in dog training that people don't understand. Everybody makes the assumption that punishment has to be aversive. And the reason for this is, the hundreds of thousands of learning theory experiments that were done years ago were all performed by computers, training rats and pigeons in a laboratory cage. Well, how can a computer reward a rat? Simple, right? It goes click and out comes a treat from a little food dispenser. How can a computer punish a rat? It can't go, 'Ha-hem, excuse me, rat, hello, I don't like what you're doing.' So, you know, electric shock. So the point was that in the laboratory where learning theory was created, punishments were always aversive. They always caused pain. However, when people train people or when people train dogs, we realize that of course punishment doesn't have to be painful or scary."

Aversive or Non-Aversive?

Webster's dictionary defines *aversive* as "tending to avoid or causing avoidance of a noxious or punishing stimulus." *Noxious* means something that causes harm or pain. So when we ask how we can stop unwanted behavior, what we really want to ask is: How can we do it without causing pain or fear? Ian Dunbar proposes a new quadrant to address this. "If on one side you put 'Is this thing I'm doing punishing, i.e., does it reduce or eliminate the undesirable behavior? Yes or no.' And 'Is this thing aversive? Yes or no.' Meaning, is it painful? Is it scary? We find that two of these quadrants are overflowing: 'non-aversive, nonpunishments' and 'aversive nonpunishments,' whereas the other two are virtually empty: 'aversive punishments' and 'non-aversive punishments.'"

Many of the things dog owners do to get their dogs to obey may be non-aversive, but they are also nonpunishing, which means that they don't get the behavior to change. "For example, nagging," says Ian. "Someone says, 'Oh, don't do that, Rover. Rover, please, will you sit down. Rover, Rover, Rover! Sit down!' And then they give up when the dog doesn't do it. So this wasn't aversive, but it didn't change the behavior and so wasn't a punishment. The dog thinks it's a riot. The bichon says, 'I love it when she talks to me that way.'

"On the other hand," Ian continues, "people are frequently aversive without effectively reducing unwanted behavior, and so this isn't punishment either. People all too frequently jerk the leash, shout at the dog, and shock it, but you know what? They're still doing it next week. The dog doesn't learn, and therefore by definition the aversive stimuli were not punishments either."

Ian Dunbar describes all this in scientific terms, but I would explain it in a slightly different way. The fact is that no animal ever responds positively to angry, frustrated, or fearful energy. If you are trying to correct your dog and you are not in a calm-assertive state, your dog will react to your unstable emotions and be unable to understand what you want to communicate to him. At the same time, if you are nagging your dog and being ineffective, not only is your energy just nasty, negative, and unhelpful, but you are probably not 100 percent committed to changing your dog's behavior either.

"The use of aversive punishment is actually quite rare," Ian says. "When a trainer who's using his voice, using a leash correction, or maybe even using an electronic collar does it correctly, you only see the trainer use it once or twice. Then they don't need it anymore because now the dog never runs away. Once, twice with the collar, and he never chases sheep again. Aversive punishment only needs to be used once or twice. However, this is not what you see most of the time. Instead, what we see is people who have the dog on-leash, and they're jerking at it all the time, they never stop shouting, and they never take the shock collar off. This is not punishment. Depending on the severity, it is either harassment or abuse.

"The quadrant that's virtually empty," Ian continues, "is non-aversive punishment. In reality, though, it's surprisingly easy and extremely effective to eliminate undesirable behavior with softly spoken instructive reprimands."

Ian Dunbar very successfully teaches people to use voice commands as effective non-aversive punishments, a method he describes in detail in Chapter 6. By this definition, I would describe the way I use body language, energy, and sound (such as "Tssst!" or "Hey!") as also being forms of non-aversive punishments. I might add the use of touch to this category if it is firm, not harsh, and does not cause pain, although there are those who definitely disagree with me here. I happen to believe that physical touch is an important part of the way dogs "talk" to one another. Touch is the very first sense that a dog develops.[9] My observation is that dogs use firm touch—not violent or aggressive touch, but assertive touch—with one another as a follow-through to a warning given by eye contact or body language and energy, and that to speak their language, it helps if I use it too. If the touch is neither severe nor done in anger or frustration—for example, an insistent touch on your friend's shoulder to get her attention in a dark movie theater—then, to my mind, it is simply a method of communication, not an "aversive" punishment. Of course, the removal of something a dog likes is also a form of non-aversive punishment (technically, negative punishment)—such as the withholding of attention, a reward, or a favorite activity or claiming a space or an object that a dog likes.

The rule of thumb in operant conditioning is that positive reinforcement, not punishment, is not only the most humane but also the most effective way to create or shape any type of new behavior.

"I have never had to use punishment to ever *get* a behavior. Never. I mean, that's a zero," states Bob Bailey emphatically. "I have used punishment to *suppress* behavior that I didn't want. But only in circumstances where it would be high-risk behavior or somebody's going to get hurt or the dog is going to get hurt or it's really going to cause damage to property or something like that. Instead of punishment, I have tried to modify the environment in such a way that the animal can't do bad things. And by proper reinforcement, I've gotten the behavior I want, and I've made the game worthwhile enough for the dog to play the game. In that way, the punishment issue just didn't come up.

"If I am going to use a punisher," Bob continues, "I am going to use a punisher that I am absolutely sure is going to stop the behavior dead. If you have to use a punisher any more than roughly three times to stop the behavior, you're not doing it right."

The bottom line is that aversive punishment isn't something to mess around with. It should work right away or you shouldn't do it. If you are pulling or poking at your dog more than once or twice and she isn't getting the message, then you can't blame the dog. You need to stop and completely rethink your strategy, not to mention your own state of mind, which, in my experience, is most often the heart of the problem.

Where does this leave leash pops or side pulls? There are those who are totally opposed to them, and I respect that. But many trainers do employ them. I use them and teach owners to use them correctly, but I want them to be a means to an end, not something that goes on all the time, every day, for the rest of your dog's life. When properly used, the leash pop—which administers a physical sensation that is not meant to hurt or "jerk" but instead to get a dog's attention—communicates to the dog that something he is doing needs to be changed. If timed exactly with the unwanted behavior, and if the correct solution (what you want the dog to do instead) is offered concurrently with the correction, popping the leash can be a teaching tool, not a lifelong crutch to use in order to "nag" your dog into good manners.

TEACHING WITH REWARDS: THE PIONEERS

It wasn't really B. F. Skinner who "invented" the modern art of rewards-based animal training. It was his two young graduate assistants, Marian and Keller Breland. Bob Bailey kindly gave my co-author and me a copy of his educational video *Patient Like the Chipmunks*, which chronicles the history of Skinner-based operant conditioning and the fascinating story of Animal Behavior Enterprises, which was founded by the Brelands in 1943. Back then, Bob recounts, Marian and Keller weren't even sure there was a living to be made training animals. But they were certain they knew how to do it. Using operant conditioning methods, the Brelands first discovered the concept of "shaping." Instead of waiting all day for an animal to perform a behavior and then "capturing" it with a reward, they began rewarding the animal for every small step it took toward the desired action—kind of like that party game Hot and Cold that we used to play as kids. Eventually, the animal would hit the jackpot and perform exactly the behavior the trainers had been looking for.

Their next big discovery came in 1945. "While shaping tricks, the Brelands noticed that the animals themselves seemed to be paying attention to the noises made by the hand-held food-reward switches," writes Patrick Burns, a trainer of working Jack Russell terriers, in *Dogs Today* magazine. "Keller and Marian Breland soon discovered that an acoustic secondary enforcer, such as a click or whistle, could communicate to an animal the precise action being rewarded, and it could do so from a distance."[10]

The Brelands called this a *bridging stimulus,* which their colleague Bob Bailey shortened to the term *bridge* when he was director of training for the U.S. Navy's Marine Mammal Program. That bridge was usually a clicker or a whistle. In this way, the Brelands and Bailey actually practiced an early form of clicker training long before it was popularized by dolphin trainer Karen Pryor in the late '80s and early '90s.

"All the clicker does is tell the animal that it's done what you want it to do correctly and there will be a primary reinforcer coming, which is food or a toy. But you have to make it worthwhile for the animal," Bob Bailey explained to my co-author. "That's one of the things that I try to get across to people. It has to be worthwhile for the animal to play our silly little game. Whatever the silly little game is, to the animal it's nothing that it probably would have done if the animal were living two million years ago out in the bush. It wouldn't be sitting in front of somebody or retrieving a little toy for a kid or something like that. It would be out earning a living. But the animal got secondary reinforcers back then too. When it did something, something happened, and as a result it ended up with food, and so it would change its behavior to do that more often and solve problems that way. So it was really nature that used the bridge first. The rest of us, we're all Johnny-come-latelies."

Over the next thirty years, the Brelands and Bailey taught hundreds of animals to perform in everything from corporate demonstrations to theme park shows to commercials, television shows, and movies. They also trained other animal trainers who went on to work at such venues as Busch Gardens, Disney World, and Sea World. Animal Behavior Enterprises contracted with major amusement parks such as Marineland of Florida, Marineland of the Pacific, Parrot Jungle, and Six Flags.

The ABE training sessions were never more than twenty minutes at a time—usually less, says Bob—and took place one to three times a day, depending on how much time the company had to produce a finished animal show. Timing and the rate of reinforcement were the secrets of ABE's success. Interestingly, the vast majority of times Bob and his team didn't end up actually working with the animals they trained. They'd get hired to do a show, produce the show, and train the animal actors so that anyone could work with them.

"Our trainers changed animals about every two to six weeks depending on what they happened to be working with. They would be rotating all the time so that the animal worked for many people, as long as they followed the same protocol. All of our trainers trained exactly the same way. We had one method of training, and it evolved over time. If somebody came up with a better way of doing it, then by Jove, we're going to use that new way, but they had to prove that it was indeed a better way."

Bob explained to us that he believes trainers who are truly dedicated to their craft are guided as much by philosophy as by procedure, and his personal philosophy is to choose reward over punishment whenever possible. "I believe the least intrusive procedure needed to get a behavior or to stop a behavior is best for the trainer and for the animal; a belief which does not preclude my using whatever punishment or force necessary to stop dangerous behavior. I think trainers philosophically oriented toward 'correction,' or other punishment euphemisms, can default under stress to coercive procedures which, in my view, often create more problems than they solve."

"I don't believe much in ideology," Bob added. "If I found an ethical method faster than behavior analysis or operant conditioning, if someone sent me an e-mail that opened a new door, I would drop what I'm doing and never look back. I'm not wedded to an ideology. It's the science. It's the technology."

THE CLICKER REVOLUTION

Since the early '90s, the clicker has become one of the most popular tools in dog training circles. I've never used a clicker because I always perceived it as more of a training tool for building new behaviors than a tool for rehabilitation. In doing research for this book, however, I've witnessed people do incredibly creative things with this very simple tool. It has been used for everything from teaching simple obedience to behavior modification to training working dogs in specific tasks to training dogs to detect cancer in human breath, which you'll read about in Chapter 8. Many of the professionals we interviewed for this book were enthusiastic about the clicker's many uses.

Kirk Turner has been training dogs professionally for more than twenty years and came to the clicker out of a desire to not use physical force on animals. He took the time to explain why he prefers to use this versatile tool. "I like it because basically you're expanding the dog's mind," he said. "You're making the dog actually think in a positive way without putting any negatives in the situation. He has to think about what it is that's actually going to get him some kind of reward.

"The thing to understand about the clicker is it means three things," Kirk explained. "It means 'That's what I'm looking for, right there'; it means the reward is on the way; and the click means end of the exercise." The clicker also works great from a distance. "I do recall exercises with families," Kirk explained. "I have them all stand around in a circle. I point at one person in the family and tell them, 'Do anything you can to get the dog to you.'" The rest of the family has to ignore the dog completely. Kirk stands on the outside of the circle and operates the clicker. This way, when the dog goes to the person who is calling him, the behavior is marked immediately from a remote distance.

Clickers can also be used to phase out food for dogs that are food-centric. "Once you've trained the behavior, you want to go into an intermittent reward system so that you're not rewarding them every single time," Kirk said. First he rewards the dog with a treat every time it performs the desired behavior, then he will ask the dog for the correct behavior three times before he will give a treat, and then maybe seven times. "Over a period of days, I can really lessen those rewards and eventually not do any kind of reward at all."

"A clicker is a wonderful tool for shaping behaviors for obedience, tricks, scent discrimination, and service dog tasks," Bonnie Brown-Cali shares. "I teach a dog that a click means food is on the way. Once a dog understands this, then I can use a click to train behaviors. The timing of the click is critical, as it tells the dog that the last behavior performed is going to be rewarded. For instance, if I have a dog that is showing aversion to a scent that I want to train on, I can use the click to change the dog's perspective. Now this scent means something good. From there, I can shape an alert for the dog to perform when he locates the scent. If the dog already knows the command 'sit,' I can tell the dog to sit at the scent and then click when the behavior is performed. Since the click means that food is on the way, I can click from a distance to tell the dog that what he did is correct, and the reward is coming. Then, once the behavior is shaped, the command 'sit' and the clicker are phased out."

"I'm not a clicker trainer per se," says behavior-based trainer Barbara De Groodt. "I use them for some fast-moving dogs and for some people who have disabilities and want to teach a service dog to do something. I also use the clicker for people who are way over the top with their praise or corrections. I can bring them to sort of a normal level, instead of the person who goes, 'Great dog!' all the time. The clicker brings them into a more normal range. The clicker doesn't have emotion and always has the same consistent meaning."

As Barbara points out, too much praise or excitement can often block your dog from learning what you are trying to teach him. I always recommend calm-assertive energy. In his informative and sometimes controversial blog Terrierman's Daily Dose, writer Patrick Burns makes the argument that clickers work for so many people because they help to create a calm-assertive state of mind and body that paves the way for clear communication.

"When Millan talks about being 'calm and assertive,' what he is really talking about is making *fewer* signals and making *clearer* ones," Burns writes. "Let's look at clicker training. What does a clicker do when put in the hands of a new wanna-be trainer? When a trainer has a clicker in hand, and is focused on getting the noise timed exactly right, is the trainer flailing around with his or her hands? No. Is he or she talking? No. In fact, they are not supposed to be moving at all. And in clicker training, it is the *clicker* that does the talking, not the human. Is the clicker assertive? You bet! The clicker sends just ONE clear signal—a signal that says 'We could use a little more of that.'"[11]

TO CLICK OR NOT TO CLICK?

Some trainers we interviewed found the clicker to be a little too constricting in their efforts to shape a dog's behavior. "I rarely use clickers anymore," says Joel Silverman, who started out as a clicker-based marine mammal trainer at Sea World and transitioned into dogs as the host of *Good Dog U* on Animal Planet. "People who think clickers can solve every behavior problem in every situation are fooling themselves. You take a high–prey aggression dog that wants nothing more than to go after somebody, and I'm telling you, treats and clickers and cookies and kisses are not going to do it."

Mark Harden is a thirty-year veteran of professional training, having worked with nearly every variety of animal there is for movies and television. "I don't use clickers with dogs. I hate them for dogs. Now, I'm a clicker wizard with cats, monkeys, birds, parrots, anything like that. The clicker works so well with cats, for example, because they're not as focused on me. They're more about the food. They want food and ritual. They're not reading my face. Maybe one in a hundred cats actually looks at my face. When they do, it really creeps me out."

In working with dogs, however, Mark feels that the clicker can block the flow of trainer-animal communication. "The clicker is a waste of a perfectly good hand. I mean, when I work, maybe I've got a look stick in one hand, I've got a bait bag, and I'm trying to get food. I'm trying to time my pay. My theory is that the dogs I'm working with are very in tune with me. Dogs have a way of reading my face. My vocals. My body language. They read everything about me. So to me, the clicker becomes this sort of anonymous noise that I have to teach them to understand. And I can do everything and more with my voice. Personally, I find that most people don't use the clicker correctly, and then it screws up your timing like crazy."

"The Brelands pioneered the use of the secondary reinforcer as a methodology," Bob Bailey reminds us, "but now this notion of the clicker kind of caught on, and I'm afraid there's a lot of people who have decided that there is magic in a clicker. Of course, that's just not true."

INSTINCT: AN INCONVENIENT TRUTH

It was the Brelands themselves who first began to realize that the science of operant conditioning had some built-in drawbacks that

would need to be overcome and understood for their animal training business to flourish. In fact, those drawbacks came from Mother
Nature herself. In a 1961 paper entitled "The Misbehavior of Organisms," Keller and Marian Breland described their first experience with
the failure of reward-based operant conditioning:

> *It seems that when working with pigs, chickens and raccoons, the*
> *animals would often learn a trick and then begin to drift away from*
> *the learned behavior and towards more instinctive, unreinforced,*
> *foraging actions.*[12]

Calling this syndrome "instinctive drift," the two researchers were
shocked to discover it because it went against all the laws of 1950s-
era positive reinforcement theory. The Brelands had been basing their
previous work on what they thought was a hard-and-fast rule—that
behaviors followed by food reinforcement should be strengthened,
while behaviors that prevent food reinforcement should be elimi-
nated. But some animals dared break these rules when their instincts
reared their ancient heads. The Brelands discovered that some instinctive behaviors can even hold a hungry animal back from choosing
food reinforcement!

"The Brelands did not overstate the problem, nor did they quantify
it," writes Patrick Burns. "They simply stated a fact: instinct existed,
and sometimes it bubbled up and over-rode trained behaviors."

In their landmark paper, the Brelands took the first step toward
incorporating the concepts of the animal ethologists—scientists who
study animals in their natural environments—into their operant conditioning and training work, which made their methods even more
effective. They turned out to be light-years ahead of their mentor,
B. F. Skinner, in this regard. "He taught that all you needed to study
was behavior," writes Temple Grandin in *Animals in Translation*. "You
weren't supposed to speculate about what was inside a person's or an

animal's head . . . you couldn't talk about it. You could measure only behavior, therefore you could study only behavior."

The now-famous Grandin was just a college student back in the 1960s, when B. F. Skinner was God and the science of behaviorism was Gospel. "Behaviorists thought these basic concepts explained everything about animals, who were basically just stimulus-response machines. It's probably hard for people to imagine the power this idea had back then. It was almost a religion."

When Grandin finally got the chance to visit her idol at his office at Harvard, they had a very revealing conversation. "I finally said to him, 'Dr. Skinner, if we could just learn how the brain works,'" Grandin chronicles. "He said, 'We don't need to learn about the brain, we have operant conditioning.' I remember driving back to school going over this in my mind, and finally saying to myself, 'I don't think I believe that.'"[13]

As it turns out, the Brelands didn't believe it anymore either. They wrote:

> *After 14 years of continuous conditioning and observation of thousands of animals, it is our reluctant conclusion that the behavior of any species cannot be adequately understood, predicted, or controlled without knowledge of its instinctive patterns, evolutionary history, and ecological niche.*

DOG TRAINING VS. DOG PSYCHOLOGY

What the Brelands discovered using repetitions and statistics and the scientific method mirrors my own very unscientific message that dog training is something that was invented by humans, but dog psychology was invented by Mother Nature. This is why I urge you to think of your dog in four ways, in the correct order: animal, species dog, breed, name. The early behaviorists were thinking *animal* only. The early ethologists were thinking mostly *species* and *breed*. Many Kennel Club people are thinking *breed* first. And most American pet owners are thinking either *breed name* or just plain *name*—for example, "My dog is Fluffy, and Fluffy is my daughter." The Brelands' paper back in 1961 was the beginning of putting it all together to understand that we have to honor and respect the whole being of a dog or any animal before we can clearly communicate with it.

I first learned that others were thinking along these lines when I read *Dog Psychology: The Basis of Dog Training* by Leon F. Whitney, a veterinarian and hunting hound breeder and trainer, and *The Dog's Mind: Understanding Your Dog's Behavior* by Dr. Bruce Fogle, a British veterinarian and a founding member of the Society for Companion Animal Studies in the United Kingdom and the Delta Society in the United States. This past spring, sixteen years after first opening his book, I had the opportunity to have lunch with the venerable Dr. Fogle in Cannes, France, and to thank him in person for letting me know that my ideas and observations about dogs weren't crazy after all. The good doctor is sort of a hero of mine, and we were both delighted to find out that we share many views, especially the observation that many dog behavior issues—even some "psychosomatic" medical issues that show up in Dr. Fogle's veterinary office—can be traced back to a dog's unhealthy interaction with its human owners.

"You know, operant conditioning is such a valid way of training," says Kirk Turner, a big believer himself in operant conditioning, clicker training, and positive reinforcement. "What gets in the way is life for many people with dogs. As you know from your TV show, Cesar, the problem isn't usually the dogs. They are a piece of cake. It's usually the owners that you really have to figure out."

Like Kirk, I've discovered that before we even think about rules to train our dogs, we need a better set of rules in order to train ourselves.

4

CESAR'S RULES FOR A
TEACHABLE DOG . . . AND
A TRAINABLE HUMAN

Cesar trains owners Adir and Anastasia Ionov.

"I tell people, 'You know, we all have baggage, and some dogs do too. No dog is going to be perfect,'" says veteran trainer Joel Silverman. "People constantly come up to me and say, 'Joel, you know I want to get a dog, but gosh, I just don't want to go through it barking and lunging and running out the door. I mean, I just don't know if I want

to deal with all this stuff.' I say to them, 'You know, I have a great suggestion for you.' They perk up, 'What?' And I say, 'You need a potted
plant. Put a potted plant in the corner, water it, it will grow beautifully
for you, and I promise you it will stay right there.' A dog, like a human,
comes with baggage, and you need to understand, and be prepared
for that."

Dogs are social, living beings—animals with a history and an
evolution so closely intertwined with our own that they can read our
faces and gestures better than our closest genetic relative, the chim-
panzee, can.[1] But you can't forget that they are a separate species,
with their own individual psychology. Just as you can't expect a dog
to be as predictable as a potted plant, you can't expect him to be a
furry human with four legs either. And you really can't expect a dog to
read your mind. To teach your dog anything, from simple manners to
complicated tasks or tricks, you need to build a relationship with him
that honors the animal-dog that he is.

And most important, you need to look within yourself and follow
some basic rules whenever you work with dogs.

RULE #1: BE CALM AND ASSERTIVE

As any regular viewer of *Dog Whisperer* knows, I credit the power of
calm-assertive energy as the key to many of my own successful interactions with troubled dogs. Though calling this steady, confident,
relaxed way of being "calm-assertiveness" may have been my idea, it's
not some sort of New Age concept that I just pulled out of my hat.
Throughout the years I've been informed by professionals in many
different fields—from biology to psychology to medicine to management science to law enforcement—that what I'm talking about has a
very real basis in science.

"Calmness and assertiveness are the energies of the two main branches of our autonomic nervous system," writes Sung Lee, MD, of the BrainWell Center in Sedona, Arizona, a clinic that specializes in cutting-edge, computer-assisted biofeedback therapies. "Assertive energy is the energy of our sympathetic nervous system. This is the energy of our 'fight-flight' response, which keys up the heart rate and blood pressure, releases energy stores, and prepares us for action or to handle a perceived threat. Calming energy is the energy of the para-sympathetic nervous system. This is the energy of our 'rest-digest' response. This system builds up our energy stores, and also regulates and fine-tunes the fight-flight response. It allows us to manage our assertive energy in the appropriate way for a given situation.

"Many researchers have concluded that imbalance between the sympathetic and parasympathetic branches is a major contributor to human disease including heart disease, digestive disorders, chronic pain, immune dysfunction, psychological and neurological disorders, and others. It seems we can add 'more likely to have an unstable pet' to the list of challenges associated with imbalance in the autonomic nervous system."[2]

To project calm-assertive energy to your dog, you must be aware of how you are feeling and what energy you are projecting in every interaction with your dog. Every aspect of your relationship with your dog is determined by your own integrity and your connection with your own true self, because dogs are nature's best lie detectors. Your dog is watching you every moment, noting the subtlest changes in your expressions and smelling every change in your body chemistry. Your dog knows who you really are, inside and out, weak and strong, good and bad.

"Dogs can read owners like a book," Ian Dunbar agrees. "If an owner gets out of their armchair, the dog can tell in a second whether they're going to the bathroom or going to get his leash. They just read the demeanor and they say, 'Oh! We're going for a walk.' Or, 'He's going to take a leak again.' So they don't have to get up that time. And it's so important to realize how different the dog's brain is from ours. Because it is a source of a lot of frustration, and when dogs don't behave, people do get frustrated, and that's when dogs get a lot of abuse."

Bob Bailey may have trained thousands and thousands of animals over the years, but there was one animal in particular he tried to avoid having to work with. "I have seldom worked with pet dog owners," he told my co-author. "My hat is off to anyone who wants to spend the time and effort working with pet dog owners, because they don't always tell the truth. I have worked with quite a few pet dog trainers over the years. And it has always been the case that it's not the animal that has the problem; it's the trainer working with the animal, because they haven't taken time to actually analyze the behavior and what they are doing in response to the behavior."

The moral of the story: if you want to teach your dog anything or influence her behavior in any way, then, "trainer, train thyself" first.

RULE #2: BE SELF-AWARE

Like children, dogs are always watching us and learning from our actions and reactions. If you shout at your spouse or the kids, your dog will learn about you and how you operate from that behavior, even if it isn't directed at her. If you feel irritable or sick and take it out on your dog, she will remember the body language and the repercussions.

"It is important when we are with a dog to realize that they are always learning," says Martin Deeley. "They are watching our movements, listening to our sounds, and, I am certain, sensing our emotions. So if you are feeling a little under the weather or getting a little irate, put your dog somewhere she cannot get into trouble and not be the recipient of your mood. Or if she is the one that can calm you, sit nicely with her, breathe deeply, and let each of you find calmness together."

"To me, anger has no place in dog training, no place at all," Ian Dunbar insists. "If you're angry, go and hit or bite a pillow, or hit the wall with your fist or something. But don't take it out on the dog, because you'll go backward in training so fast."

It's important that you be yourself when you are with your dog, especially if you are trying to influence her behavior. You cannot lie to a dog about who you are or how you are feeling. So don't try to copy my way of being or that of someone else you've seen on television or even at your local dog park. Learn your skills from the best teachers, from as many teachers as you can, and practice these skills thoroughly, but when you are applying them, be yourself. In the words of Hollywood trainer Mark Harden, "Be your *best* self." Think about it this way—the chance to share your life and work with an animal that can bring out the best in you is a wonderful opportunity!

RULE #3: POSITIVE REINFORCEMENT BEGINS WITH YOU

I am constantly amazed at the attitude of some "positive reinforcement only" trainers who say hateful things in the press about those they don't agree with—including, and sometimes especially, me! I try really hard not to take it too personally because I believe America is all about being entitled to your own opinions . . . but come on! Aren't these the same people who are supposed to be all about changing behavior through rewards and not through punishment? Doesn't that apply to human beings as well as dogs? I believe that when you use positive reinforcement or any kind of behavior modification method with your dog, the key to your success always starts with your own state of mind. *To influence your dog's behavior, you must always begin by being a positive, confident, calm, and assertive human.* This is the definition of true leadership.

One of the most important things I want my clients to understand is that true positive reinforcement should not just be considered food rewards. It is also a matter of being in the right state of mind—a positive, open state of mind—whenever you work with a dog. You must be mindfully aware of your own feelings and energy, as well as the dog's emotions. You should touch the dog only when she's in a calm, receptive state—and reinforce her positive state with your own. If you are starting off with any kind of frustration or anger or negativity, if you are putting a stopwatch on your dog when she is trying to learn something new, then you are not practicing true positive reinforcement, no matter how many treats you might throw.

Positive reinforcement and the many different things that motivate your dog can come from anywhere in the environment, not just from a kibble box or a packaged toy. In Chapter 6, Ian Dunbar talks about his concept of "life rewards," which I love. As a reward, you can use a tree or a bush that a dog loves to explore to shape her mind. A tree doesn't have to be just a thing that a dog uses for peeing, if you choose to see the tree's potential. A simple stick lying in the backyard can easily become a dog's favorite thing in the world, and that can become your reinforcement and the dog's motivation in that moment. In this way, you are honoring who your dog is and what she really wants and needs, not just trying to manipulate or bribe her to get your own needs met.

The ultimate positive reinforcement is using other dogs—the power of the pack—to reinforce or to create a behavior. In Viper's case, I used Daddy to inspire a formerly terrified Belgian malinois to want to come out from hiding and join me and my pack. Later I used not only Viper's dog pack but his temporary human "pack"—my sons—to help him get through his fears in formerly scary situations. In one *Dog Whisperer* episode, I used a parrot to help me influence both Maxwell, an aggressive Welsh Sealyham terrier, and his owner, since the parrot was the only one in the whole animal-human pack that was practicing calm-assertive energy. When you draw on your creativity and find ideas from the world around you, you are empowering yourself to believe that you can influence your dog no matter where you are or what you have to work with—even if you have forgotten your clicker or your pouch of treats or left all your leashes and collar back at home.

Our dogs can teach us a thing or two about how true positive reinforcement works. Here's an example that most dog owners can relate to. Your dog wants to go outside and pee. He sits by the door. You open the door. The dog walks out, but as he passes by you, he looks up at you for a moment and makes eye contact.

He just rewarded you. But he didn't give you a cookie.

To me, positive reinforcement means the human-dog bond is so strong that we each do things to make the other happy, but we don't have to give each other a cookie.

RULE #4: START WITH THE BOND

Although we don't have to have an emotional bond with a dog in order to teach it something, the fact is that our close connection to our dogs can be a unique advantage and a motivation in itself. Building a bond takes time and patience, however, and trainer Joel Silverman finds that some dog owners attending his seminars don't want to fit that part into their busy schedule.

"People can be impatient," he says. "They'll say, 'I need to be the leader,' and they want that to happen right away, but I tell them that the most successful dog trainers across America are the people who understand that the best thing you can do to build a great relationship with your dog is to get to a place where your dog really wants to please you and wants to make you happy. Then training is a hundred percent easier.

"I suggest taking two to four weeks," says Joel. "And there are three steps to that process. That first step is getting to know your dog, just like a human being. You didn't become best friends with your boyfriend or girlfriend, husband or wife, in a day. You're just going to live with your dog and expose her to all these different situations, places, toys, and treats. Does she have a high prey drive because she's going crazy over the treats? Does she like certain toys? Does she like taking walks? Does she like people? Does she like other dogs? Those first four to seven days you're also going to see the things your dog does not like. Maybe she gets scared around moving objects, for example. Just observe and take note.

"The second step is developing a relationship. It's real simple. You're just going to incorporate the things your dog likes. All those things your dog liked, you just pick out those activities, treats, and toys, and people, but things she doesn't like you just eliminate for the next week and a half, two weeks.

"Which gets you to the last phase, which is building the trust. That is where you actually begin dealing with some of those issues, maybe those fear situations like moving objects or people. You start gradually—thirty feet away from the moving object, and maybe we'll hang here for like twenty minutes, but tomorrow we'll go twenty-five feet away, and the next day we'll go twenty feet away. And this works you up to get ready to actually start training your dog."

As I wrote in Chapter 2, to my mind, balance is a more important element for a dog than training, and a balanced dog is a dog that is ready to be easily trained.

"Many times when I get a dog in for training, the first few days are the days I am working to find out what I have in my 'canine student,' and many times I find it is a complete mess of emotions and understandings," Martin Deeley relates. "The dog does not know how to react, when to react, or who to even react with. This is usually a result of the mixture between the dog's personality and the 'training' interaction with people and other animals it has had before. I work at building routine, understanding, relationship, and clarity of command for four days. This is done to clear the mind of all past incorrect learning. After about four days I often smile and claim, 'Now we have a true dog. We can begin to build a real dog.' Nervous dogs become more sure; aggressive dogs become more accepting and confident of being able to handle situations without resorting to aggression. But most of all, they get confidence in me guiding and leading them. Consistency throughout is essential, and a fair, patient approach, with understanding of their balance problems, is the way forward."

RULE #5: START YOUNG AND PREVENT PROBLEMS

Back in the 1970s, veterinarian and behaviorist Ian Dunbar was doing postgraduate research on dog behavior with Dr. Frank Beach at the University of California–Berkeley. In this work, Dunbar observed a puppy named Sirius go from being a total bully with other puppies in one-on-one situations to an easygoing, socially appropriate pup when placed with a larger group of puppies and twelve adult dogs. Sirius's transformation taught Dunbar that what might first appear to be fixed personality traits in a dog can actually be quite malleable in young pups. This means that early temperament training can go a long way toward creating a dog that is people-friendly, dog-friendly, and safe (acquired bite-inhibition), with the canine social savvy to become a relaxed, confident, and well-behaved adult dog.

In 1981 Ian got his first puppy, an Alaskan malamute named Omaha Beagle. Armed with his scientific knowledge of dog behavior, he set out to find a class for his young pup to attend. He was appalled to discover that every obedience school he visited made the claim that they never trained pups under six months old. Ian set out to change that ridiculous practice and designed his own class in conjunction with the Marin Humane Society. Thus, SIRIUS® Puppy Training, the first off-leash behavior class for puppies, was created.

For all dogs, what's called the socialization period—from about three weeks old to twelve weeks old—is a crucial window for learning. During this time, social play with littermates and guidance and discipline from the mother (or human pack leader) help to shape the proper behaviors for a well-behaved adult dog. Dogs that are handled and petted by humans regularly during their first eight weeks of life also make the best pets and have the best lifelong interactions with humans. Those trainers who turned Ian Dunbar away were dead wrong—puppies can begin learning commands and tricks as young as eight weeks of age.

According to Ian Dunbar, there are three important reasons for puppy classes:

1. To teach bite inhibition, or gentle jaws—hence the puppy play sessions and dog-dog socialization
2. To teach a puppy to enjoy interacting with and being handled by people, especially children, men, and strangers, and thus be safe in people-dog socialization
3. To teach reliable off-leash obedience so that the puppy promptly and willingly responds to verbal commands even when distracted—hence the many training interludes integrated into puppy play sessions

Unlike so many commercial puppy classes that are just free-for-alls—a group of unrelated puppies and owners get together in a room and play in an unstructured, undisciplined way—Ian Dunbar's puppy

classes are fifty-five-minute play sessions that are regularly interrupted (every minute or so) by short training interludes. The goal is for
the puppies to learn to respond quickly, reliably, and happily to their
owners' requests. Every time the play session is interrupted—perhaps
by a sit-down-sit sequence or a ten-second down-stay—the puppy is
then told "go play" again as a reward. Thus, playing with other dogs
is used over and over as a reward for training, rather than becoming
a distraction that works against training. Ian warns against the tendency some people have to just let their puppies play in their presence
without some sort of structure; he feels that this approach leads to a
dog that won't reliably obey in adolescence or adulthood.

"What I'm doing with puppies is so blindingly simple," Ian Dunbar
told me. "Prevention is a million times easier than cure. Prevent the
problem when your dog is a puppy."

"A critical time in a puppy's mental development is between the
ages of seven weeks and approximately twelve months, depending
upon the breed," says Bonnie Brown-Cali. "This period shapes the
puppy's responses for survival. Whatever he learns during this time
will affect him for the rest of his life. I teach a head-start class for puppies between the ages of ten and twenty-four weeks. There's a little bit
of a calculated risk because the puppies have not completed their vac-
cinations, but all puppies are required to be under veterinary care. The
training class is indoors, on a clean tarp, and the puppies are allowed
to socialize freely for short durations. This gives me the opportunity
to teach clients about dog body language: when to ignore their puppy
and let them figure life out, or when to step in and redirect behaviors.
It is crucial that a young puppy learn how to 'speak dog,' interact with
a wide variety of people and other animals, and feel comfortable in a
variety of environments.

"Over the years I have trained numerous dogs with overly reactive and potentially dangerous behaviors. A dog that has bitten has
learned that he can control a situation by biting. It is self-rewarding,

and when it happens a few times, it becomes a shaped behavior. Do I think that means the dog is a lost cause? No. Can I take away the fact that he knows he has made people go away by biting? No. But, I have successfully taught dogs what are acceptable behaviors and what behaviors will exclude him from the pack. By teaching the dog that his owner is in control and that it is less stressful to perform an alternate behavior, I can help the dog be less likely to be reactive and bite. But, I can never take away the fact that he knows he can bite. He will always have to be managed."

TRAINING SUCCESS STORY: BOOT CAMP

MPH Entertainment vice president of finance Catherine Stribling—who's also a *Dog Whisperer* writer—always thought she was a good dog handler until she got Duncan. This hyperactive yellow Lab, now five years old, has been a challenge since Catherine got her at nine weeks. Walking on a leash was

Catherine and Duncan with Jill Bowers

never a problem until Duncan came along. A hardheaded bundle
of energy and nerves, Duncan forges ahead even if she doesn't
know where she's going, impervious to direction or correction,
exhausting Catherine mentally and physically without ever tiring
out herself.

Frisbee throwing, treadmilling, doggie day care—Catherine
tried everything. Duncan may have been tired after these activities, but she was no better at understanding her owner's rules,
boundaries, and limitations. "Duncan wants so much to please,"
Catherine says, "but she never could figure out how to do it.
What we had was a failure to communicate."

Fast-forward six months. "Everyone in the *Dog Whisperer*
office notices how much calmer and more obedient Duncan is.
When they ask how, I say, 'Thank Dog! Bootcamp.'" Owned
and operated by Jill Bowers in Burbank, California, Thank Dog!
Bootcamp marries human boot camp to basic dog obedience.
Jill is a certified human trainer and dog trainer, incorporating
basic obedience commands such as "sit," "stay," "come" from a
distance, and "go to your place" into heart-pumping cardio routines; the dogs learn to sit quietly by the owner's side during the
weight-training portion of the class. "Once I matched the activity
to Duncan's energy level, she began listening."

Catherine is the first to admit that she's a calmer owner now
that her own nervous energy has an outlet. "Energy really does
travel down the leash." Because Thank Dog! Bootcamp has a
revolving group of dogs and owners, Duncan has the ideal place
to learn how properly to socialize with other dogs. Most important, Duncan and Catherine have forged a bond with their shared
activity. "Whenever I would walk Duncan, my other dog, Rupert,
would come along. Thank Dog! Bootcamp is our special thing.
It's where we learned to work as a unit."

RULE #6: OLDER DOGS LEARN
NEW TRICKS TOO

Of course, it's ideal to catch a dog when she is in puppyhood and we can mold her into the perfect dog, but what about older dogs, especially those that end up at shelters or rescue organizations? Can they learn too?

"Older dogs are no less teachable than older people!" says Kelly Gorman Dunbar, dog trainer and founder of Open Paw,[3] a program to help educate pet owners so that fewer dogs are relinquished to shelters, but also to help shelter dogs become more adoptable. "Behavior is always in motion, always adapting, changing. Older dogs may have formed habits or certain associations that must be overcome in order to progress, but with a basic understanding of how dogs learn, it is possible to change behavior."

Kelly is passionate about educating people about the unique issues that shelter dogs face. "A shelter dog might get passed over for

Older Daddy

many reasons: it might not be as cute or as dynamic as a younger dog, it might be depressed to find itself in a shelter at this point in life, it might be frightened by the environment and not displaying its true personality, it might not be house-trained and therefore sitting in its own excrement in the kennel, or it might be coping with the stress by outletting—by barking, pacing, growling.

"All of the roadblocks to adoption mentioned above and more can be addressed by classical conditioning and basic training. Shelters can be overwhelming for both the resident dogs and the humans who come to visit them. If dogs in the shelter are clean, calm, quiet, approachable, and pro-social, the shelter will be more pleasant for everyone involved. Realistically, dogs only have fifteen to thirty seconds or so to make a good first impression on a potential adopter, to draw them in, so they'd better have the skills to impress the heck out of people!

"First on Open Paw's agenda is to lower the stress level of the resident dogs as much as possible, which enables them to learn. A dog that has pent-up energy or is stressed and in fight-or-flight mode will have a very difficult time learning, as taking in new information is nearly impossible under those conditions. Teaching dogs to offer pro-social, human-desirable behaviors such as approaching the front of the kennel, wagging, soft eye contact, sitting politely, play bow, shake, gently raising a paw to the fence via reward training is low-stress on the dog [shelter dogs do not need more stress or pressure in their lives] and increases the likelihood of the dog catching the eye of passing humans."

I've seen dozens of cases in which an older dog surprises everybody with its ability and eagerness to learn. My late best friend Daddy was learning new things and helping me with problem dogs right up to the day he died at sixteen years of age. When Daddy began developing the many unique issues related to canine aging, I made sure to carefully document every stage he went through, so I could learn to help others with senior dogs in the future. The Senior Dogs Project is a wonderful organization that promotes and educates dog owners about the special needs of senior dogs and, more important, the many wonderful things older dogs have to offer.[4] The Senior Dogs Project maintains that dogs can be taught complex new behaviors at any age, and they share many case studies to prove it.

One example was a husky/shepherd mix named Autumn, who was the ripe old age of ten years when she was adopted by Laura Eland in Ontario, Canada. "When Autumn was turned over to me, I was told that she had no training, had never worn a collar or leash, and that her nickname was 'Stupid,'" Laura wrote the Senior Dogs Project in 2001. "At first, when she came to live with us, she would sit in a corner most of the time, staring at the wall. She would also growl when I touched her or her food dish. I called a local trainer, who designed a program for Autumn and me to follow at home. After just the first session, I could see Autumn's personality changing. She stopped staring at the wall and started to trust me as a leader. The nickname Stupid was replaced with comments like, 'Autumn's the smartest dog of the whole pack.' At fourteen years of age, Autumn behaves like a six-year-old. She's the oldest in her class, but also at the top of it."

RULE #7: LEARNING ISN'T A RACE

Just like people, dogs have different learning abilities. Some dogs learn quickly, some learn slowly, and some learn at different rates depending on many factors, including what you are attempting to teach them.

You should never compare your pup to another of the same age. Even if they are from the same litter, their learning ability can be very different. The most important thing you can do is spend time with your pup and watch how she learns and is developing. Watch for a willingness to work with you, watch for independence and willfulness. Look for sensitivities, and identify what pleases and rewards her after a behavior.

"There will be times when your dog will be distracted, times when she will decide not to obey, and times when she will not understand what you feel is a familiar command because of the situation. Believe that your dog really wants to be good and do as asked and help her through it," says Martin Deeley. "Even the most clever dogs can encounter difficulties which slow down the learning process. These can be caused by disruption, the particular activity you are teaching, or the tools you are using, because of unfamiliarity, fear, frustration, or simply distractions that take the dog's attention away from you. Even dogs that pick up certain commands quickly may have problems with others."

Consistency throughout is the secret. Even if you are not doing much formal training, you can think of every activity as an opportunity to teach. "If you do this as a matter of routine," Martin promises, "one day someone will say, 'What a well-behaved dog,' and you will say, 'Yes, she was a natural.'"

RULE #8: TAKE BREED INTO ACCOUNT

You will sometimes hear an owner brag about his dog by saying something like, "She's a collie, and that's the world's smartest breed." Everybody wants to think that their dog is "smarter" than any other dog, but what do we mean when we say "smart"? How do we know what makes one animal smarter than another? We can't give animals IQ tests or ask for their SAT scores. Even if we could sit a raccoon and a pig and a crow all down at three desks, give each animal a number-two pencil, and start them answering questions on a timer, we still couldn't compare their responses because, practically, they would all need to take different tests. Nature built a raccoon for a totally different purpose and ecological niche than it built a crow or a pig.

It's no different with dogs. Although breeds of dogs are all the same species, *Canis familiaris,* human beings have genetically engineered most dogs for specific purposes as well. So we can't really compare the imaginary IQ test scores of a greyhound to those of a beagle or a Labrador retriever. These three breeds are genetically designed to do different jobs in the world, so they have different built-in strengths and weaknesses that usually have very little to do with "intelligence." Is a car mechanic smarter than a Nobel Prize–winning poet? Maybe the poet has a higher IQ on paper, but if your car breaks down, you don't call the poet to come fix it.

Intelligence is a matter of perception, and the question to ask is: What does "smart" mean to you right now, for the job you need to have done? You may think your high-energy, agile Australian cattle dog is the most intelligent dog in the world, but if you are lost in the mountains and rescued by a slow-moving, sad-eyed bloodhound, then I promise you that you will be wanting to give that bloodhound an honorary PhD while your cattle dog is still going around and around in circles trying to find you. It's all a matter of figuring out what your needs and perceptions are.

In terms of obedience and trick training, of course, herding dogs tend to do very, very well, and people perceive them as smarter because of the way their intelligence manifests itself. These are the dogs that can learn "math"—as in one finger means one bark, two means two, and so on. But the capacity for understanding "math" is part of the herding dog's genetics. Herding is an incredibly complex task that involves acute awareness of movement and distances, spatial learning, lightning-quick responses, and even the ability to strategize. A herding dog is very sight-oriented and is always on the alert for visual cues and movements coming from the humans and the nonhuman animals around them. When people say to me, "The herding dogs are the smartest breeds," they are also saying that the intelligence those dogs display most closely resembles human intelligence. To my mind, the jury is still out on whether human intelligence is all it's cracked up to be.

Of course, training is all about helping our dogs flourish and become the best they can be, using all the skills and smarts that come built into their DNA. For instance, to watch a group of well-trained cattle dogs work a herd of sheep is to witness an intricately choreographed performance that is better and more seamless than the most amazing ballet ever staged at Lincoln Center. But you are not going to see a border collie looking for bombs. Their best assets are not their noses but their eyes, their acute perception of movement, and their reflexes. As a breed, they're not going to be able to perform as sniffers as well as breeds such as the bloodhound, the basset hound, the German shepherd, the Belgian malinois, and the Labrador.

Likewise, when we returned to check on Viper the cell-phone dog—a Belgian malinois—after his two months of rehabilitation with us, Harlen Lambert gave us a demonstration of how well the new, balanced Viper could work. When I watched him do his thing and find all those tiny hidden electronic components, I felt like I had a ticket to the best detective film Hollywood ever made. You may not be sending a Newfoundland to sniff for drugs, but if you want to see one of the most heroic feats in the world, watch a well-trained Newfie do a search-and-rescue in the water. It's like an action movie. Witnessing any dog work at the peak of its abilities is better—for me anyway—than any man-made form of entertainment on earth. And that's what training a balanced dog can do for you—give you a free lifetime pass to Mother Nature's multiplex.

Choosing the wrong breed for the job can definitely get in the way of the training you want to do. "Here's a little war story," recounts Bob Bailey with a chuckle. "We were doing work for a military group, and one of the animals they selected for us to use was the American basset hound. Now, his was a pretty high-energy job of having to go out and detect mines, and you had to go through obstacle courses and that kind of thing. If you know an American basset, I mean, they look up at you with those sad eyes, and they just give you this look of agony. Anyway, we could not believe their choice, and we said right from the very start, 'This is not a good selection. You must have meant the English basset.' There's a world of difference—the English basset is definitely a working dog. It turns out that really was the problem. But we worked six months with those American bassets, and we were in hysterics, because they ended up doing what we wanted, but it took a long, loooong time."

A skilled trainer, however, can overcome such obstacles, in Bob's opinion: "A lot of people would say, 'This is going to be a slow-moving animal,' so they themselves move slowly. And the dog just moves slower, and so the person moves slower, and then the dog moves slower, and that's not the way it should be. You can almost always perk up these supposedly slow dogs by working faster. If you don't do it within a certain period of time, the bar is closed. You can't expect too much at first, but over a period of time the animal changes what you might call work ethic."

Beyond specific breed-related abilities, all dog breeds are capable of learning basic obedience. They can all learn to respond to commands and even to do tricks, depending on the limitations of their bodies, of course.

Bonnie Brown-Cali trains dogs to do search-and-rescue and to identify environmental scents for conservation work. She takes breed-related characteristics into account in selecting candidates for training. "For search-and-rescue, I look for a dog that's a little bit obsessive," she says. "One who likes repetition, has a lot of play drive and a little bit of prey drive, but a lot of just work drive, and who likes to interact with the owner.

"A simple test is to see if a dog will have the drive to search for a treat or a toy, first without distractions, then with distractions. I prefer to work with Labradors because of their retrieving instinct. They are happy doing repetitive work. However, there are many dogs, including mixed breeds, that are driven to do the same work over and over. It is not about the breed, but about the instinctual behavior and the task to be performed. A dog that is play driven but easily distracted by prey is not going to be focused on the work at hand."

In other words, there is a training exercise and even a job just right for every dog—including yours.

TRAINING SUCCESS STORY: ANGEL'S AGILITY

"I got miniature schnauzer Albert Angel from Cesar when he was about eight months old," says SueAnn Fincke, *Dog Whisperer*'s producer and director. "Raised for the book *How to Raise the Perfect Dog,* Angel was all that and more. But after a couple of

Angel and SueAnn on an agility course

months I wanted to pursue an activity with Albert that would not only challenge him but also strengthen the bond between us." When SueAnn asked me about agility, I told her it was a great idea. Terriers like Angel can make wonderful agility dogs, and having raised Angel from puppyhood, I knew him to be a dog that needed lots of mental and physical challenges to be happy and fulfilled.

SueAnn called Cara Callaway, the owner of Jump City Agility in Van Nuys, California, and registered for a series of beginning classes. They met once a week at a local park.

"The course looks a bit like a circus ring—with tunnels, A-frames, tires, and teeter-totters," SueAnn recounts. "Agility training is all about positive reinforcement. Albert Angel gets rewarded every time he completes one of the obstacles on the course. You simply keep trying to do the obstacle until you succeed, and you always end with a reward. Since Albert and I are still beginners, his reward is food. But I don't just give him dog treats. Albert gets the real deal—small pieces of meat or maybe salmon. And because he is rewarded so much in the two hours we are training, Cara recommends not feeding him dinner on our training day."

Agility training is all about you and your dog progressing as a team. Patience is key. You work one obstacle at a time—over and over again, always motivating and encouraging your dog along the way to finish the task. "You learn voice commands, so that once you have advanced to doing the whole course, your dog knows what obstacle you want him to complete," SueAnn says.

"Cesar was right, Albert Angel *loves* agility. And it turns out that he is actually very good at it. We are still in the beginning stage, but I look forward to running a whole course with him someday."

RULE #9: SMALL SUCCESSES BUILD
BIG REWARDS

The brain of a puppy, and even that of a mature dog, will get tired more quickly than the body. Training and practicing new behaviors can be a great way to drain energy, which is another reason training your dog is a great way to keep her life challenging and fulfilled. But to build a solid foundation of learning, it's best to work gradually in small increments, keeping sessions short and sweet. "Too often we expect our dog to be in university when she has not even graduated from kindergarten," says Martin Deeley. "It is better to succeed slowly in small steps than to try big steps and fail."

Nothing succeeds like success. Not only is it important to end every training session on a winning note, but it's up to you to always be thinking ahead to find ways for your dog to be successful. Doing the wrong things could be self-rewarding, or you could indirectly reward without knowing it. "One good example," says Martin, "is we love puppies to run up to us and jump at us—we then pick them up and cuddle them. Next they are sixty pounds of muscle and doing it to everyone. What was okay as a pup quickly becomes not okay as a big dog, or even as a small one which is overexcited."

Ian Dunbar agrees. "What's the dog's only crime? It grew up." It is far easier to instill good habits right away than it is to try to break them down the line, no matter what age your dog is.

RULE #10: BE CONSISTENT

The objective of this book is to offer you a wide variety of techniques and tricks for creating a well-behaved dog. Once you have chosen the way that feels right and doable for you, it's best to stick with your strategy until you can make it work. "When I first began training dogs, there was one training standard, the Koehler Method," explains Bonnie Brown-Cali. "With the advances in animal behavior studies, we have a better understanding of how dogs learn. I travel all over the world to learn from and work with a variety of trainers. I have found if you pick a sound training philosophy that fits your dog and your goals, and you stick with that program with repetition and consistency, you are going to have positive results. But if you start bouncing from one training idea to another, you are going to be confused, and so is your dog."

5

HONOR THE ANIMAL

Lessons from Hollywood Animal Trainers

Chico

This isn't a book for professional animal trainers; it's for dog owners who want to give their pet the healthiest, happiest, most fulfilling life ever. But you don't need to take your dog to a casting call to learn from the current generation of humane professional animal trainers working in Hollywood. A great animal trainer is a problem-solver and someone who understands that the best way to get the behavior you want from a dog is to honor the animal by first concentrating on what makes that particular dog happy.

When it comes to animals in entertainment, there is always a lot of controversy. Even the American Humane Association, which since 1980 has been issuing the now-familiar trademarked end credit "No animals were harmed in the making of this film," gets its share of criticism. But in the hands of a great trainer, and working under the AHA guidelines, doing movie work can be a brilliant and exciting challenge for the right dog. I always remind people that as much as dogs need patterns and routines in their lives, they also need adventure. Dogs are an incredibly curious species, and if they're treated right, the kind of daily stimulation that movie work provides can help fulfill them psychologically and lead them to be the best dogs they can be.

Karen Rosa is currently the president of the No Animals Were Harmed® Hollywood division of the American Humane Association and has worked in the Film and Television Unit program for the past eighteen years. "When people say, 'Oh, it's such a shame that these dogs are in entertainment,' I say, 'But they get to travel. They get incredible psychological enrichment. They get exercise. They get all kinds of affection. They get rewarded for doing it. They have a great deal of fun, quite frankly, much more fun than that poor lonely pet alone in the condo for twelve hours while the owner is at work.' Plus, we love the fact that so many of the dogs and cats, especially, in film and television are rescued animals.

"Our main tenet is reward and repeat," says Karen. "Reward the behavior you want, and repeat to encourage it. Any animal on a movie set has to do a lot of repetitions, so this formula is what works best."

Most people don't realize that professional animal trainers do what I do: they check out a dog's energy level—or personality—and make sure it's a fit before casting the dog in any role. And since the fictional dog in any scripted movie may have to show a more multi-faceted personality than any one dog possibly could, sometimes it takes a team of animal actors to flesh out a single character. When I first came to America, I remember how shocked I was when I learned there was more than one Lassie!

"Usually, you have many dogs playing that main character," Karen explained. "So you might actually have five Lassies. You'll have herding Lassie, running Lassie, stunt Lassie, glamour Lassie, and then maybe a red carpet Lassie for live appearances—because their temperaments are all very different. So when a trainer reads a script, he'll think, 'Hey, I've got a dog that can do that. And I've got another dog that can do this. And then where do we fill in the gap?' It's really quite amazing that they are able to get the performances they do from the live animals and get it humanely. It is brilliant to watch them."

It's been a dream of mine since boyhood to watch those Hollywood celebrity animal trainers at work. I believe that these pros with their creative solutions to both building new behaviors and blocking old ones have a whole arsenal of secrets that can help you think of new and ingenious ways to turn your own dog into a happy, obedient pupil.

BE YOUR BEST SELF

On a blustery Saturday afternoon up at my ranch in the Santa Clarita Valley, I invited movie animal trainer Mark Harden to come show me some of the ways he teaches his dogs to perform behaviors on cue. Mark was recommended to me by the American Humane Association as one of its most professional, compassionate, and experienced trainers, and as soon as I met him I could see why they respect him so much. He's a wiry, agile, upbeat man who clearly loves his animals and who even after thirty years on the job remains wildly passionate about what he does. Like me, he could discuss dogs all day. Mark brought four of his best dogs with him to help illustrate the way he works with different animals. I wanted to talk with him about how he gets animals to do amazing things for movies, but I also wanted to find out how some of his secrets could be used by the average dog owner.

One of the first things that Mark said was advice I also give to my clients. "Be yourself first, but be your *best* self. If you're not yourself, the dog will know. I'm a little, quiet guy. I know trainers out there who are really loud and dramatic and expressive. If I tried that, my dogs would laugh at me. If you're a big, loud guy who does best using your voice and making big, grand gestures, then if you try to be like me, the dog just won't believe you. Whereas if you go ahead and be yourself and adapt your techniques to who you truly are inside, the dog will learn, 'Okay, this is who I'm working with,' and adapt himself to that. But you have to stay consistent. You can't be one way one day and another way the next. Be who you are, but be consistent."

I've never been on a movie or television set where there hasn't been a lot of intensity and pressure. There's always a clock ticking, the meter's running, and someone's trying to get somebody else to hurry it up. When I asked Mark about his state of mind when he goes on a set, he told me, "I have to be calm. There's times when I know it's going to be stressful and I'm nervous about getting the action that the director wants, but I have to put myself in a place where I can relax and just breathe. I breathe, calm myself, and say, 'Okay, the dog's not going to do anything if I'm the one freaking out.' I have to be calm, centered, and in control of my emotions."

MARK HARDEN'S TOOLS OF THE TRADE

Bait Bag A bait bag is a simple bag that attaches to my belt and holds the treats I use.

Treats I use treats of all kinds. My current favorite is Natural Balance Rollover. It is a complete and nutritious diet in a convenient log. I can cut it into bite-size pieces and feed it all day without feeling like I'm giving the dog junk food. I am not above using biscuits or hot dogs on occasion. Frequently, I'll boil liver or cook chicken if I need extra drive. I often have my animals working for their living. I measure out their daily diet and try to work them for it.

Beanbag Marks We call the little beanbag disc we train our dogs to stand on a "mark." I use the little nylon discs because they are handy. I have them made in my own unique colors so I don't lose them or confuse them with the marks of other trainers. Our training marks are often replaced on the set with rocks, sticks, leaves, matchbooks, paper plates, or anything that blends into the set.

Apple Boxes An "apple box" is a filmmaking tool we've usurped for animal training. I begin their mark training with apple boxes and start teaching them the basic concept of direction. When on set, I use my apple boxes "out of frame" to give my animals a very specific place to either start or end the scene.

Look Stick I use a Lucite rod with a Kong toy on the end of it. The idea is to teach the dog to look at the toy, not the treat. I train this trick because I can rarely be where the dog is supposed to look. When effectively trained, I can stand in one place and direct the dog's look (or eye line) to another place.

Clicker A clicker is a little plastic box with a metal tongue in it. I use a clicker to communicate with animals less attuned to my vocal inflections and body language, like cats and rats and monkeys. I don't use a clicker with dogs.

Toy Rewards Some dogs are better rewarded by using a favorite toy. Set work can be monotonous and boring, so it becomes important to vary the reward, and toys work best for many high-energy dogs.

The first dog Mark brought out to show me was a Turkish breed— a magnificent Anatolian shepherd named Oscar. With his perfect cream-colored coat, black highlights around his ears, and mastiff-like muzzle, it was a little embarrassing for me, a short guy, to stand next to Oscar, who practically came up to my shoulders. At 160 pounds, he was a stunningly impressive specimen of dog. The first trick of Oscar's that Mark showed me was "get up"—this massive animal jumped up and "hugged" me, with his feet on my shoulders. The trick took me by surprise and made me burst out laughing.

"Oscar was a livestock guardian for a herd of miniature horses," Mark recalled. "And I felt like I'd fallen through the rabbit hole, because his owner had six of these and a dozen miniature horses, and all of the dogs were bigger than the horses. She and her husband were elderly and were downsizing, so they gave me Oscar for the movie *Cats and Dogs 2: The Revenge of Kitty Galore.*"

MARK WORK: THE CONTROLLED STAY

Mark wanted to use Oscar to demonstrate for me how he teaches "mark work": training a dog to go to a certain mark on the floor and to stay there, either to perform a specific behavior or until he's released. Because of the intricacies of camera placement, focus, and lighting on a movie set, sometimes a dog has to move from one mark to another mark in a single shot or "take." The shot will be wrecked if the dog doesn't hit the exact mark. Now, few dog owners need to micromanage their dog's movements this way, but Mark's formula for mark work with movie dogs incorporates some smart suggestions for getting a dog to stay until released.

"Mark work teaches you to be able to control your dog from a distance," Mark explains. "Our goal is always distance, because we have to be somewhere behind the camera and we can't always be right on top of the trick. It's a big challenge for a dog, especially when you've been teaching him from close up to that point, baiting him and rewarding him."

Mark brought out a white quarter–apple box and put it on the ground. Then he guided Oscar to it. Oscar immediately put his two front paws up on the box.

"I start off with something big and obvious, like this box. Later I'll get specific and ask him to be on a part of the box." Mark threw down a round beanbag-filled disc, about four inches in diameter, and Oscar immediately moved his paws onto the center of the box where the disc had landed.

"I start by asking him to get on his mark, and I reward him for staying there," Mark tells me. "Then I ask him to stay on his mark while I move away. I need to be able to stay at a distance and move anywhere while he stays on the box. But there's also what I call the 'yin and the yang' of training. Many people forget that if you teach a dog to stay, you need to give him the command to release him from that stay. If you teach him to lie down, you need to give him the command to get

Oscar on his apple box mark

him up on his feet. If you only teach him one-half of the behavior, then he isn't going to respond to you with consistency."

CAPTURED TRICKS VS. FORCED TRICKS

A trick is "captured" when a trainer sees a natural behavior that a dog is already doing and rewards it, reinforcing him to do it on cue. A "forced" trick isn't supposed to involve force—in the hands of a caring trainer, it's more like a "guided" trick. Mark's example of teaching Oscar to sit is one of those. He gently guided Oscar's butt down to the ground and rewarded him just as it hit. Then he partnered the movement with the verbal cue. "I don't teach 'sit' to my pet dogs," Mark wanted me to understand. "I think it's something that just grows out of our relationship—the way we move, the way we live. With a working dog, it's a little bit different, so I've got to get it on cue, got to get it from a distance."

THE YIN AND YANG OF THE SIT

"Then there's the yin and yang of the sit," says Mark. "So I say, 'On your feet.' To do that, I gently put my toe between his legs, and it prompts him to stand up. So I'm controlling both things—when he sits and when he gets up from the sit. I want to teach the cue, and then the opposite. 'On your feet, stay,' at the same time. So this way I teach both behaviors together."

Mark told me that after a couple days of working with a dog on a big mark like a box, he starts working the mark down in size, until he gets it to something as small as a dime. On movie sets the mark often has to be as small as a rock, or at least small enough that the camera won't see it. In operant conditioning terms, this process is known as "shaping": "The next step is for me not to lead him to the mark, but to teach him to go find it. And I'll reward him for that. So he starts thinking about looking for where that mark will be. I want to teach a dog to think."

Mark starts by using constant positive reinforcement—in this case, paying with treats. "But you have to wean them off that constant reinforcement, because on the set you can't always control when he gets paid. So he has to move to mixed-variable reinforcement, which means, once I know that he knows to hit the mark, I hold off on the pay. I'll just say, 'Good'—that's reinforcing, right? And then maybe I'll use food to pay for the second trick, also bridging it with my 'Good.' And I have a lot of different 'Goods' in my tone of voice. I have 'Good' like 'Okay, you got it, but barely,' and 'Good!' like 'Amazing, what a great job!' I use my body, I use everything I've got, to communicate. Dogs are amazingly intuitive."

PAY FOR WHAT YOU WANT, NOT FOR WHAT YOU DON'T WANT

It's from the mark point that an advanced trainer like Harden teaches his animals to respond to his signals and to perform what are called "micro commands." Those are the behaviors that you'll see an animal express on camera. I watched in amazement as, from a distance, Mark directed Oscar to turn around on his mark like the hands of a clock by saying, "Get around, Oscar." "I used to train elephants when I was younger," Harden explains. "So when I started working with larger dogs and I couldn't physically move them myself, I thought it made sense to just teach them commands the same way I would teach an elephant." As Oscar turned, Mark would sometimes tell him to "look away"—an important command in movies, since animals sometimes have to appear to be looking at something happening on the other side of the screen. Watching Oscar perform his 360-degree turns on command was truly a jaw-dropping moment. For me, it was a lot more interesting than watching a whole movie!

As he worked with Oscar, Mark showed me that *what* you reward is just as important as *when* you reward. "I say, be very specific with the trick, and never pay for what you don't want." He illustrated a common mistake: after asking Oscar to go to his mark, he backed up and, as Oscar reflexively followed him, shouted, "No, no, no," until Oscar hit his mark again; then he said, "Good boy," and paid Oscar with a treat.

"What did I just teach you? You missed your mark, you cheated forward on your mark, you backed up, and then I rewarded you. What I taught you was to take three steps forward and then one step back to get my reward and approval. That's a common mistake people make. So I say, be specific with the trick, pay for the trick, and not the other stuff. So I'll go back and do it over. I'll do it over one hundred times. Eventually he'll learn exactly what it is that gets him paid."

BREAKING THE TRICK

If you shout "Good boy!" after your dog does something and your dog can learn to work through it, fine. But beware of breaking the trick. If you want your dog to sit and then stay, yelling "Good boy!" after his butt touches the ground rewards him before he's finished. You've broken the trick.

"With me," Mark says, "whenever my voice gets excited, it's a cue to my animals that we're done for the day, work time is over, and playtime is about to begin. That's why I remain calm, with less overt emotion, during work hours." Dogs recognize the difference between working and not working—that's how guide dogs, assistance dogs, and security dogs do it. That's why there's usually a sign on their vests saying, DON'T PET OR PLAY WITH THIS DOG—HE'S WORKING. Save your unbridled enthusiasm for pure playtime; don't blow it all when you're trying to teach. Too much enthusiasm can create too much excitement, with the result that you lose the lesson.

Mark stresses that the hard work is rooted in teaching the basics, or the building blocks of the tricks. "I start it all by teaching him to go to his mark, and stay there, and learn that there's a point to all this—that I'm not just a crazy person asking him to do random things. Once he gets that, then the tricks come really fast. The dog has to learn to learn. So start with cause-and-effect tricks—tricks where they do something that makes something happen. 'Give me your paw' is a good one. You start with the seed of a behavior and then shape it into the trick you want it to be, such as first the sit, then the sit-stay, then the sit-stay with distance, then the sit-stay when I can get behind you."

That's an important lesson for all pet owners who teach their dogs commands. Start with the basics and make sure those lessons are ingrained. Once you do that, you've got a solid foundation for any future training you want to do.

BAD DOGS ARE "WINNERS"

Mark's next dog, Finn, had the appealing scruffy face and compact body of your classic lovable terrier mutt. "Look at him," Mark said. "This guy fell right out of a Disney movie. He may have been on death row, but the way he looks—if I can't get this dog a job, forget about it." Finn was a last-chance dog who had been returned to the animal shelter in Agoura, California, three times.

I asked Mark what he looks for in a shelter dog such as Finn, whom many previous owners may have not been able to handle. "I look for the dogs in the shelter that I call the winners. The people in the shelter might not think of them as that. They think of them as losers and feel sorry for them. But to me, this is a dog that has succeeded in everything he's tried to do. He's succeeded in escaping from the yard. He's succeeded in tearing up the living room. He sees himself as a winner. He's in this strange environment, the shelter, and he's still happy. I see him as a dog with a great giving personality who's going to try and try and try until he wins. My job is to challenge him with new things to succeed at and then to pay him for what I want."

When Mark first brought Finn home, Finn, who was a biter, went right for Mark's face. "Within three months I had him on the set, perfectly happy and working. Kids were picking him up. I just had to let him know what was acceptable and what wasn't. Biting any part of my body, that's not cool. He's a terrier with a ton of energy, and the point is to put that energy to work for him instead of against him."

I noticed that when Mark first brought Finn out, the brown-and-white terrier mix was excited and jumpy, until Mark changed his demeanor from a casual one to a working one. I was amazed at how quickly Finn picked up on Mark's cue that, "Okay, now we are getting serious here." The split-second interval that it took for Mark to switch his energy cues from playful to serious was impressive. I wanted Mark to break down for me what exactly he was doing there.

"I practically grew up with wild animals," Mark said, "and one of the things that I learned was, humans are the only animals that play as an end in itself. Most animals use play as a means to an end. I use play that way. I play with them, and then I stop. I understand a little mouthiness in dogs. That's who they are, that is how they communicate. But I would be foolish not to let them know when they are getting to be a little much. So I control it, I start it, I stop it. It allows me to have some dominance without forcing anything on them."

When Mark used the word *dominance*, I stopped him immediately—that's a word that has constantly gotten me into trouble. I wanted him to explain exactly what he meant by it.

"The best dominance is invisible; it's an aura, and the better a leader that you are, the less it is seen," Mark told me. "I've been with wild animals virtually all my life, and this is just a part of all social behavior. In the wolf packs I worked with, the real pack leaders weren't ones who had to do very much at all. They could control everyone with a look or a body posture. It goes to show that the real leaders are the coolest guys in the group."

The word *control* is another hot-button word for some people. I believe we should always have control over our dogs, but it should be a voluntary kind of control in which the pack followers happily and willingly want to please the pack leader. Mark sees it slightly differently. "Well, yes, I do want control of the dog on the set. But what I really want is the animal's attention," he said. "I need him to be paying attention to me and looking to me for the cues as to what he should be doing. But it's a partnership. We're working together on this. I have to earn any control I have."

Sometimes the animals Mark can't control are the other people who work on the busy and chaotic movie sets. He offers some great advice for pet owners who are uncertain about how their dog might react around strange people or animals. "Create a bubble of safety around your dog, especially a learning dog. Make sure the dog is calm and on the leash, and that you are prepared for how he might react. It's up to you, the owner, to keep your dog safe."

THE MOVIE RECALL

"I would never let a new dog off a leash until I have a relationship and a consistent recall," Mark told me. "I learned that the hard way. Someone gave me a rescued briard, and I brought him home and turned him loose in my backyard and said, 'Oh, look at the pretty dog.' And then suddenly it was like I had a coyote in my backyard—I couldn't get near this guy for five days. My kids were terrorized. I asked myself,

'Why would I do this?' This is a totally strange environment, and I've known this dog for all of five minutes. I realized, 'Liberty is earned. This dog has no point of reference for how to behave in my environment.'"

I agree with Mark on this point. Often the first thing people do when they bring a rescued dog home is to set the dog loose in their home. They mean well and are thinking something like, "I want you to know that it's all right, that I love you, and that this is your home now, and that you are free." But these owners are overlooking the fact that the dog has been given no instructions as to how to behave in this new environment. The dog is looking to pick up cues from the owner, but the owner is not giving any. So naturally, the dog is going to improvise—and usually his solution is not going to be one that accounts for your grandmother's wing chair being an heirloom and your carpet having just been shampooed.

"In movie work, a recall is a 'treat' thing. The dogs come for food. With my pet dogs, it's just manners. They come because I call them and we have a relationship and I've trained them to come when they're called. But for a movie dog, I have to know that he will run, across a street, through a field, out a window—every time I call, he's got to reliably come to me."

The movie recall is actually a great exercise that any family can practice at home as a fun game, something to strengthen their dog's desire to respond when his name is called. It is usually done with two trainers as a release and a call. "It's called an 'A to B,'" says Mark.

We started the exercise with me holding Finn off-leash, as the "A," and Mark running all the way across the field. Then he called, "Finn, come!" and Finn took off like a shot toward him. Finn ran from "A" to "B" and got a treat. Of course, Finn already knew Mark. To train him to come back to me, a perfect stranger, Mark brought Finn closer to me, gave me some bait, and then let me call him at close quarters. When Finn reached me, I rewarded him for it. We repeated that exercise again and again, with each of us moving farther apart each time.

"We'll do that all day, going back and forth, back and forth," Mark explained. By the end of the exercise, Finn was coming to me when I called him from all the way across the field.

"The next step in creating a consistent recall would be, one of us might go around a blind corner and call him, so we'd be out of sight and he'd be coming to our voice. When we have that down, we might run around your ranch here and hide and do the 'A' to 'B' from various hiding places at the ranch, to get him to come look for me. I'd start by paying him all the time, and then break it off. I only do that once I feel they've got the trick. This guy—Finn—he doesn't need treats because he just loves to run. I've got to admit that sometimes the treat payoff is really for me, not the dog—because it makes me feel good to give them something."

THE HARD-TO-REACH DOG

Right after Mark finished telling me about how important it is to create "professional relationships" with the animals he works with, he admitted to me that he had a secret. "This is my favorite dog," he said coyly, as he slipped a martingale collar around the neck of one of the most magnificent Akitas I've ever seen in my life. "I use the martingale with him because I don't have to make the loop with it every time. I can just go up to Chico on the set, put the collar on, move him, slip it on, slip it off.

"I got this dog when he was two, worked with him for six months, then worked with him on the movie *Hachiko: A Dog's Tale*. Since then, I've had him for almost three years. He was initially a failed show dog because he was so shy. Why was he shy? Again, I don't really care. It could have been birth order for all I know. People say, 'Oh, that dog must've been abused,' but he came from an excellent breeder, and I think birth order can play as much role in a dog's personality as anything else. Where was he in that original pack? Was he the last one out, the one who got kicked away from the teat all the time? Was he stepped all over by the other puppies? I don't know, but even if I did, that really doesn't help me. I have to help him work through those issues in the present, not the past."

Mark is a man after my own heart in this philosophy. When I rehabilitate a dog, the owners often want to tell me the long, long story of the terrible life the dog lived before they stepped in and saved him. Well, that may be the truth, or it may be their imagination. But because it's in the past, it's history. And history is, by definition, just another story. I have to work in the now, which is the reality. I want to look at the dog before me as he is today and figure out: Who is he at this moment, and what does he need from me to be able to help him?

The story of how Mark broke through to this incredible Akita and not only trained him but created a lasting bond with him is incredibly beautiful. It choked me up a little bit. It brings home one of the lessons I hope you are getting from this book—that in order to teach a dog to be obedient to your wishes, you've got to reciprocate by sharing something that also matters to him. Mark told me, "I love Chico so much probably because I really had to work for it.

"When I got him," Mark recalls, "the breeder said, 'He really likes you,' because I took him out and he came right to me. 'He never does that,' the breeder says. And Chico went to me, and I walked him. I brought him home. He came out of the crate to me—it's very important to me to be the first one to open the crate door. And he came right out. Everything was good."

But then Mark tried feeding Chico. Not only did the dog refuse to take food from Mark's hand, but he even refused to eat in his presence! "It was almost like a humiliation. It just was verboten. 'No, I'm an Akita. I don't eat out of your hand.' And I was like, 'Dude, you got to eat.' And I couldn't find anything that gave this dog pleasure or joy, and I'm going, 'Well, this isn't going to work. Not if you don't enjoy this.' But I had no choice because we're doing an Akita movie, and he's the lead dog, and this is our livelihood. I mean, if I can get a leopard to hit a mark, I can get this dog to hit a mark. I just have to figure out how to communicate with him."

Mark's relationship with Chico finally turned a corner when he started doing agility work with him. "Pretty soon he was doing the full agility course, no treats, no rewards. Wouldn't look at me at first, but he got it. There was a purpose to my training. 'Oh, he wants me to go from here to there. And then from here to there. Now I get it.' It made sense to him. Mostly, he enjoyed it. And then after that, a couple of other things started making sense to him, and then pretty soon he was gobbling food out of my hand. He got his whole diet out of my hand."

After a month of not getting any response from Chico, Mark finally found his "in" through the agility work they did together. In six months, Chico was doing the lead role in a movie with Richard Gere, performing on cue in front of huge film crews, lights, and machinery. Akitas are traditionally very difficult to train. Many of the more ancient breeds seem to be more aloof and less inclined to want to please humans than retrievers, herding dogs, or terriers, for example.[1] "The Akita breeders were shocked that I got so much work out of this dog and so much reliable repetition. After the movie, I took him home as a pet, which I'd never done before."

It's important to note why Mark was so successful. He wasn't just thinking about what the dog could do for him. He was thinking, "How can I find something that really turns this dog on?" Making the experience fun and challenging for the dog was the most important element in their relationship. "I wanted him to get joy out of the work. Otherwise, I would have none," Mark says.

DIFFERENT DOGS, DIFFERENT ABILITIES

The last dog that Mark brought out to show me was absolutely gorgeous—a brown-and-white English shepherd named Dusty. Dusty was half of a duo—Dusty and Duffy, two lookalike English shepherds who together make up the character of Sam the shape-shifter dog in the HBO vampire series *True Blood*. One of Dusty's special tricks was lifting his leg on command.

I watched as Mark called Dusty to his mark, then commanded, "Lift!" The leg went right up, and Mark gently whispered, "Hike, hike," as the dog continued to hold it for a good ten seconds. Mark released Dusty by saying, "All right!" and giving the dog a treat from his pouch.

"This is a kind of 'forced trick,' the same idea as 'give me your paw,' except it's 'give me your back paw,'" he explained. Mark's assistant, Tracy Kelly, brought a white half–apple box to help Mark show me how the trick had been shaped. He used a pointer to guide Dusty's leg up onto the box, then rewarded him. "You start by rewarding him for just a touch. So he gets the idea. You start with a small box and then lift it higher and higher."

Of course, an English shepherd has the agility and physical body type to be able to do this. Another dog might have a harder time. That's why Hollywood animal trainers often use multiple dogs to play one role.

"Different dogs have different abilities and different personalities," said Mark. "For instance, Dusty did the leg lift faster, he caught on to it better, than Duffy, so usually, if we need a leg lift, I'll use him in the scene. He's also more people-oriented than Duffy, so if there's a scene where he has to run into a group of people and get hugged, we would go to him. Duffy is a little more trick-oriented, a little more precise, so if it's something real specific, we'll go to Duffy. Duffy also has a more serious look to his face. This guy"—he gestured to Dusty, mussing up his fur—"kind of has a more open and youthful look. Duffy's a little more serious, a little sleeker, so if it's a scene involving aggression or something where he has to be ominous, he looks a little better, so we just balance it out. One time they got to work with each other because they play Sam, the character's dog, but they also play the dog that Sam shape-shifts into. So in one scene Sam shape-shifts into a dog, and he and his own dog go swimming together. That was a fun one."

When we shook hands at the end of the day and Mark and Tracy piled his dogs into his truck for the drive back to his ranch in northern Los Angeles County, I felt like I'd been talking to a kindred spirit. While Mark's work involves getting animals to do behaviors solely for human benefit, he clearly approaches his job from the dog's perspective and looks for ways to make movie work fun and rewarding for the dog. This is a man who begins every task by reminding himself to honor the animal first. In my opinion, that's why he has been getting such great results and having fun at his job for over thirty years.

MARK HARDEN'S HOLLYWOOD TRAINING RULES

1. Be clear and simple in what you want from the dog. Start with small, basic tricks and don't move on until you are certain that the first behaviors have been consistently mastered.
2. Every dog is different, and different dogs are motivated by vastly different things. Have a lot of options in your tool kit, and don't give up until you find that special reward or activity that allows you and your dog to communicate with each other. And make sure the experience is fun!

(continues)

3. My "yin and yang" rule: when you teach any behavior, also teach the opposite of that behavior—for instance, "sit" goes with "get on your feet!"

4. Use mixed-variable reinforcement—once the dog has the basics of the behavior you are trying to teach, don't reward it every time and alternate rewards, from food to praise to toys. Eventually, having successfully completed the behavior becomes a reward in itself.

5. Be specific. Pay for what you want, not for what you don't want. If the dog gets only part of the behavior right, don't reward. Otherwise, you are teaching him to get only part of the behavior right! Let him figure out what it is he needs to do to get paid—that's part of the challenge.

6. Be yourself when training—your best self—and be consistent.

LOSING THE LEASH

Dr. Ian Dunbar and Hands-Off Dog Training

Dune in the park

Our van filled with the scent of freshly blooming spring flowers as we wound our way up the picturesque streets of the Berkeley, California, hills. At the crest stood Ian and Kelly Dunbar's house—a charming Italian-style villa from the 1920s, set above a lush garden that looked out on the park and the college town below.

When I first learned about Dr. Ian Dunbar and how he had pioneered off-leash training for puppies, I had immediately wanted to meet him. Ian and his lovely wife, Kelly Gorman Dunbar—also a dog trainer—had met me for a casual dinner two years earlier. We all got along famously, but never really addressed the "elephant in the living room," which was the very different ways each of us worked with dogs.

The purpose of this second meeting was to share ideas and information and for Ian to show me, hands-on, how his off-leash training methods work. By inviting me into their home, the Dunbars knew they would draw flak from some in the positive training community who criticize and often misinterpret what I do. And I knew that I would be spending the good part of two days as the student of someone who doesn't agree with me in a few key areas. But I had been looking forward to this meeting for a very long time. As a father, it is very important for me to show my kids by example that we need to dialogue with people who might not agree with us instead of being defensive or shutting them out or labeling their ideas as wrong. I want my sons to make a difference in the world, not by staying away from people who don't share their exact point of view but by talking with them and, most of all, by listening to them. This is how we learn and grow and how we make a difference as human beings, not just as dog whisperers or dog trainers. By sharing information and opening our minds, everybody benefits, and we open a door of hope for the world. I believe that world transformation begins with self-transformation, and that was the spirit I carried with me as I prepared for the opportunity to work with one of the most respected and influential men in modern dog training.

"Mind the wall," the neatly dressed, snowy-haired Ian Dunbar chirped helpfully as we backed into his narrow driveway. Pointing to a pale yellow stucco barrier that bordered the front of the house, he casually added, "My son Jamie and I put that up ourselves."

That homemade wall was my first hint that Ian Dunbar and I had a whole lot more in common than it might appear on the surface. After all, I am an earthy Mexican guy with a high school education who came across the border with only the clothes on his back. He is a proper Englishman with a wall covered in diplomas—a veterinary degree, with special honors in physiology and biochemistry, from the Royal Veterinary College of London University and a doctorate in animal behavior from the psychology department of UC Berkeley—and spent a decade researching olfactory communication, social behavior, and aggression in domestic dogs. Ever since I appeared on television in the United States, my critics have compared me unfavorably with Ian Dunbar, who had his own television series in the United Kingdom for five years. What could the two of us possibly share beyond our interest in dogs?

Well, it turns out that we are both country farm boys at heart—a couple of simple guys who want nothing more than to be able to plant trees in our gardens, build our own walls, and wander the countryside with our dogs. Ian's cordial, easygoing manner put me instantly at ease.

"I grew up on a farm," Ian sighed. "When I was a kid, I roamed the fields with my dog. I was always with the dog. And it was wonderful. I didn't even own a leash until my first dog show."

I nodded and wistfully drifted back to my own days on my grandfather's farm, trudging through pastures and down dusty roads, always with a pack of dogs trailing after me. No leashes involved there either.

"And people don't get to enjoy that today, you know?" Ian continued. "There's not so many places now you can go with dogs off-leash. It's happening in countries all around the world now. When I was a kid in England, if you went into a pub, there were three dogs in there: two lurchers and a Jack Russell, all drinking beer from a saucer. Now you go into a pub, you don't see a single dog."

"Why do you think that is?" I asked him.

"We're becoming much more restrictive now because people are worried about dog aggression," Ian answered. "But ironically, the increased restriction means it's more difficult to socialize a dog now."

The rise in the problem of antisocial, out-of-control dogs is the place where the lives of a British veterinarian and a Mexican immigrant converge. While unruly dogs drove my career path from becoming the trainer of the next Lassie to being the Dog Whisperer, the same problem inspired Ian Dunbar to develop his own original view of how to train puppies—as well as grown dogs—to become obedient off-leash. His goal is to use basic training to prevent all those behavior and communications snafus that end up with the crazy, out-of-control situations that make my television show so dramatic.

"I teach mostly noncontact techniques, and there's a good reason for that," Ian explained. "Most human hands can't be trusted. Of all the humans who can't be trusted with their hands, I guess men and children are probably the worst. They do a lot to dogs that spook dogs out. If they have the leash on, and the owner's touching the leash, they're usually going to end up jerking it. So I just say, 'Well, we'll take the leash off, solves that problem.'

"It's one thing if you're an experienced animal handler like you or me, 'cause you know which animals you dare touch and how you can touch them," he continued. "The training methods that I would prescribe have nothing to do with the way I would train a dog or you would train a dog. It has to do with the fact that this is a family and there's two children in it. They're not necessarily going to have the observational skills that we have, or the speed or the timing, and certainly not the dog savvy. But they still have to learn to live happily with their dog.

"Most people use the leash as a crutch. It's become a training tool which is very, very difficult to phase out. Food is easy compared to that."

Working with dogs off-leash is my own preference as well, though the tools I'd usually employ would be my energy, body language, touch, and a couple of simple sounds. Ian Dunbar doesn't agree with my way of using touch to correct a dog. Although he also uses body language to communicate, his tool of choice is his voice.

"I keep my hands off the dog. I never use my hands to get him to do stuff, but the hands do go on him to say thank you, to say, 'There's a good dog.' But I use my voice, because the voice is the only thing we've got with us all the time."

I've always preferred silence when working with dogs. To my way of thinking, that is how they communicate in their own world—using scent, energy, body language, eye contact, and then sound last of all. Learning Ian Dunbar's method of training would be a new challenge for me, but an important and exciting one. Many of my clients dream of being able to use verbal commands to communicate with their dogs.

"With my malamute, I used to be able to talk to her in a complete sentence. 'Phoenix, come here, take this, and go to Jamie, please.' So she'd take a note and run down and find Jamie in the garden. It's binary feedback: reward the dog when he gets it right, reprimand him when he gets it wrong, but always use your voice. Use it instructively because that's what you want to teach. The main criterion of training is that we have verbal control when the dog's at a distance and distracted and without the need of any training aid whatsoever. No leash, no collar, no food treats, no ball, no tug toy. When you say sit, that dog sits."

I had brought along my trusty pit bull Junior, then two and a half years old. Like all of my dogs, of course, he was totally "balanced," yet not what I would call trained. "I have raised him since he was two months old," I told Ian. "I can't take the credit—my dog Daddy, who passed away a few months ago, did most of it. Junior pretty much took over Daddy's way of being, and I just guided them a little bit. And so Junior has no 'sit', no 'down,' no 'stay.'" I demonstrated for Ian the two command sounds that Junior knows: a kissing sound that means "come, yes, good," and my "tsssst" sound, which means "I don't agree with what you are doing." "Those are the only sounds he knows, but I would like you to show me how you would teach him commands."

Welcoming the challenge, Ian invited Junior and me into his airy, light-filled living room and offered me a seat on a thick-cushioned chocolate leather sofa.

JUNIOR LEARNS ENGLISH AS A SECOND LANGUAGE

"Before we start," Ian began, "my grandfather taught me that touching an animal is an earned privilege. It's not a right." I smiled, feeling even more at ease. There was one more thing that this charming Englishman and I had in common—grandfathers who shared with us their wisdom in the ways of Mother Nature. "And the most dangerous part on a dog is that red thing around his neck." He gestured at Junior's collar. "About twenty percent of dog bites happen when the owner touches that. Happens when an angry owner grabs a collar and gets in the dog's face—'You bad dog.'" Ian had spent several years researching the causes and effects of domestic dog aggression, so he knew his statistics.

To avoid that potentially volatile situation, Ian uses a treat in hand as a temperament test. "I take a little time. See, I don't know Junior. He has no reason to like me. So I want to make sure he's okay. If Junior here takes the treat, I say, 'Gotcha. We're off and running. We're gonna work with you today.'" As Junior took the treat from his hand, Ian took Junior's collar in the other, then repeated those two motions a few times. Ian was conditioning Junior to associate his hand with the pleasant experience of getting the treat. This kind of association can also be a lifesaver, he added.

"You know, we could have an emergency: he could be jumping out the car window on the freeway, and I grab his collar quickly.

He's not going to react by biting me; his first thought is, 'Where's my treat?'"

Ian explained to me that his process begins with a very simple four-part sequence: (1) request, (2) lure, (3) response, and (4) reward.

"So we say, 'Junior. Sit.' That's number one, the request. And then we lift the food up." Ian bent his arm at the elbow and lifted the treat lure up above Junior's head. "Now his butt goes on the ground. That's the response. So now, 'Good boy. Take it.' We reward."

Ian then asked Junior to stand, moving his hand with the treat slightly over to the side. "When he stands, we say, 'Good boy,' and then we give him the treat." Ian repeated this sequence one more time, with Junior responding nicely.

I noticed that Ian would hold the treat right up against Junior's teeth but wouldn't give it to him right away. "The longer you hold on to it," he explained, "you reinforce this really nice, calm, solid sit-stay."

Junior was doing just great with the sit-and-stand routine. Next, Ian gave Junior a much tougher assignment—the "Down." Saying the word *down,* Ian moved his hand holding the treat to the floor. Junior followed with his eyes but didn't go into the down position.

"It's all right," Ian said kindly. "This one is a little harder." He started the routine again with "Sit," using just his arm movement and not producing a treat reward.

"See, I'm already phasing out the food lure for the sit signal. That's really important. Phasing out the food is the most important thing that you do in training, and this is what a lot of people aren't doing. So the dog learns: if my owner has food, I'll do it; if he doesn't have food, I won't. Just like there's no point in having a dog trained that is only obedient if he's on-leash, there is no point in a dog that's only obedient if you've got food on you. We've got to make sure that he will listen to us even when we don't have food."

I looked over at Junior proudly. There he was, attentive, alert, in perfectly poised pit bull posture. He was just waiting for the next command.

"Look at Junior," Ian said, echoing my thoughts. "He's thinking, 'What do I do next?' So nice and calm. So we'll try with the down again." Ian moved his arm down, and this time Junior followed with his whole body, but very awkwardly. Ian still rewarded him with the treat and encouraged him in a warm, comforting voice: "Good dog. Good boy. There's a very good dog. I'm very impressed by that. Junior, sit." When Junior sat right up again at only the verbal command, I couldn't help but pump my fist in the air.

Ian laughed. "You're proud of him, aren't you? Okay, Junior, down." Down Junior went, folding into the floor one clumsy body part at a time.

"Good dog," Ian said, "even though that was more of a collapse than a down. I'll reward you anyway. What we're doing here is teaching Junior ESL—English as a Second Language. We're gradually working on these three commands: 'sit,' 'down,' 'stand.'"

As he continued to work Junior with the three commands, Ian explained to me that by teaching a dog these basic commands—most important, a reliable "sit"—he can solve 95 percent of potential behavior issues that could arise with his dogs. That foolproof off-leash "sit" is at the core of Dunbar's training philosophy. "If he's about to run through the door, jump up on you, chase the cat, get on the couch, jump out of the car before you want him to . . . 'Junior, sit.' End of problem. If he's about to chase a little girl in the park because she's got a hamburger, even though Junior's just playing, because he's a pit bull, imagine what people would think. 'Junior, sit.' End of problem."

Ian went on to explain that, even though the fail-safe "sit" is the most important thing to shoot for, he works a dog with the three different commands so that the dog actually learns what each word means. If he just does "Sit, stand," or "Sit, down," the dog can outsmart him by predicting what command will logically come next. By switching up the commands, from "Sit, stand, down," to "Stand, down, sit," in as many variations on the sequence as possible, he forces the dog to actually listen to the sounds coming out of the trainer's mouth and figure out which sound attaches to which behavior.

"It's not the words themselves that are important," Ian explained. "Kelly teaches her dogs in French. You could use Spanish. I use words so that the owners understand the meaning. But for the dog it doesn't matter. After just half a dozen or so associations, a dog can understand the meaning of a new sound or word."

"How do you do the transition from him expecting the food to not getting the food?" I asked Ian.

"First we phase out food as a lure, and then we phase out food as a reward," he responded. "Okay? Junior, down. So, you see, I don't have food in my hand. He's following my hand, but he went down, so I'll give him the reward from the other hand." Ian continued working with Junior, demonstrating the many different ways he phases out food lures. First, he would change the hand in which he kept the food so that the dog was responding to the hand signal but not the food. Next, he'd put the food in his pocket or on a nearby table and use it as a distraction and a reward. Junior knew the lure was there, but he couldn't focus on it because he had to pay attention to Ian's commands and signals. Ian even gave me the food lure to hold, which was an even bigger distraction for Junior, since I'm his owner and the one he is used to listening to. Also, Ian rewarded Junior with the food only intermittently, and only for Junior's best responses, so Junior never knew when or if a reward was coming. Throughout all these variations in how he used food as a reward, Ian continued to reward Junior verbally. "Your dog knows what 'Good dog!' means. Not necessarily the words, but your tone of voice, and your face, and your body language. 'Praise your dog when he gets it right,' I tell people. Too many people only talk to their dogs when they get it wrong. Dogs do so many more things right than wrong."

Though Ian advises dog owners to phase out treats for training as soon as they see the dog making the connection from a command or hand gesture to the desired behavior, he thinks that treats still have an important place in an overall plan for socializing a dog, especially to strangers and guests. "Keep treats in the house for guests, so that your dog always associates new people coming in with good things happening. Your guests can practice teaching commands too, which is good for the dog. And absolutely save the best, tastiest treats for kids to use. That way, when your dog sees a child, he associates it with the absolutely most wonderful reward."

As Ian repeated the three-command sequence, Junior was definitely getting the hang of the process, but his body was moving too slowly for Ian's tastes. "I feel like we're in slow motion. I want to show you a really fast dog doing this."

"Junior, buddy, what are you doing to me?" I thought to myself. He wasn't doing anything wrong, of course, but for my own ego reasons, I wanted Junior to be the most perfect dog in the world for his lesson with Dr. Ian Dunbar! I mean, how would it look if the Dog Whisperer's number one right-hand dog was deemed "slow"?

"He's a smart dog," Ian replied, sensing my dismay. "And a smart dog can be harder to train. I mean, he was outthinking me in a number of ways. He says, 'No, you don't have food in your hand, it's in the other hand.' I was trying to move too fast with him. So, yeah, he's got a good IQ. He's a smart dog."

"Thank you, God!" I exclaimed.

HUGO AT LIGHTNING SPEED

Ian's wife, Kelly, brought in Hugo, a happy-go-lucky, high-energy French bulldog with huge, expressive brown eyes. Kelly is the founder of Open Paw, an international humane animal education program for pet owners and shelters, and Ian says that she is a far better trainer than he is. My observation was that these two top trainers share the same overall training philosophy but have different personal styles. While Ian is effusive, a bit goofy, and gives lots of continual verbal feedback during a session, Kelly is a little more like me in that she is quiet and reserved until she feels she's achieved her objective 100 percent. She works with subtle gestures and very few words. I thought about Mark Harden's advice to trainers to "be yourself first, but be your *best* self," concluding that both Ian and Kelly are absolutely their best selves working with the dogs that they love. That is the mark of a great handler—maintaining personal integrity at all times.

Calling Hugo over to the sofa, Ian said he would show me his training routine with a dog that had much faster reflexes than Junior. I swallowed my ego and tried not to take the comparison personally. "This is just like I was doing with Junior, but faster," Ian said. "So, first we work with food in hand. Sit. Down. Sit. Down. Sit. Good. Stand. Good dog! Down. Sit. Yeah, you're missing it, dude, I'm sorry. Sit. Down. Sit."

I was blown away by the feisty Frenchy's speed. Ian rattled off the words in rapid-fire succession, and Hugo moved like lightning. "So," Ian continued, "once we get him as fast as this, I know I can cause the behavior just by moving my hand. Now watch this." Ian called out six quick command sequences, and Hugo responded perfectly. At the end of the long sequence, Ian rewarded him.

"Now, this is his first treat he's getting after all that behavior. So I was using the food as a lure to teach him how my hand moves, but now that he has learned the hand signals, I can put the food in my pocket and use it only occasionally to reward him for faster or more stylish responses. Then we go cold turkey on the food and phase it out completely. We use verbal commands and hand signals to get him to respond and then reward him with life rewards. For example, 'Hugo sit,'. . . . and then we throw a ball. 'Hugo, down,' . . . and we pet him. Or we ask him to sit lots of times while playing tug-of-war. We use food as a lure to teach him what we want him to do and to get the speed, and then we totally phase it out, first as a lure and then as a reward. From then on, we use life rewards to motivate him to want to comply."

The next level of Ian's training involves phasing out the hand signals so that the dog responds only to the verbal commands. "Now, this is the hard bit," he told me. "Because, as you always say, Cesar, body language is the way dogs read us. They sniff, they see life through their nose, or watching the movement of people or other dogs or animals, and so we think, 'Oh, he's learned what 'sit' and 'down' and 'stand' mean,' but he hasn't, he's actually learned what the *hand and body movements* mean.

"So this is where the timing is really important. We have to say the word, a very short pause, and then [do] the hand movement. So it has to be like this: 'Hugo, down. Good.' Now there, he was going down before I did the hand movement, which is showing he does have some comprehension. Eventually, he will anticipate the hand signal and he will respond when I ask him to verbally, and that's when he's starting to actually learn the meaning of words. And that's so important for dogs, because at home they're off-leash, their back is turned, they're in another room, and so verbal communication is the only way to go. You can't touch the dog's collar or give a hand signal—he can't see it. So that's why verbal control is really important, but it's the most difficult thing to teach. It takes usually about twenty trials before he can make the connection. So you can see the learning in progress."

I observed that when Ian commanded "down" to Hugo, while he was phasing out his hand signals, he made a tiny, unconscious movement of his head. He laughed out loud when I busted him. "That's bad, but we all do it. What I meant to do is do this absolutely still. 'Hugo, sit. Good dog. Hugo, down. Good boy!' So I was better there, was I?" he asked.

"Good boy!" I told Ian.

"You have to minimize the signals you are sending, with your body or even your eyes. And that's where, when the dog doesn't do it and people think, 'Oh, he's dissing me, he's being disobedient,' then they start to get frustrated, and they get mad at the dog, and the relationship goes downhill. But that's not what's happening. I mean, look at Hugo now—is he being disobedient? No, he's sitting right in front of me, looking at me, but he just doesn't understand yet because I haven't done sufficient training with him."

Kelly, who was standing by quietly watching us with Hugo, added her own thoughts on the subject. "I think it's an important point that people don't realize all the signals they are giving their dog with their bodies and their heads all the time," she mused. "So then, when the dog isn't looking at them, they're saying 'sit' or 'down,' and the dog doesn't respond, now the dog is bad. Or they may be saying one word, but their body is saying something else. So that's why verbal commands are so important, but so few dogs have adequate verbal comprehension. They're just so very good at observing us."

"And I should say," Ian added, "Hugo is much better trained in French. Kelly uses French, and he is a well-trained dog, it's just he doesn't know English when I speak it very well."

"Is it because of your accent?" I asked him with a wink.

"No, no." Ian laughed. "Actually, I try not to train him that much so I can use him as a demo dog, because he'll be more likely to make mistakes. One of the most endearing things about dogs is that they are individuals. They're not robots, and to me, when they do it their own way or make a mistake, it's almost as endearing as when they do it right, as long as it's not dangerous. The reason I like working with Hugo is to show to people that just because your dog doesn't do it, doesn't mean to say he's bad, or not smart. It means you need to train him more and keep working at it, because it's the learning process."

Before we moved on to the next stage of training, Ian offered me a go at teaching Hugo in Spanish, to demonstrate how dogs learn words. "Just use your hand signals, okay? 'Cause Hugo knows those."

I raised my arm, saying, "Hugo, *siéntate*, Hugo, *siéntate*. Hugo, *échate*. Hugo, *párate*." He responded quickly to every command.

"We have a multilingual dog!" Ian cheered. "This is his first Spanish lesson. He speaks French, he speaks English, and now he speaks Spanish. And that is what training is all about. It's teaching our languages as a second language to the dog. Whether it's Spanish as a second language, English as a second language, or French as a second language. Then we can communicate to them what we'd like them to do."

"But again, it's really not the words themselves the dog understands, right?" I asked.

"Whether they really understand the actual meaning of a word—we can have a discussion about that for hours," Ian responded. "What we do know is, you can teach a dog if you say a word: he will do a certain thing to a certain amount of reliability. But dogs learn differently from people, of course; they don't generalize. For example, I taught my son how to travel in an airplane by sitting ourselves in chairs in front of the TV and strapping ourselves in. And we did a practice run before we got on the plane to London. That way, we could work out all the things that could go wrong, like, 'This is boring,' 'I want to pee,' 'I want to go to the toilet,' 'I want to eat,' 'I'm thirsty,' 'I want to watch a movie,' 'I want to read a book.' So we rethought it all together, and then when we did the real plane flight it was great. Humans can do that. On one trial they can generalize. Dogs can't. If Kelly teaches the dog in the kitchen, what you've got is a good kitchen dog with Kelly. I come in the kitchen, the dog won't listen to me.

"The dog has to be trained by everyone in every situation. That's why the very best training exercise you can do is, when you're walking your dog, every twenty-five yards stop and ask him to do something. 'Sit' . . . 'Down' . . . 'Speak' . . . 'Let's go.' And so each little training *episodette* is in a different scenario, outside a schoolyard, a basketball pickup game, a leafy street with squirrels, lots of skateboards, and kids and what have you. And after a while, you know, one three-mile walk, the dog comes back and realizes, '*Oh*, you mean sit always means sit? Everywhere? Never would've guessed that!'"

LIFE REWARDS

The next step in Ian Dunbar's training process is to transition from food rewards to what he calls "life rewards." Life rewards can be anything and everything that gives a particular dog's life meaning, the things that bring him the purest joy. "We start with food as a reward because it's convenient. But it doesn't compete with the dog's real interests, whether that's playing at tug-of-war, sniffing, or playing with other dogs," Ian explained. "Here's the secret to a highly reliable dog: make a list of the dog's ten favorite activities; you put it on the fridge. And that's when you train the dog. You let him outdoors to sniff, then teach 'Come here, go sniff. Come here, go sniff.' Or 'Sit, go sniff.' You let him play with other dogs. That's probably the biggest. And then you just say, 'Come here,' or have him sit, then release him to go play again. And at that point, these wonderful activities—they're part of the dog's life, the dog's quality of life; rather than becoming distractions that work against training, they now become rewards that work for training."

I immediately fell in love with Ian's concept of life rewards, because it is such a clear way for people to understand and honor the animal nature of their pets. It is also a way to practice a kind of leadership with a dog that can blossom into a true partnership.

"Ninety percent of training is not teaching the dog what you want him to do; it's teaching him to *want* to do what you want him to do," Ian continued. "So eventually you end up with a self-motivated dog. And you say, 'Come here,' and he says, 'Yeah, I'll do that.' Why? 'Because Cesar called me. I'm not doing it to please him; I'm doing it to please myself.' Because it's a dog and a person living together, it's a relationship. I look on training like basically tango. You're dancing tango. And the two of you have this beautiful, exquisite choreography, and one's meant to be leading, but often the other does. You're following each other, you're changing roles, but you're enjoying doing something, living together. And that to me is what dog training is."

Throughout his training session, with both Ian and me, I noticed that Hugo had been looking yearningly toward Kelly. "So a life reward for Hugo would be to go see Kelly?" I asked.

"You got it," Ian agreed. "Let's try it. Hugo, sit. Good dog. Go and see Kelly!" Immediately after sitting, Hugo sprinted across the room and jumped into Kelly's arms.

"Good dog! See?" Ian asked. "That makes him really happy. So running to Kelly, looking for odors, playing tug-of-war, those are the biggest rewards for the dogs in our house."

"It's like, honor nature, honor your house, honor your family, and think of them as a reward," I mused.

"That's a very nice way to look at living with people and dogs, isn't it?" Ian agreed. "They are the reward."

GAMES PUPPIES PLAY

Dogs love challenges, and they love playing games. I've always believed that training and even rehabilitating dogs should become a game wherever possible. Ian Dunbar has come up with an endless assortment of creative ways to use games as both training tools and life rewards for his dogs.

First Dog Down

One of the first exercises Ian demonstrated for me made use of the playfully competitive nature that comes naturally to dogs in order to teach and improve their responsiveness to commands. He brought in Dune, their magnificent purebred American bulldog with a lean, sinewy body the color of burnt sienna and an enormous head that reminded me a little of Daddy. Ian called Dune and Hugo to him so that they both sat poised in front of the couch while he held up a treat. Then he tested their knowledge of a verbal command while making it a contest.

"So I say, 'First dog to . . . down!'"

Both dogs hit the floor, but the larger Dune made it first. "Oh, Dune won that. Hugo had a start on him. Okay, 'First dog to . . . sit!' No, I didn't say 'scratch,' Hugo, I said 'sit!'"

Ian always left a long, dramatic pause before the actual command word, so that the dogs couldn't anticipate him. Instead, they stayed at rapt attention until they heard the cue. It was a wonderfully creative and fun way of making sure the dogs knew the actual words for the commands, not just the body signals.

Controlled Tug-of-War

I always warn my clients about playing tug-of-war with their dogs, particularly powerful breed dogs like pit bulls or rottweilers or insistent dogs like bulldogs. If you don't understand how to control your dog's intensity, a tug-of-war game can become a power struggle between you and your pet that you don't want to encourage. Ian Dunbar, however, has conditioned both Dune and Hugo to be able to play this tricky game, while he retains total control of the "on-off" switch. In this way, he does several things at once: he reinforces his leadership position with them, he polishes their understanding of verbal commands, and he gives them a fun life reward that they relish.

Kelly brought Ian a toy that they fondly call "Mr. Carcass": a stuffed replica of a rodent carcass, it resembles a fuzzy piece of roadkill. Ian placed the toy in front of Hugo, who waited politely until Ian said,

"Okay. Go take it!" Immediately, Hugo dug into the well-worn toy and began to pull with all his weight, while Ian continued to encourage him: "Pull. Good dog. Okay, pull. Okay, good dog, good dog. Okay, Hugo, thank you." The moment Ian said, "Thank you, Hugo, sit," Hugo backed off and went right into a sit. Right after Hugo complied, Ian repeated the command—"Take it!"—and Hugo dug right back into Mr. Carcass again. "That's the reward. You see, it's much better than a food treat. Go on, pull. Thank you, guys. Dogs, sit.

"I really want them to enjoy this, because this is the reward for the sit. But then I very calmly say, 'Thank you. Good dogs. Dogs, sit.' When you're playing tug, you've got to have lots of rules; you can never touch it unless I say, 'Hugo, take it.' The learning process would be like this: 'Take it,' and then we'd tug, and then I'm going to say, 'Thank you,' and go absolutely still. And when the dog lets go, 'Good dog . . . there's a good dog' . . . maybe a food treat to begin with. And then of course, the bigger reward, 'Take it.' But the rules here are, you can never touch my hand. If you touch my hand, it's finished, the game's over. They never touch the tug toy until you say, 'Take it.' And they always let go when you say, 'Thank you.' You can see how much the dogs enjoy this, so they're never going to touch your hand. This kind of exercise takes a lot of patience to perfect. What I'm interested in is, I can start the activity and I can stop it. Once again, it's a trick in dog training where you take the distraction that's working *against* training and you turn it into a reward that works *for* training."

The flip side of this game was another toy Ian produced called "Mr. Mousy." Compared to the ratty, ripped-up Mr. Carcass, Mr. Mousy looked brand-new and had the kind of high-pitched squeaker inside it that can make dogs go crazy. "This toy isn't for tug. It's for teaching limits. So I let them touch Mr. Mousy, 'kisses only.' And this is training a dog that there are things they can touch but are not allowed to bite." Ian squeaked the toy but carefully controlled the interaction so the dogs gave it gentle respect. "You can use this exercise in preparation to bring a kitten or a new puppy or even a baby into the house, when you've got to practice on something. So this toy will live forever."

I asked Kelly how she controls the intensity of the dogs' play— how intense is too intense? "You do keep an eye on the intensity, but from a training perspective, the frequent interruptions keep playing and training from becoming mutually exclusive. So you use frequent interruptions if your goal is to use play as a reward for right behavior, and then less frequent interruptions if they're just having a good time and everyone's cool."

PUTTING MISBEHAVIOR ON CUE

The Dunbars use the "tug" play session as both a training exercise and a game, and that is also the basis of how they teach owners to control a dog's bad behavior—by making the behavior its own reward, and then putting that reward on cue.

"Everything that people think is a problem—'Oh, my dog barks,' 'My dog tugs at things,' 'My dog jumps up,' 'My dog runs away'—they aren't problems anymore. They're just games that you play with the dog to always reinforce the 'sit.' And once you've got that one emergency command, 'sit' or 'down,' you can stop anything that's going on. You just say, 'Sit'—end of problem. And we're back in control again, so we can then praise the dog."

For instance, if a dog is compulsively barking, you can put barking on cue. "You use the same one-two-three-four formula—request, lure, response, reward," Ian explains. "For example, say, 'Speak,' have an accomplice knock at the door, and when the dog barks, praise and reward. So then the dog learns, 'Aha, when he says, "Speak," someone knocks on the door,' so they learn to speak when you say so.

"It's difficult to teach a dog 'shush' when people are at the front door because the dog is so excited. But once you've got 'speak' down, you may teach 'shush' when it's convenient for you. You can drive somewhere in the middle of nowhere where you're not annoying anyone, tell the dog to speak, and then, when you want the dog to shush, say, 'Shush,' and let him sniff a food lure. When he sniffs the food, he'll stop barking. As soon as he goes silent, praise him gently for a number of seconds and then give him the food as a reward for shushing. Then you can practice it at the front door with the same basic one-two-three-four sequence. Say, 'Speak,' lure him to speak, knock-knock-knock on the door, he barks, 'Good boy, there's a good boy,' then say, 'Shush,' waggle the food in front of his nose so he sniffs, and as soon as he goes quiet, 'Good shush, good shush,' and give him the reward. Now you have a dog that will inform you when someone is on your property, but he will shush when you ask."

"So you are being proactive about it," I said. "Before the dog drives you crazy."

"Exactly," Ian replied. "They like barking so much, I can now use that as a reward in itself. I remember once I was driving back from San Francisco and the bridge was all blocked. I was there for two hours in the traffic, and I had my malamute, so I opened the sunroof, and I said, 'Omaha, ooww!' and he put his head through the roof and went, 'Oooouuuuwwww.' And there was a guy in a BMW next to me. He comes through his sunroof and he howls. And everybody on the bridge got out of their cars and howled. It was just a moment in time when everyone howled. And so you use barking as a reward."

HEELING WITH LETTUCE

Ian describes his oldest dog, Claude, as a "big red dog." "We think he is a cross between a rottie and a redbone coonhound," says Ian. Claude is about twelve years old and wasn't raised from puppyhood by the Dunbars, as their other dogs were. "Claude was asocial when we got him. So he plays and breaks a lot of rules. He's the top dog here."

Claude has another interesting quirk—he's crazy for lettuce. This senior dog used to have a habit of putting his nose down and ignoring his human on the walk, but once Ian made the lettuce discovery, he realized he had a brand-new motivating tool. "When I go for a walk with him, I'll bring a little bit of lettuce, and while I just stand still and bring the lettuce out, he sits and looks at me, which otherwise he never does on a walk. So, you know, you need to be inventive—if kibble isn't working, if praise isn't working, find something else that excites him."

By using his creativity and finding that special something that turns his dog on, Ian created a whole new technique, "heeling with lettuce." He let me try it. While holding the lettuce, Claude worked perfectly by my side, then heeled when I turned and looked at him. "Sit," I said, and obediently he sat. I gave him a bite of lettuce, and we continued on.

"It's a Cesar salad!" I said.

"And this is how all training should be," Ian remarked. "When you're heeling your dog, it should be like you're walking hand in hand with your kid, or arm in arm with your spouse."

NOSE WORK WITH DUNE

I was thrilled to discover that the Dunbars are as enthusiastic as I am about giving nose work to their dogs—as a game, a physical-psychological challenge, and a training exercise. Scent is the most primal of a dog's senses, and by making sure a dog stays connected to his nose, you are honoring the deepest part of the animal-dog in him. You, the owner, are showing your dog that you care about his doing the things that matter the most to him, not just what matters to you as a human.

Ian Dunbar has done extensive laboratory research into the olfactory abilities of dogs. "Their sense of smell is so unbelievable, we can barely comprehend all they can smell," he said. "I mean, they can come into a room and figure out, 'There's eight people here, and one of them is scared.' They know that immediately. You can be twenty-five yards away, and they would notice it. Nose work is when all the training comes together and there's no need to reward him doing this."

"Your dogs get to use their favorite sense," Kelly added, "and they get so much joy out of it, and it really exhausts them, just like exercise. And it gives them a job too. Pet dogs don't have jobs anymore. It gives them a little work that any dog can do at any age. It's not something like agility, where they have to be in great shape."

"People in New York might say, 'Well, my house is very small,'" I remarked. "But this exercise—it doesn't matter how small your house is, right?"

Kelly nodded enthusiastically. "You can do this anywhere: you can do it indoors, you can do it outdoors at the park. Even small rooms can become more challenging because the odor really pools, so a small room is actually a good challenge for a dog."

While the dogs looked on excitedly, as if they knew that their favorite game was coming up, Kelly explained to me their method of doing nose work. They take a piece of birch bark—an herb with a root-beer-like scent—in a tiny aerated metal container, and then they hide it somewhere in the room while the dog is outside.

Then they let the dog in and show him his reward. "For Claude, it's lettuce. For Hugo, it's food," Ian said. For Dune, a tug game fanatic, the ultimate reward is a huge green stuffed crocodile—CrocoBob. Next, they give the command, "Find it." When the dog finds the odor, they reward him with whatever his treat of choice may be.

"The way we prepared Dune for this was, we had to transfer that

Dr. Dunbar's Four-Part "Sit"

PART 1: REQUEST
Dr. Dunbar holds a treat in his outstretched hand and says, "Junior, sit."

PART 2: LURE
Dr. Dunbar quickly raises the treat above Junior's head, luring his nose upward
and causing his butt to move toward the ground.

PART 3: RESPONSE
Junior's butt hits the ground in a proper "sit."

PART 4: REWARD
As soon as Junior is in a proper "sit," Dr. Dunbar praises him
("Good boy, take it") and rewards him with the treat.

Dr. Dunbar continues to work with Junior off leash.

To teach "down," Dr. Dunbar brings the treat to the floor.
Hugo, the French bulldog, did this at lightning speed.

Dr. Dunbar improves responsiveness to commands by having
Hugo and Dune compete in "first dog down."

Hugo plays a game of controlled tug of war with "Mr. Carcass." If an owner
doesn't understand how to control a dog's intensity, this game can become a
power struggle that should not be encouraged.

Oscar the Anatolian shepherd approaches his mark.

Oscar waits on his mark.

The "get up."

Finn practices the first part of the A-to-B recall, coming to Mark when he calls.

Mark Harden helps shape Dusty's leg lift.

Dusty the English shepherd's leg lift.

Although all his dogs are "working dogs," such as Dusty, star of the HBO series *True Blood*, Mark shares a close bond with each animal.

association with the toy to the odor," Kelly explains. "So first we taught him to search in general with just looking for his toy. And then we paired the toy with the odor, so he learned that the odor meant the croc."

When they were ready to do the exercise, Ian let the dogs out of the room while Kelly hid the scent box among some books on a side table. When Dune came into the room, it didn't take him more than a minute to home right in on it. On the second go-round, they hid the scent under a pillow on a chair by the large open fireplace. This location was a little more challenging, Ian explained.

"This is kind of hard there, because all the air will be going into the fireplace and up there, so it'd be sucking the odor out, so he may be getting a scent of this, far away from where it is," he said. "One of the biggest mistakes people make when they're doing scent training, they use too much scent, and then it goes, whooom, and floods the room."

The first place Dune went when he came back into the room was the place where he'd found the odor on the last go-round. "There's a lingering odor there," Kelly said, "but he's got to find the odor where it is in the highest concentration." We all watched a very focused American bulldog try to figure out where the scent was coming from. "It tells you a lot about how the air travels in the room," Kelly said, watching all the places Dune traveled on his quest. I could see the intensity of his search and the pure joy of the challenge. He was in the zone. "This is a good way for owners to learn how to read their dogs," Ian commented as Dune began to hone in on the location. "We can see that he's hit the scent but he can't quite work it out." Just under two minutes after entering the room, Dune hit on the scent and got his reward.

"The wonderful use of this is, once you train the dog first to find what he likes—Hugo finds food, Claude finds lettuce, and Dune finds his tug toy—then the next step is, now they can find the remote control for the telly, they can find your glasses. I mean, I'm always losing them. I can say, 'Where's my glasses?' They can find your car keys, and now you can take your dog for a ride in the car. So it has great uses, and I think it's the best mental exercise for a dog. I would put it above a treadmill in terms of exercise. I would say sniffing and working out the olfactory puzzle is more important than physical exercise on the treadmill."

As my viewers know, I believe that there is no substitution for a dog getting primal, physical exercise by walking outside with its owner. But as Ian points out, mental exercise is every bit as important when it is a structured challenge like the Dunbars' nose-work drills. This kind of challenge can keep a dog from getting stressed or bored on a rainy day, a hot day, a snow day, or any day when the owner can't physically be outside with the dog. It can be done by dogs of any physical ability, or even any age. I thought back to Daddy. When he was so old that he barely had any eyesight or hearing left, his nose was still as active as ever.

"You can see that the task is the reward," Ian pointed out. "It's not a job anymore. This is kind of like watching movies for the dog. The activity now becomes the reward. He's just so happy using his nose, the best part of his body, and it's a training exercise, yet it's a thrill for him. It's what all training should be, the very reward."

OFF-LEASH IN THE REAL WORLD

Where the strength of your off-leash training really comes into play is in the real world, out on the street or in a park. To demonstrate the practical applications of everything he'd been explaining to me at his home, Ian took me with him and Dune down to the lush Berkeley Codornices Park.

"Training has to be stronger than instinct, stronger than any urge, stronger than any distractions. And there are a lot of distractions out here. Scents especially. I mean, the dog's nose is amazing. I did research on what they smell. They can obviously tell male from female, neutered from intact, individual dog from individual dog, strange male urine from males that they know. It's their form of pee mail. That's basically how dogs communicate. Like we have e-mail, dogs have pee mail, right? And it's just as important to them. They're social animals."

Ian pointed to Dune, who had wandered over to a plot of leafy groundcover and was sniffing away with abandon. "He is checking up on all the guys he's met on his walks. He's not been to this park for probably a year. And he's smelling now, thinking, 'Oh, that's Joe! I met him way up on Shasta just three weeks ago. Wow.' You know? And it's like you've been away for a holiday, and now you've got all this e-mail to check.

"The thing is," Ian continued, "it's so important to dogs that it will become a distraction. And that's why we have to turn it into a reward in sessions like this."

Ian showed me what he meant by turning the distraction of the park and Dune's intense sniffing into a "life reward" that works for his training, not against it. The first requirement is that the owner have a reliable "sit" down pat. The sit, as well as the recall, should be rehearsed at home, starting in a small area.

"They should practice this in the bathroom, in the living room. They should do this in the backyard, or in a smaller area where they can control it. Then they bring in a friend's dog, so now the distraction is the off-leash area and the other dog is the temptation. And then all of these things which were distractions, which cause the dog not to behave, and so make the owner so mad and cause them to punish the dog, become a reward instead."

Ian demonstrated with Dune how his method works. He let Dune off-leash to wander around at his pleasure, but kept an eye on him. If Dune started to wander a bit too far, Ian called out, "Dune, sit." The faster Dune responded, the more quickly Ian would release him from the sit to give him his "life reward" of sniffing in the brush afterward.

He'd release Dune by saying, "Go play." I noticed that Kelly used the word *free* to mean the same thing. If Dune did not sit right away, Ian would increase the urgency in his tone of voice until Dune sat, and then he would call the dog toward him and instruct Dune to sit again. "If the sniff's out there, then when he sits immediately, he gets the reward back immediately. However, if he doesn't sit immediately, he's going to have to come towards me and repeat the exercise until he sits following a single command before being allowed to resume exploring once more. So eventually, the dog learns, you know, if you just sit when they ask, you can have a great time out here."

Ian and I both agree that when you are with your dog in the outside world—be it at an off-leash park or sitting with your dog on-leash at a sidewalk café—your dog should have at least a part of his attention focused on you at all times. Since Dune and Ian hadn't been doing walks in the park together for some time, at the beginning of our excursion it was clear that Dune was not complying on that front. "He's not totally with me yet. So there'll be more training than play. But once he's on the ball, and when I say, 'Sit,' he sits. Well . . . then it's all walking and sniffing."

One of the reasons this exercise is so challenging is that a dog's sense of smell is so strong that when he's smelling something, he often won't even hear or see you. And it's challenging for a human because it's easy to become impatient or emotional when you think your dog is ignoring you.

"The ears are turned off. The dog literally doesn't hear you if he's sniffing," Ian asserts. "I liken it to my son or my wife. They don't always do what I ask them to do right away, but I don't want to get annoyed or upset with them. I love them. And the same thing with the dog. Okay, so you didn't sit on my first command. It's no big deal. But you're going to do it. And once you've done it, you're going to repeat the exercise until you sit following a single command. I look on training as a lifelong process."

Dune searches for a scent.

DOG CON ONE, TWO, AND THREE

Ian Dunbar maintains his hands-off philosophy whenever possible, even in the park. "I use my voice in training, and I use my voice as a reprimand as well. It's a form of punishment, but it is a non-aversive punishment. But you can do a lot with your voice, different variation of tone, which the dog understands. And I have a method that is really useful, in that I always code to the dog how important each command really is."

That coding can be done with energy level or tone of voice. I witnessed Ian varying his tone and volume a lot during the course of our time together, all with the intention of getting a different response. One of the creative ideas he suggested was to practice shouting at the dog in an urgent tone of voice in a normal, calm situation at home, and then rewarding him lavishly. "You simply shouldn't train if you're in any way upset. It's not going to work. However, you should train the dog to listen to you if you *are* upset or frightened. The first time an owner uses the 'sit' command as an emergency, they might shout,

'Rover, sit, *sit, SIT!!!*' And the dog says, 'I don't think so—you're shouting at me!' The dog just panics and runs off. So we do practice commands delivered when the owner uses a loud voice, but all it means
to the dog is, you're going to get a better reward. That way, if you are
outside and your dog runs into the street, when you call him back in
a loud, urgent tone of voice, he doesn't think you're suddenly mad
at him; he understands the urgency and that there is a bigger reward
coming if he obeys."

The other way Ian accomplishes "coding" is what he calls "dog
con one, two, and three." He uses both tone of voice and the name he
calls the dog to indicate the importance of what he's asking the dog
to do.

"So, by saying to Omaha, 'Ohm, come here,' he understands that
it's not a command but a suggestion. And I live with dogs about
ninety-nine percent of the time at 'dog con one.' For instance, we're on
the couch. 'My buddy,' I say. 'Ohm, settle down. Ohm, move over on
the couch.' And he has the option of refusal. Whereas if I really want
him to do it, I say, 'Omaha, sit.' And as soon as I call him 'Omaha,' he
knows he must follow the next instruction. No exceptions. There's no
argument, there's no bullying, there's no physical forcing. But if I say,
'Omaha, sit,' the next thing that will happen before life as he knows it
continues, he will sit, and then he will repeat the exercise until he sits
following a single request. And then I'll let him continue on with his
life again. That is, 'dog con two.' Letting a dog know that he can relax
most of the time increases his reliability when you really need it.

"You find a lot of parents do it too. Especially in multilingual families. They will suddenly change from English to Spanish. You know
they're saying, 'Johnny, put that down,' 'Johnny, don't touch that,'
'Johnny . . . Juan, *siéntate.*' And as soon as they change languages, the
little kid responds pronto."

I cracked up at that—because that's how it works in my own
family.

"Then finally we have 'dog con three,' which is what we do when we're on TV or in the obedience ring. When I call Omaha Wahoo, he knows it's showtime, so he's got to be looking at me, smiling, with his tail up. There are times when you want really good obedience, the best you've got. And so we can signal those times to the dog, by using a different name or a different command."

SIT VS. THE RECALL

While we were in the park, Ian demonstrated how he uses a reliable "sit" at a distance to communicate with Dune off-leash. He prefers teaching pet owners to have a totally reliable sit before he teaches the more difficult recall. "My major goal is to get an owner to be able to perform a reliable sit in all situations. I teach an emergency sit or down. Say the dog's roaming, and here comes a child. If one parent says that this dog jumped on the kids, he becomes a legal entity right there. So I'll say, 'Dune, sit.' I can leave him there until the child leaves. He sits and stays because he knows that this is our routine—'Ian tells me sit, and I always do this. I'll sit because I always do this—sit and go play, sit and go play.' So the distraction, playing, running at large, is the reward I use to get my reliable sit."

But beware of overconfidence, says Ian, even if you've done a great deal of training. "When people say, 'Oh, my dog's totally reliable,' I just pull out my wallet and say, 'Right. I have a test here, a hundred bucks.' And as yet, no one has ever passed this test. All it involves is asking the dog to sit eight times in a row . . . but in weird situations. I'll have the owner lie on their back, or have the owner out of sight. And it's just a test of the dog's comprehension of 'sit.'

"So the point is, most people cannot control their dog if their back is turned and the dog is just one yard away from them. Well, what if the dog were forty yards away, but his back was turned, and he's chasing a child or a rabbit, you see? So the problem can be shown right here. Your dog doesn't know what 'sit' means if he can't see you. So I like to take people and show them, no, your dog's not reliable. And we can do a lot of work right here before you push the dog too far, too fast, and have him off-leash in the dog park where he's too far away from you. Because you don't want to set the dog up to fail. You want the quality of life, the experience for the dog, to be so much better."

As we left the park with Dune, Ian remarked on what a special relationship each of us shares with our dogs and lamented the fact that more people don't have the same wonderful off-leash experiences. "There's not many people that can wander around, dog tagging behind like you with Junior or me with Dune or Hugo. We know these dogs are really totally safe around people, but we both put a lot of work into it."

SIMILARITIES AND DIFFERENCES

Before our two-day visit was over, Ian and I opened a couple of beers and sat down to talk about the things that brought us together—as well as some of the issues that might still separate us. We definitely share a deep affinity for dogs and the desire to train humans to be better humans to their dogs. We both want to show humans how to understand the world through a dog's eyes, even though we have our own ways of doing things that may not be the same and may even conflict in some areas. Now that he had spent time with me and seen firsthand how I interact with dogs, Ian shared a few specific things that he wished I would do differently, especially on the *Dog Whisperer* show.

"You know, we may have disagreements, and there aren't really many," he mused. "I would like to see you slow down with some dogs, but I do understand what's coming behind you. You know, you have a director, a producer, cameraman, they get in there, 'Solve it, get in there, solve it! Let's get some action.' And you've got fifteen minutes. But I would just like to see, hey, take a few minutes, toss a few treats. See if you can get the dog to take a treat from your hand. And I think that would be some extra magic to show people. And because you've got great dog-reading skills, when the dog is upset, learn from the dog. I mean, the great things I've learned about dog training haven't come from books. They came from the dogs where I royally screwed up and got into situations and thought, 'Well, I won't do that again.' "

For my part, I truly admire Ian Dunbar's incredible range of knowledge about and skill with dogs, and I learned many things from my time with him that I will take back and assimilate into my own work. Yet there are some areas in which our personal styles are far apart. Working quietly with dogs is such a part of me that I could not try to be the outgoing, exuberant, verbal person Ian is around dogs without the dogs knowing that I was faking it. His techniques work so well for him because he is totally, 100 percent genuine; these are the methods he invented, and he accomplishes them brilliantly. They are who he is. I also believe that dogs communicate with one another using touch, so that when I give a firm—not harsh—touch in a calm-assertive and not frustrated or emotional state, I am using a very natural way of redirecting a dog's attention. Ian, on the other hand, feels that most human hands cannot be trusted and that using touch carries too high a risk of abuse.

But all these different ideas highlight the message of this book, which is that it is crucial to have knowledge of and exposure to many different ideas, many different theories, and many different methods. You have to find one that works for you—for the person you are, for the values you hold, and for the dogs you own.

I felt as though Ian Dunbar and I accomplished something important together by opening a line of communication and showing the world that there are many options, and many possibilities, and that we both want the same thing, and that is peaceful, balanced dogs and peaceful, balanced humans.

"We have to talk to each other. Because what you and I have to teach, Cesar, is really special. When you look at the biggest foibles people have, it's in getting along with other people. Well, that's the skill we can teach, because we have to get along not only with another living being but with another species. I think the most important thing is talking to people who may not see it your way, and if you want to change things, that's everything. I've never been one to shun someone because they don't see it my way. They are the people I want to talk to rather than limiting my audience and preaching to the converted. It's all about dialogue. And you know, if we take this little field of dog training, there's an analogy for the world. The world is all different people who all see things differently."

THE RETURN OF "FLASH" JUNIOR

Before I ended my two-day visit with the Dunbars, I felt that I had to correct one important misconception. No, it wasn't about me, my methods, or my philosophies about working with dogs. It was about Junior. I just couldn't leave Berkeley with Ian Dunbar thinking my brilliant right-hand pit bull was slow!

A lightbulb had gone on in my head when Ian brought out the lettuce that motivated Claude and when he spoke about finding that special thing that turns your individual dog on. There's one thing that Junior always responds to, and that's a tennis ball. He'll jump as high as a kangaroo, dig in the dirt like a bulldozer, dive underwater like a dolphin, and churn up dust like a racecar—all to get control of a coveted tennis ball. What if I asked Ian to do his request-lure-response-reward sequence with Junior again—except this time use the tennis ball instead of the treats?

"Well, this is a different dog today," Ian said after working with Junior for a few minutes using my new tennis ball strategy. Junior was doing his sit-stand-downs in rapid-fire succession and in perfect form, never once taking his eye off the ball. "Yes, he's supremo. I think the fastest dog I've ever seen."

"Yes, sir," I told him proudly. "That's 'Flash' Junior."

IAN DUNBAR'S SEVEN RULES

1. When selecting a puppy at eight weeks of age, make sure that he or she is house-trained and chewtoy-trained, has been taught to come, sit, lie down, and roll over on cue, and has been socialized and handled by at least one hundred people.

2. When adopting an adult dog, make sure that all family members "test-drive" the dog. Take plenty of time to handle the dog and take him or her for a long walk. The right dog is waiting for your family, so make sure you consider your selection carefully. Selection! Selection!! Selection!!!

3. From the very first day your new puppy or adopted dog comes home, implement an errorless house-training and chewtoy-training program—to prevent house-soiling and destructive chewing, to help prevent excessive barking, and to prepare your dog to enjoy spending those inevitable times when left at home alone. For guidance, see "Puppy Playroom and Doggie Den" at Dog Star Daily, http://dogstardaily.com/training/puppy-playroom-amp-doggy-den.

4. Socialization never stops. Always have visitors offer your puppy/dog a treat and show them how to instruct the dog to come and sit when saying hello. Similarly, carry a few

(continues)

treats on walks in case a stranger would like to greet your dog. Praise and give your dog a couple of treats whenever children pass by, or anything scary happens. Thus, your dog will grow in confidence and relish the company of people.

5. Do *not* feed your dog from a bowl (until you are convinced that your dog is perfect for you). Weigh out your dog's daily allotment of kibble and use these valuable food lures and rewards for teaching manners and behavior training. At the end of the day, moisten the kibble, stuff the mush in hollow chewtoys, and put them in the freezer overnight to give to your dog for breakfast. Feeding dogs from chewtoys reduces barking by 90 percent and lessens hyperactivity and anxiety.

6. Train off-leash with lures and rewards from the outset. Never use a leash or touch your dog to force him to comply. Otherwise, your dog will respond only when on-leash or within hand's reach. Instead, use your hands to pet (reward) your dog once he or she complies.

7. Integrate short training interludes into walks and play. Every couple of minutes, ask your dog to sit when walking, or to come when playing, offer a treat, and then say, "Let's go" or "Go play." This way, your dog won't pull on-leash and both the walk and play will become rewards that work for training rather than distractions that work against training.

A WORLD OF WAYS
TO BASIC OBEDIENCE

Step-by-Step Instructions

The pack takes a walk at the new Dog Psychology Center.

THE WALK

Anyone who watches *Dog Whisperer* knows how seriously I take the concept of the walk. Walking is about much more than giving your dog exercise, although exercise is the first and most important element in my three-part fulfillment formula and a big part of why we walk our dogs. To me, however, walking side by side is also the activity that forges the deepest kind of bond between human and dog. It is the primal core of that relationship. Thousands and thousands of years ago, humans and dogs first walked, hunted, and migrated together and thus became two species that would evolve side by side as interdependent partners. It's a beautiful story—one of Mother Nature's miracles—and when I walk with my pack of dogs in the hills behind the Santa Clarita Dog Psychology Center, I can hear thousands of years of human-dog history echoing in every step we take together.

This is why one of the first things I do when I work with a client is to make sure that he is walking his dog correctly.

Cesar's Rules FOR MASTERING THE WALK

1. Leave and enter your house in front of your dog. Position in the pack is important.

2. Don't let your dog leave the house in an overexcited condition—make sure she is calm-submissive and in waiting mode before you open the door. Make sure you are the one to invite her outside and to trigger the activity.

3. Walk with your dog behind you or next to you, not in front of you (though there is a time and a place for that), and definitely not pulling you or creating any tension on the leash.

4. Make your walk a minimum of thirty minutes for older, lower-energy, or smaller dogs and forty-five minutes for larger or higher-energy dogs.

5. Walk like a pack leader—head up, shoulders back. Your posture is part of the body language that your dog reads when assessing your energy. Keep your arm relaxed and the leash loose, as if you were holding a briefcase or pocketbook.

6. Alternate between the formal, structured walk and short breaks for your dog to pee, sniff, and explore, which may

> even include short bursts of walking ahead of you. The key is
> for you to be the one to start and stop the behavior.

To me, the ideal way to walk with a dog is off-leash. I love it when I walk with a pack of dogs off-leash and they all fall into formation behind me or at my side. I can't describe what a wonderful, connected, harmonious feeling that gives me. I agree with Ian Dunbar that the off-leash experience is something all dog owners should be shooting for. But that isn't possible for everybody, and we do live in a world of leash laws and potentially dangerous distractions. So mastering the walk on a lead, or a "walk to heel," as it's traditionally been called, is a crucial skill for every dog owner to develop.

THE WALK: WALKING ON A LEAD

Before taking your dog for a walk on a leash, you need to know that she is accustomed to the leash and feels comfortable wearing it. Some dogs seem not to notice the presence of a leash and collar; others exhibit fear, annoyance, and even anger at being constrained in this way. The first experience of a lead can change some dogs into bucking broncos.

If you are starting with a puppy, the solution is easy. Start the puppy young with a loose, short leash, and let her wear it during pleasant experiences such as feeding time, supervised playtime, and times when you are giving her affection. Get her used to you putting the leash on and taking it off and the sensation and the weight of the leash, so that the tool signifies nothing except happy experiences and a way for the two of you to bond. Since puppies are programmed to follow you, a leash isn't always necessary in the first months of life, but you can keep a loose rope or nylon slip lead clipped to your belt as you walk around the house and go about your routine to help your dog build the association that a leash means "follow me." If a leash is what a puppy knows and becomes accustomed to in her first eight months of life, then it should never be a big deal to her, even when she enters her rebellious adolescent period.

For older dogs, especially shelter dogs that may have had bad experiences with tools in the past, it's your job to make sure that any leash you use has only positive associations. Never bring a tool to a dog—always allow the dog to come to the tool. Use a treat or a toy or something that attracts the dog, then lightly rub the leash back and forth on top of the dog's head while she is playing or munching. Do this a few times, with no pressure. (In other words, don't do it five minutes before you want to take your first walk!) Once the dog seems comfortable with the leash, gently place it over her head, allowing her to provide the momentum of pushing through. With an older dog that has leash aversion, you can practice what I suggested for puppies: let her do some normal, pleasurable activities with the leash on. (This goes for any tool you might want to use.)

When you start walking your dog on the leash, start with small distances in comfortable, familiar areas before you venture out for the real thing. Viper, the fearful Belgian malinois I wrote about in Chapter 2, had attached extremely negative associations to every tool that had ever been used with him, so I had to go through this routine from scratch with all the leashes and collars he feared.

The great thing about dogs is that they can let go of the past much more completely and easily than humans ever can. If you are gentle with your dog and don't rush things, it should take only a few sessions of this type of positive conditioning for her to feel comfortable wearing the leash or collar you have chosen for her.

THE WALK: PRACTICING THE WALK

I'm not a big one for the command "heel," since my rules for a good walk, outlined earlier, are very basic. Still, these rules must be practiced daily to become perfect. Problems that can arise on the walk range from pulling forward to wandering off to the side to sitting down and refusing to budge. Another problem that is all too common occurs when a dog becomes distracted by or even aggressive with another dog or person walking by.

I have found through my experiences with hundreds and hundreds of dogs and their owners that the owner's attitude and state of mind often present the biggest problems on a walk. Why is it that I can take a dog that an owner insists has never been able to walk on a lead, and in five minutes I'm walking perfectly calmly and happily with her? It's not that I've done anything to "fix" the dog in that five minutes. But I simply cannot imagine having a problem walking a dog. I've never had a problem in my life with it, so I can't imagine failing. The dog reads my confidence in my face, my body language, and my emotional state, which she may be able to sense by smelling the tiny changes in my chemical and hormonal balance that indicate whether I am calm or nervous, happy or depressed. When owners dread a walk with their dog, the dog knows it; when owners anticipate awful events, the dog anticipates right along with them.

Beyond the psychological and spiritual aspect of the walk, there is the purely mechanical part of it. Traditionally, dogs are walked on the left-hand side. Personally, I feel you should find the side that feels right for you, teach your dog to walk on that side, and stick to it until you are certain that you and your dog are totally in sync during your walks and that controlling her comes easily. Then teach her the same routine on the other side. Thus, you'll be able to walk her on whichever side is more convenient for a particular situation or environment. Being able to walk your dog on either side is yet another way of establishing your leadership in many different situations. The instructions in this section are based on a left-hand-side walk; reverse the instructions if you want to start on the right.

Some trainers and owners still like to use the command "heel," so I asked my colleague Martin Deeley, executive director of the IACP, to share his advice for teaching this behavior.

THE WALK: MARTIN DEELEY'S INSTRUCTIONS FOR THE WALK

"The handle on your lead should be in your right hand, and your left hand should act as a guide for the lead down to the pup," Martin begins.

"If you are left-handed, do this the opposite way round: handle in left hand, guide with right hand, and keep the puppy on your right-hand side. Walk slowly forward, and if she is on the left, set off on your left foot, encouraging your pup to follow—give the command 'heel.' If your pup enjoys being around and following you without the lead, this should be relatively easy, but be ready for a few 'battles' if she decides that the lead is constraining. If she runs ahead, stop and encourage her back alongside you before walking on again. If she stops, encourage her to keep up with you and to keep moving forward. If your pup likes treats, then these can help with the encouragement, but don't let her train you to give her treats by stopping or running ahead!"

Martin offers an interesting solution to the pulling scenario. "If a pup forges ahead," he continues, "I find that stopping, waiting for her attention, and then doing a number of 180-degree turns makes her look to me to find out what I am going to do.

"Initially I may command 'heel' each time I turn, but after a while I say 'Heel' only at the beginning or if we have stopped for a short while. The reason is, I have given a command, and when she understands it, that means to do that command until I give a different one. Also, some dogs learn to pull and then do so, waiting for the command to stop pulling and change direction. If they do not know when that change in direction is coming because you do not give a command, they are more likely to watch you and be attentive for the change of direction."

Martin recommends practicing your walks on sidewalks or narrow country paths to provide a framework for your dog to walk in straight lines beside you.

Rehearse your about-face turns here as well, so that they become second nature.

THE WALK: TO POP OR NOT TO POP?

Some trainers don't agree with using leash corrections on a walk. Martin and I are not among them. If a dog walks ahead of you, a quick, split-second "pop"—not a jerk but a "pop"—is a good, non-aggressive way to catch his attention. I use a leash pop, a quick touch, or a foot tap (*not* a kick—tap by bending the leg farthest from the dog to prevent the tap from carrying any force) in the same way I would tap my son on the shoulder in a dark, loud movie theater to get his attention to see if he wanted some popcorn.

Properly applied, a leash pop merely reminds your dog to pay attention to you. When you are first practicing the walk, you can im-

mediately turn and go in the opposite direction after a leash pop, encouraging your dog to come with you. In this way, you are always leading and she is following.

"In training a dog to walk," Martin says, "you go no distance unless she is alongside you. Therefore, it does not matter if you never go more than a few yards, or even get to the end of your driveway at first. After a while, your dog will realize, unless she walks on a loose leash with you, she isn't going anywhere.

"As soon as your dog begins to walk comfortably on the lead, you can concentrate on getting the positioning right. You can use many different aids to achieve a close 'heel.'" Martin suggests going along narrow country paths or walking close to the side of a wall or a fence as ideal ways to practice positioning. "With the dog between yourself and the fence, you can concentrate on keeping her from going forward or dragging backwards. As she begins to walk more with you, if she pulls forward, tap your thigh and turn sharply to the right, or do a complete about-turn so that she is behind you again.

"If your dog starts dragging behind you," Martin continues, "tap your thigh and encourage her up to you. Increase the patterns that you make with your dog at your side by turning left and right and doing complete about-turns. If she is not concentrating, turn without warning and then tap your thigh to bring her up to it—it will encourage the dog to keep an eye on you. It may help to have two trees or posts or any objects that you can walk around and do a figure-eight path. In this way, you are turning right and turning left around these obstacles. Make sure you encourage her and make the exercises fun; being serious at this stage can create concerns. The relationship you build is the most important."

Also vary your walking speed during these exercises—sometimes walking normally, other times fast, even trotting, followed by slow walking. Slow walking can teach your dog to pay more attention

to you and to concentrate on what you are doing. Putting a lightly weighted backpack on a higher-energy dog is another way to slow the process down so that the lesson becomes clearer.

"When you stop," Martin suggests, "ask your dog to sit.

"If the lead is held in your right hand, you can slide your left hand downwards and guide the dog's backside to the floor as you stop and say, 'Sit.' It does take a bit of practice to do this well, and sometimes you will find that your dog anticipates and moves forward more quickly than your hand can push.

"A useful method of training your dog to walk correctly at heel is to have the lead in your right hand but behind your body rather than in front. Again, your left hand can guide the lead, but if your dog tends to move forward, the lead comes up against the back of your legs and their movement actually gives the dog a small pull backwards. I have also found it easier using this position to achieve the sitting when you stop. The dog cannot move forward and your left hand is relatively free, enabling it to guide the dog's backside to the ground."

The aim should be always to have your dog on a loose leash at any time in any place, even when there are distractions. So when you're stopped, put your dog in a sit and keep the leash loose.

THE WALK: VARY YOUR ROUTE

Martin has one last little tip for all your walks. "Change the route you take on walks. [Your dog] will often pull more on the return to your home than leaving it. So don't be predictable, and if she does begin to pull at any stage, about-turn and go in the opposite direction until you have her attention once more. And always work to keep the leash loose. It should hang loose when your dog is in the right position alongside your legs."

Changing your walking route is also essential to keeping your dog interested in walking with you. Dogs love patterns—a walk at the same time every day, food at a regular hour—but they also crave adventures. If you walk the same three blocks and back every day for six months, your dog may exhibit symptoms of boredom or engage in frustrated, destructive behavior, even if you are giving her the required thirty to forty-five minutes of exercise, twice a day. Just like humans, dogs need a change of scenery now and then! The more you change your walking routines, the more exciting the challenges you offer your dog's mind and the more you establish your leadership position with her in many different environments.

THE WALK: LEASH-FREE WALKING
WITH A CLICKER

Using a clicker can help you teach a dog to heel off-leash—if you have a safe, enclosed area to practice in and a lot of patience. Kirk Turner is a dog trainer with over twenty years' experience who uses clickers among many other techniques to train pets as well as working dogs. "The first thing to know about clicker training is that you are not 'making' the dog do anything," Kirk stresses. "You are simply marking a desired behavior with a click sound and immediately supplying a motivator like food, a ball, or maybe a small squeaky toy for just a second or two. So I first figure out what is extremely motivating to a particular dog, and that will be what I use."

Kirk gives us the example of Sparky, a miniature dachshund who is incredibly motivated by Duck Jerky treats.

"Once I've established my great relationship with Sparky by teaching him the relationship between the clicker and the reward, I can start walking around, and he will follow me and catch up with me. I wiggle my fingers on my left side, and when he is right there I will click and give him his treat. I change directions frequently and look at the ground about four feet straight in front of me and just notice when he comes into heel position with my peripheral vision. As he is there, I will say, 'Heel,' and walk a couple of steps, then click and treat. I love to start this process when the dog is off-leash. Randomize the clicks and treats as he gets better at it."

THE WALK: TOOLS

Tools—leashes, collars, and other aids that dog owners use—are inanimate objects invented by humans to help humans handle dogs. They are neither good nor bad—they just are tools. In my opinion, it's the energy behind the tool—that is, the attitude and state of mind of the person who's using it—that can transform a tool that was intended for good into a device that causes a dog discomfort or fear.

If you are raising a dog from puppyhood in the manner I describe in *How to Raise the Perfect Dog*, you may never have any need for an advanced tool at all. Your puppy is born with a built-in leash, and if you take full advantage of that during her formative months—while establishing a firm foundation of leadership, of course!—your walks should come easily, and a simple nylon or rope slip collar or light, flat collar with a clip-on leather strap or rope should be all you ever need. Mr. President, Angel, Blizzard (aka Marley), and Junior, the four pups I raised for that book, are all adolescents now, and their respective owners—MPH Entertainment paralegal Crystal Reel, *Dog Whisperer* director SueAnn Fincke, Dog Psychology Center director Adriana Barnes, and myself—can take these dogs anywhere, anytime, with the most minimal leash available. Anyone can walk them, and they understand the concept that the leash means to follow. They are also all great followers in off-leash situations. Recently, I was in a busy, crowded airport with Angel, and people would stop and stare, amazed at how calm and perfectly obedient he was as he followed me through crowds and up escalators and through the security lines. This is the huge advantage of early conditioning and preventive training. If your pup never experiences anything bad about a leash, your chances of having any future problems on the walk are greatly diminished.

However, some older dogs, shelter dogs with serious issues, or dogs that are too large or powerful for their owners to control with just a slip leash may need more advanced tools, usually on a temporary basis, but sometimes for longer. Here are some of the many tools that are available to today's dog owners.

The Flexi-Leash

Pros: The flexi-leash allows a dog to wander and explore while not being confined to one particular leash length. It lets a fearful dog have a less structured walk, which can work to build trust, while an owner slowly introduces a shorter leash over time. An example of a great use for a flexi-leash was in my strategy for building Viper's confidence in stressful situations, encouraging him to solve his own problems without my interference (see Chapter 2).

Cons: By not providing much structure, the flexi-leash does not convey the message that the owner is in charge on the walk. An owner can end up being pulled in whatever direction the dog wants to go. The flexi-leash also offers only minimal control over a dog and should not be used with high-energy, dominant dogs.

The Choke Chain or Training Collar

Pros: Despite its negative name, there is no choking involved provided that this tool is used correctly. When a dog wanders away, the split-second tightening of the chain around the neck sends a message of correction. There is an instant release once the correction has been heeded. Its sole purpose is to get the dog's attention and to motivate her to self-correct her behavior.

Cons: If used incorrectly, the choke chain can in fact choke a dog and cause harm. The owner should have a professional give hands-on instruction in how to properly use the choke chain.

The Martingale Collar

Pros: Designed to help a dog stay comfortable while remaining securely on the leash, this tool has a longer, wider section, usually made of leather, chain, or nylon, that is joined through two loops. The larger loop falls loosely around the dog's neck; the smaller one is clipped onto the leash. If the dog pulls away from the leash, the tension pulls the small loop taut, tightening the larger loop around the neck. The wide section prevents the collar from becoming so tight that it cuts off the dog's airways.

Cons: In my experience, martingales are a good alternative for happy-go-lucky dogs that don't need a lot of correction and for dogs that are basically well behaved and just need an occasional reminder. Martingales are not as effective in dogs that are just learning to walk on a leash.

The Illusion Collar

Pros: This collar is an original design that keeps the leash at the top of the dog's neck, which is the most sensitive area. It also gives the lower part of the neck support, while allowing the owner to correct at the more sensitive upper neck. The idea is to give the owner more control over the animal during the walk while keeping the dog's neck safe from constriction.

Cons: I'm biased, but I love this tool as a method to teach an inexperienced owner the proper way to walk a dog. Some owners may feel, however, that the collar is too limiting for their laid-back or already well-behaved dog.

Harnesses

Pros: Harnesses were originally invented for tracking or pulling. The harness allows the dog to use the entire weight of his body as leverage. It also allows a dog more freedom, including being able to keep his nose against the ground, which is necessary for tracking.

Cons: For many dogs, the harness triggers an instant pulling reflex. I'm always surprised at the number of people who use standard harnesses on their dogs and then wonder why their dogs are so out of control on the walk. As Hollywood trainer Mark Harden puts it, "When I want to teach a movie dog to pull, I put her in a harness."

The No-Pull Harness

Pros: Designed to gently squeeze a dog's chest when he starts to pull, this harness causes discomfort that encourages the dog to stop pulling.

Cons: Dogs can actually still pull in this harness, but they have to contort their bodies to do so. This harness will not prevent a dog that is hard to handle from finding a way to pull.

The Halti and the Gentle Leader

Pros: Also called the head collar. Fits around the dog's face, positioned far down the nose. When a dog pulls, the halti tightens around the dog's mouth, and then it loosens when the dog relaxes. If a dog is too strong for you to control, the halti can give you a more direct way to keep him from pulling you around. Some people who feel uncomfortable or insecure managing a neck collar are happier with a head collar.

Cons: Some dogs feel automatically uncomfortable wearing a head collar—it's not natural for them to have something blocking their mouths. It is also an easy device for the dog to revolt against . . . and win.

The Prong or "Pinch" Collar

Pros: Made up of chain or plastic links that are pointed toward the loose skin around a dog's neck, when tightened, the prong collar gives a quick startling correction—like a bite. The idea, as with the choke chain, is for the dog to self-correct to stop the unpleasant sensation. If used properly, the prong collar should never be painful—the objective is pressure, not pain.

Cons: Repeated, violent corrections can puncture a dog's skin, especially if the collar is not fitted correctly. If a handler is not trained in its proper usage, it can cause pain and injury.

As Ian Dunbar has shown us, there are successful techniques for working with dogs that don't involve leash corrections. But many positive- and rewards-oriented professionals still use this method in a safe, humane manner. "As dog trainers, I think we have to be honest and try not to pigeonhole ourselves into one training camp or definition," says Bonnie Brown-Cali. "It limits our training tools and closes us off from ideas that may help a dog. Using purely positive training techniques is almost impossible because there is always some form of correction. If a dog is being trained on a six-foot leash and runs to the end of the leash, the dog is corrected simply by the fact that he hits the end of the leash. To use purely positive techniques, the dog would have to be off-leash in a closed environment, like a dolphin in a pool, and be motivated to want to work with the handler because there is no other option. On the other hand, using purely compulsive techniques can have the adverse affect of teaching avoidance behavior. I want dogs and their people, whether it is an elderly client with a Cavalier, or a hunting dog and his handler, to be happy and confident in their work. If you pull ideas from a large bag of techniques, you have the tools to train a diverse dog population."

"There is no nice way to deal with prey aggression," says trainer Joel Silverman, who also prefers a positive approach whenever possible. "For people who say they can deal with prey aggression using treats and clickers, I would get them on TV and say, 'Here's a hundred thousand dollars. Make it work.' Maybe they can make it work, but I don't see them being able to teach it to somebody else. You take a high–prey aggression dog that wants nothing more than to go after somebody, and I'm very open about this. I say this at my seminars. You need to bring in specialists that deal with prey aggression or deal with aggression."

e-Collars

The electronic collar (the e-collar, or "shock" collar, or its milder cousin the vibrating collar) is not a tool designed to aid owners on the walk, though I'd like to say a few words about the myths and realities surrounding it. First of all, it is *not* a device suitable for basic obedience training, and since it is a punishment-based device, it should never be used for creating or adding a new behavior. In some countries, it has become illegal because of past misuse and misunderstanding of its purpose. For the record, in 317 *Dog Whisperer* cases, there have been only 8 that featured e-collars. (The owners were already using the collar in 4 cases, and I simply instructed them in its proper use. In 4 other cases, I introduced the e-collar myself to solve a specific problem.) Remember also, most modern e-collars have variable settings, from vibrate (and as we've seen with Viper, there are collars on the market that only vibrate) to a range of higher electric stimulation that can feel like anything from a light tap to a buzzing sensation to an irritating tickle to a tense unit vibration to a sharp, static shock. The goal of the collar is *not* to cause the dog pain or to create fear, but to startle and redirect the animal from the activity it is engaging in by creating a negative association between that activity and the decidedly unpleasant stimulation of the collar.

Martin Deeley, who does use an e-collar in training, claims that instead of seeing it as a device to be used solely for correction or punishment, the highly variable levels of the best modern e-collars make it useful as a communication aid between human and dog, analogous to an invisible leash. "I find it a very versatile tool that can be used at low levels just barely perceptible to the dog to interrupt an unwanted behavior or guide and assist the dog's learning, while maintaining a very happy disposition. The modern e-collar is not the correction/punishment tool of its terrible reputation—it is the off-leash communicator that many owners dream of. But it has to be introduced and used correctly, and that is where professional help is essential."

Although those who advocate the banning of e-collars cite studies that point to the dangers of their misuse, other peer-reviewed scientific studies indicate that properly used e-collar rehabilitation can bring about quick, effective, and permanent changes in unwanted behavior *without* causing hurt or injury to dogs.[1] I believe that, *if employed correctly and under the right circumstances by a trained professional,* an e-collar can save the life of a dog with a minimum of time and stress. However, there is no question that it is an advanced tool that can be abused or mishandled by an uneducated person.

The primary use of the e-collar is to block prey drive. Hardwired into a dog, prey drive can cause a dog to try to chase rattlesnakes, herd cars in the middle of traffic, or sprint after a jogger into a dangerous street. In a recent NPR interview, Temple Grandin, the esteemed advocate for the humane treatment of all animals and a champion of positive reinforcement, describes what she considers the correct use of an e-collar. "Car chasing, jogger chasing, cat killing, deer chasing—anything that's prey-drive behavior. And this is not aggression and it's not fear. It's a very special other kind of emotion that the animal has," Grandin explains. "And you'd want to put the collar on, have the dog wear it for two days, and then—because you never want him to find out that the collar did it—and then one day a thunderbolt from the sky blasts him for chasing deer. And that's one of the few situations I would use a punishment."[2]

San Francisco Bay Area trainer Kirk Turner, who uses primarily positive reinforcement and clicker techniques in his work, has used e-collars to protect coursing dogs and keep them safe. "When you send a coursing Borzoi team out after a rabbit, if that rabbit goes through a barbed-wire fence, then that Borzoi wants to go through that barbed-wire fence to get that rabbit," Kirk warns. "There, an e-collar is a totally appropriate use. Every tool I have used on dogs I have tried on myself.

I've put on an e-collar, I've shocked myself, so I do know what a level-five charge on a Tri-Tronics e-collar feels like. I have also used the vibrate setting to teach deaf dogs. You use the vibrate setting to get their attention and then use hand signals for everything else."

I don't recommend that anyone ever use an e-collar—or any other advanced tool, such as the prong collar or choke chain, for that matter—without thorough instruction from a qualified professional in the proper use of the device. For instance, Bonnie Brown-Cali teaches classes in the ethical use of correction-based tools, including the e-collar.

> According to Katenna Jones of the American Humane Association, the AHA is very stringent in its guidelines for correct use of an e-collar and recommends its use only in the following cases:
>
> - When employed by a professional who is highly educated in animal learning theory
> - When employed by a professional who is highly experienced with the tool or technique
> - In very rare, exceptional, life-or-death situations
> - As a last resort when all other options have been exhausted
> - For three or fewer trials (more than three trials or presentations borders on abuse and should end immediately)

THE WALK: WALKING WITH A CHOKE COLLAR

I find the choke chain to be a practical tool, but I almost never use it unless a client is already using it and has become comfortable with it already. In 317 *Dog Whisperer* cases, I've introduced the tool my-self only one time, because my goal is a closer connection between human and dog, leading toward the concept of an off-leash experi-ence. I prefer a simple, light leash placed high up on the neck to give me more control, as you see done by handlers working in a dog show. But many slightly built women and men are more comfortable with a choke chain, which can build their confidence when handling a pow-erful or high-energy dog. Moreover, a number of the professionals I interviewed for this book consider it a useful device to use in training, especially with adult dogs that have had no previous experience walk-ing on a lead or following a human leader.

"I'm very open about the fact that I use a choke collar in some situ-ations," says veteran trainer Joel Silverman. "And you know what? I've never had one person, not one person in thirty-five years, ever come up to me or ever write or e-mail me and say, 'I have an issue with the way you use it.' I mean, they may say, 'I prefer not to use a chain col-lar,' which is totally cool, but the point is, it's not about the tool, it's about the way you're using it."

Working with his Anatolian shepherd Oscar, Hollywood trainer Mark Harden showed me how he uses the choke chain during a walk. When used correctly, the metal choke chain, in Mark's opinion, is more humane than a cloth leash. "The thing is, it's there and it's gone. Whereas [with] a cloth collar, there's always something, there's always sensation there that they're feeling, and they can't pull or unpull, it's always there. So there's not that instant of difference. The other thing is, they have a pull instinct. They get their head stuck in something, and their instinct is to pull out of it. So you can nag them with that all the time and never make an impact, and it seems to me the people I see using straight cloth collars nag their dogs a lot more as opposed to going 'boom,' over, taught, let's go on with our day."

Mark brought Oscar close to show me the correct way to put on the collar. "So as you face the dog, it should look like a 'P,'" Mark said, holding the chain out in front of the dog's face. "And it goes over him." He slipped the collar over Oscar's head. "And then when it's applied, it releases.

"The first thing I do when I get an animal I need to train for a movie is, I'll go for days, hours, hours, hours, just walking." Mark led Oscar around the sheepherding field where we were working. "I'm saying to the dog, 'You walk the way I walk.' And I believe that all the control that I have and all the relationship I have flows through this leash. If I can get you walking, I can get you doing anything.

"There's no force. I don't pull at all. I mean, I couldn't pull this dog. This dog could pull me anywhere he wants to go," Mark said. "Oscar is like a 160-pound four-wheel-drive vehicle." It wasn't the leash or collar that gave Mark such control over the enormous dog. It was the leadership and trust he had worked to build into his relationship with Oscar.

"To me the biggest mistake people make is there should never ever, never one second, be tension on this leash except for that split second that I want to communicate with him. The rest of the time it's loose.

"I see people on their walks, and it's always like this." Mark balled the leash up in his hand, causing tension on Oscar's choke chain. "If my leash is always loose, I never have to say anything. I don't say, 'Heel'; I don't yell; I don't do anything. I just walk."

Mark continued to walk, and as soon as he didn't have Oscar's attention, he turned around and walked the other way, giving a little tug of correction. Oscar followed right behind him. Mark did this several times.

"I keep changing directions because I'm not as interested in having him stay right by my side, but I want him to check in. It's like, 'You don't know where I'm going, Oscar. How can you be in front of me?' So what I do is, it's a pop, boom, instant, so his own weight works against him."

Mark believes that the problem with choke chains lies in owners who don't know how to use them. "To me, there's no better way to teach my dog and to control him than this. It's easier, it's faster, it's not as constantly nagging as a cloth collar," he said. "This is a quick communicator, and one day, fifteen minutes, and I've got a dog that walks with me as if he was mine his entire life. People look at it like it's magic, but people aren't taught to use it properly."

Even though he himself gets great results using choke chains, he also knows that owners need to find what works for them. "If you can make a cloth collar work for you, if you can make a harness work for you, there's no judgment. I've trained hundreds of dogs—this is what works best for me. I've never hurt a dog with it. I mean, I can cut my vegetables with a knife, and I can stab somebody with a knife. It's the way it's used, it's not the tool itself."

Katenna Jones, an applied animal behaviorist in the Office of Humane Education for the American Humane Association, has a very different opinion about chain collars. "I've never used one in my life and never will. Do they work? Certainly. But are they the most 'humane' tool out there? No way. If I came to a client that was using one, I told them if they wanted to work with me, the choke chain goes. I primarily train, especially reactive dogs, on head halters."[3]

However, even more benign tools, like head halters, can be misused by an uneducated or impatient, frustrated owner. "I see people all the time jerking on a Gentle Leader like it was a choke chain," warns Kirk Turner. "And I can just imagine what it's doing to that dog's neck. The problem with the Gentle Leader, as with most tools, is that the dog knows when it's on and knows when it's not. Personally, I'd rather accomplish what needs to be accomplished with my nonverbal signals, such as the blocking technique and a calm, assertive attitude."

THE WALK: COMING WHEN CALLED

As our survey in Chapter 2 shows, the number one most important thing for pet owners is having a dog that comes when called. Nothing is more maddening to most people than a dog that ignores them and only comes when she feels like it. In many cases, a frustrated owner will reprimand a dog after she does return. Dogs live in a world of cause and effect, so that pet has no clue why she is being yelled at. Now you have taught her that there is a negative association with coming in to your call. Next time she'll be even more likely to play "keep away" when you call her to you. Catching a dog you've lost your temper with is not easy and makes you even madder, which further damages the bond between you and your dog. Thus, owners get caught in a downward spiral.

A dog that won't come can be a danger as well. If you call your dog in a dangerous public situation near a road or other potential accident area, your panic, fear, anger, or other negative emotions may spill out through your voice, and you will give your dog more good reasons not to want to come to you, even when you know you're calling your dog for her own good.

"There are many reasons a dog wants to come back to you," says Martin Deeley. "This can be broken down into two basic emotions. The first, because she wants to, and the second, because she feels she has to. She hears the leash being taken from the hook for a walk, the food going into her bowl, and abracadabra—the magic recall with tail wagging. Or she hears you call and knows, 'I had better go because if I don't there will be consequences.' Sometimes it is a little bit of both."

Consistent recall is built on the relationship you have with your dog, the leadership qualities you possess, the pleasures and rewards you provide, the limits and boundaries you have set, the consequences for your dog of not doing as asked, and, most important of all, your dog's innate desire to be with you—to be part of your team and your pack.

In *How to Raise the Perfect Dog*, I explained that raising a dog from early puppyhood provides you with an invisible leash, because all puppies are programmed to follow. Once they are separated from their mother and their littermates, they will transfer that instinct over to you, their new pack leader. The first step in creating a dog that will come to you every time is to utilize those precious first eight months of her life to develop and strengthen that invisible bond between you. One of the biggest mistakes owners make that contributes to poor recall is allowing a young pup too much freedom early on. You naturally want your dog to have times of play when you give her free rein, but while your puppy is young, "freedom" means more than just romping around in the yard. It also means being comfortable and secure knowing what the rules and guidelines of your pack are going to be and knowing that she can always trust you to keep her safe and let her know what she's supposed to do. While she's young, concentrate on conditioning your puppy to believe that the very best, most satisfying things in her life happen when she's with you—not when she's out on her own sniffing in the grass or interacting with another dog.

When you inadvertently teach your dog that her independent wandering is part of the pack "culture," then you have put coming when you call low on her list of priorities. Then your increasing frustration with her for not coming starts to show in your body language and energy. Now you're reinforcing her belief that it's definitely more pleasant to be away from you than close to you.

Martin Deeley knows retrieving dogs backwards and forwards. He has discovered that playing fetch with a puppy or a young dog is a great way to encourage outdoor play and exercise while keeping the "fun" associated with you. "If you encourage retrieving a thrown toy back to you, this will also provide the opportunity to let your dog run long distances, yet remain under control as she concentrates on the 'job.' To begin to create a name recall, say your puppy's name after she retrieves the toy and right when she starts back to you. Reward her with affection when she gets there. Never grab for the toy or snatch it from her in any way. Allow her to come to you and share it with you before gently taking it."

I always advise my clients to begin the ritual of the walk when a puppy is young, but veterinarians warn that long walks are not always good for puppies' bone development. Short walks combined with other play sessions with you can become part of the training process. "Long walks are not essential for young puppies if you use retrieving and other vigorous fun games for exercise and training," says Martin Deeley. "Exercise while training. Your dog will get as much exercise running around close to you as she does at a distance. Once your walks become longer, make your structured walk a training walk. Teach her to walk on a loose leash, sit when crossing a road, sit when meeting people, and generally be a good citizen when out on public view."

I always warn my clients that puppies are people magnets and may draw unwanted attention that will distract from your training. With both puppies and adult dogs, make sure you set limits for when people are and are not allowed to shower your dog with affection so that the structure of your walks and training time remains intact.

Until you are sure of a reliable recall, Martin Deeley advises, use a long leash or a long line so that you are always in touch with your dog. "This can be a strong ribbon type to start with," says Martin. "And then you can reduce it to a lighter line as you trust her more. The aim is to gradually remove it in small stages while she continues to obey. Take her out for a little walk around the yard or field and let her follow, tail a-wagging, around your ankles."

When your dog starts drifting away from you, use that as an opportunity to strengthen your ability to call her back. Turn in the opposite direction and call her, praising her as she returns. Very quickly your dog will begin to realize that if she goes too far, you will start to disappear. This will encourage her to keep at least one eye on what you are doing at all times. Occasionally, if the environment is a very secure one, if she happens to wander down one path, you can veer off on another, then call her to you. All these exercises reaffirm the importance of her coming to her name and heeding the recall command if she wants to find you again.

Hide-and-seek exercises are the next step in building your reliable recall. Hide behind a tree or lie down in the grass, call her, and then make a big fuss when she finds you.

Even with this foundation, some dogs still give in to the temptation to run away and explore. Shelter dogs adopted as adults have often become used to self-reliance and need to be reconditioned to understand that coming to you is an important and pleasurable activity.

"The most obvious way to have a dog returning to you," says Martin Deeley, "is for the treat reward. Always put your pup in a position where she cannot do wrong; therefore, a leash or long line is very helpful to provide control. With this attached, initially back away and call her up to you, with a light, fun voice. I use 'Here' and make myself interesting by lowering my body a little, semi-crouching or going down on one knee [not bending over], and smiling.

"When she comes up to you, give her a very small piece of a treat she enjoys. Go back to walking. Back away again, and once more call up and treat. Make it a fun game. Begin to walk around with her on

the long leash. Let her go away from you, and when she is not looking, change direction so that you are moving away from her. As you
do this, call her and once more make yourself interesting and fun and
offer the treat. If she does not at first respond, the moment you move
away and she feels the leash she will generally want to follow you."

As Ian Dunbar has shown us, when using treats as lures, it's important to phase them out of the training as soon as possible. You never
want a snack to become the only reason your dog comes to you. Once
she is responding regularly, begin to give her the treat at random intervals. The aim is to reduce the treat-giving to none at all so that she
happily comes to you even when there's no food present. Also, many
dogs, like Junior, are simply not treat-motivated. "With some dogs,
you will find the 'want to return' is related to other rewards than food,"
Martin tells us. "Retrieving or a tugger toy are examples, where your
dog enjoys the game more than anything else and sees being with you
as the place it all happens. In this case she comes willingly to partner
with you." If you do use a tugger or ball, teach your dog to let go or
drop it in your hand when asked. You start the game and you stop the
game—that is what leaders do.

As your dog learns, allow her to go farther away from you on the
long line and then call her up.

This is important because a dog that will recall at five yards will not always recall at ten. Once you've got this behavior down pat in a safe training scenario, you can begin to introduce distractions at a distance—other dogs and people walking by, cars, cats, and other interesting things in the environment. The leash will enable you to stop her doing the incorrect action and guide her into the right one. "You may occasionally have to give her a pop on the leash to get her attention back and ensure she follows, rather than giving way to temptation," Martin reminds us. "When you do this, never do it harshly. It is a sharp wrist-popping action or a short pull at the level of the dog's shoulders and neck. With some dogs, just standing on the long line

CESAR MILLAN

so she cannot move away is enough. Encourage her to you and praise her when she does come. Read your dog.

"Next," Martin continues, "we can begin to make the leash control less by allowing it to run on the ground. Follow this by replacing a heavier leash with a lighter-weight one. Once you are successful with this, in a safe area you can shorten the leash until you take it off altogether and work your dog on the recall with no leash and no treat at all."

If you agree with Ian Dunbar's theory that a leash is a crutch that is often too hard a habit to break, you can follow his prescription of practicing the recall-sit, first in an area as small as a bathroom, then the kitchen, then the living room, then your fenced backyard, until your recall is solid at least 95 percent of the time. Your voice and your connection with your dog become the invisible leash in this method.

COMING WHEN CALLED— THE CLICKER WAY

Using a clicker is another way to teach the recall command off-leash. I asked Kirk Turner to outline a clicker method for teaching a recall.

"I'm working with Sparky, the dachshund, and I know he's motivated by Duck Jerky. So I say his name, he looks at me. *Click!* Treat! Walk away and ignore him," Kirk explains. "Actually, I try to avoid him. He tries hard to get my attention, but I just wait until he is distracted by something else, and then I say, '*Sparky!*' And he looks at me and comes running. When he is about halfway to me, I click with the clicker behind my back and give him a treat when he gets to me. I also am very exuberant with my praise.

"I repeat this process several times before I use the word *come.* When I am positive he is going to come to me anyway, I will start saying the word every time. I will also start randomly clicking only when he is all the way to me, and I will vary the amount of treats he gets and the length of time I am praising him. As time goes by I will bring him to more distracting environments and repeat this process, maybe even from the beginning if he is too distracted."

All these techniques are great starting points for making sure your dog comes to you when called. The bottom line, however, is that your dog must trust you, want to be with you, and respect your leadership in all environments and situations. With a puppy, this is a piece of cake; with some rescued dogs, it can take a lot of time and patience. But patience is the key. No dog is attracted to frustrated, angry, or impatient energy. If you are having a hard time getting your dog to come, check your own attitude first. Are you offering your dog something wonderful to come home to? It's up to you, not only to establish leadership at home but to be the best thing in your dog's life, wherever you go together.

THE SIT

All dogs can sit and obviously do it all the time on their own. Teaching them to sit on command is just a matter of capturing that behavior and attaching a word to it. This should come easily, but some people do find the timing of attaching the command to the behavior difficult. "Too often pups are told to 'sit' when they are doing something naughty, and owners yell the command in anger to get them to stop," says Martin. "Unfortunately, 'sit' then becomes a word associated with a correction." We want our dogs to have a positive association with this behavior.

There are many ways to teach the sit command. Remember, when you first begin teaching any behavior, start with lessons that are short and sweet and work in an environment where there are as few distractions as possible.

THE SIT: THE NATURAL WAY

As Bob Bailey points out, the simplest way to tell any animal what behavior you want from her is to simply "capture" the behavior that the animal is naturally doing, then reward it. This takes patience, but in my opinion it is the method of training that is the closest to how dogs would learn from each other in nature. Animals learn by trial and error—but when it comes to survival in the wild, there's not much room for error. You can take advantage of this natural method and simply look for opportunities to teach many commands.

Your dog will sit on her own many times during the day. Sometimes if she is on the leash and you just stand and wait at the door, she will sit after a while. Whenever you see her moving into a sit position, say, "Sit." Do it calmly, with a natural voice and with a smile. Send her your proud and loving energy, reward or praise her immediately afterward, and you will be surprised how quickly she can learn many commands from just doing them herself. I find myself teaching my pack all the time by just encouraging good behavior with my happiness or disagreeing with unwanted behavior by using the "tssst" sound. Dogs were born to learn, and they are hardwired to learn from us. When you use Mother Nature's method to communicate with your dog, you may be surprised at how effortless and fun basic command training can be.

THE SIT: FEED TIME AS MOTIVATION

With a small puppy, feed time is a great opportunity to get the point of "sit" across without having to do very much, and with a built-in reward attached. First, prepare the dinner, then bring the pup to where you are going to feed.

Initially, you may let the puppy smell the food, but then hold it up away from her and wait. She may jump around at first, and she'll probably jump on you. If so, indicate your disapproval with your attitude and body language and slowly move yourself back or to one side . . . and then wait.

Remember, your patience as an owner now will pay off in a well-behaved dog for a lifetime.

After a while, your pup will probably begin to try to figure out what she needs to do to get her dinner. That "figuring it out" look will appear on her face, and she will lower her butt to the floor.

At that precise moment, put the food down in front of her. "After doing this once or twice," says Martin, "I find that the moment I go in with the food and wait, the pup sits automatically." Once you begin cueing the sit behavior with the food ritual, just add the word *sit* so that the pup hears this request the split second before she sits. This way, it becomes a cue.

Praise can be your secondary reinforcer. Don't overpraise with excitement, but feel your own pride and calmly tell her, "Good." This way, your pup has learned the command by association and, perhaps just as important, by a behavior that she has figured out for herself.

THE SIT: USING TREATS TO LURE

Choose a treat that your dog will enjoy. The rule of thumb I use for treats is to save the best, most delectable treats for last, to reengage your dog if she begins to lose interest in the training session. I like to save a piece of chicken or a hot dog just in case attention wanes. For early in the session, or for shorter sessions, kibble or treats made specifically for training work just fine. "I prefer to use kibble that my dog has at dinnertime," Martin Deeley says, adding, "and cut back on the amount when feeding if we have used it for training." Obviously, using treats to train a behavior won't work as well right after your dog has had a full meal as they will between meals. Some professional trainers like Mark Harden use their dog's "pay" as their whole diet on working days, so the dog is literally working for her living.

You can teach this technique off or on a leash. Hold a food treat in your hand between the first two fingers and the thumb.

Let your dog sniff so that she knows it is there, and remember my rule: nose first, then eyes, then ears! When you engage your dog's nose, you are appealing to the most important part of her brain.

Next, as she is sniffing and getting interested, slowly lift the treat above nose height and move it gradually over her head and slightly back toward her shoulders. The aim is for your pup to lift her head

up, move her shoulders back, and naturally have her butt lower to the floor.

Lift the treat slowly and easily so that your dog's nose follows it in your hand. If she jumps at your hand, take it away. Next time, have the treat hand closer to her head. The moment she begins to follow the treat with her nose and eyes and her butt begins to move to the floor, say, "Sit," calmly and easily. "Use a natural voice," Martin reiterates. "We don't want to distract, startle, or concern her." Remember one of my cardinal rules for training: don't overexcite your dog, so that she loses the lesson in all the commotion! As we saw from my session at

the Dunbars', the movement of your hands and body also provide a visual cue in addition to the verbal "sit." In the future, by lifting your hand in this manner in front of her head, you can signal her to sit.

"Learning words is not the way dogs are born to communicate," says Ian Dunbar. "Dogs are used to *watching* people. And they're so good at reading a person's body language that they pick up the hand signals in every single intention. Most people aren't even aware of their body language when they're giving commands, then get frustrated when their dog answers to what the body language is saying, not what the command is saying." So make sure your body and your words are exactly in alignment so that your dog doesn't get mixed messages.

Unlike many trainers, I prefer silence to commands when communicating with my dogs. To me, training is usually based on sounds, but dog psychology is best accomplished with silence, then simple, basic sounds. After my dogs learn from my body language and hand signals, I add verbal commands only if need be. If your dog is across the field or has her back turned to you, you're very likely to prefer that she be able to obey a range of commands expressed in human words. As we learned in our session with Ian Dunbar, the language of the words doesn't matter. It's the association of the word with the required behavior that counts, and the reliability with which the dog follows your commands. Whatever method you choose to teach the sit, make sure you practice it in as many locations and situations as possible, so that your dog knows what the word means everywhere she goes.

THE SIT: GUIDE YOUR DOG USING YOUR HANDS

Using gentle physical guidance is another way to show a dog the behavior you wish him to display. Once again, I like to have a dog figure out for himself what it is that I want, because I believe the lesson has more meaning for him that way. But if that approach doesn't work for you, there's no harm in communicating with your hands, as long as you are tender and respectful. Remember, know your dog before you train, and make sure your dog is telling you with his energy and body language that the way you are touching is okay with him. "I enjoy sitting on the floor with a small pup and having her in close to my body," says Martin Deeley. "My hands should always be friendly. I like to get the pup familiar with a gentle touch and guidance." He adds, "I especially want pups to get familiar with every part of their body being touched so that in future they can be groomed, nails can be clipped, and the vets can check everything out."

Sit or kneel on the floor and let your pup come into your body. Don't grab or force, but wiggle your fingers and encourage him to come in closer to be gently held and slowly petted. While doing this, with one hand rub on the chest and slowly move up under the chin. Slowly move your other hand down the back of the pup and apply light pressure to the butt, your middle finger and thumb resting on each hip, palm on his rear.

Gently apply pressure. Nothing hard! Once your pup makes even the smallest movement toward the floor, release the pressure imme-

diately. Do this until you can apply light constant pressure and the pup's butt touches the floor. While there, gradually stroke down his back, praising calmly, "Good."

Next, add the word *sit* as you begin to do this exercise. Timing is essential—the word *sit* should precede the action you ask for. So say the word at the very moment the pup begins to move toward the floor. With just a few days of practice, you will find your pup understanding the verbal command and responding to the sit you ask for. Again, praise calmly with your happy energy or a word you choose, such as "good."

Some dogs have a physical frame that makes it difficult to sit— greyhounds, for instance, are renowned for this problem. If this is the case with your dog, you can show her gently how to bend her rear legs to get into a sit. With your dog on a leash, kneel down next to her. Hold the leash up with one hand; if she is large, just holding her up at the front with her collar under her chin will suffice. Now run your other hand down along her back. This time, keeping your hand on her body, go past the butt, bending her tail slowly downward, and run your hand down the rear of her legs until you reach the back of her knees. Once your hand is in this position behind her knees, gently

begin to move those knees inward to have them bend. This action brings her butt down. Don't expect her to sit the full distance immediately—stop and calmly praise when you achieve small successes in the dropping of the rear to the ground. Build up the distance she descends toward the floor in small stages, until you and she are successful. Then praise her—"Good dog"—and smile.

If you have any doubts at all about your dog's physical range of motion or any disabilities she might have, check with your vet first and have him or her talk you through this exercise to make sure you are doing it correctly. With this method, your face is close to the dog's mouth, so always be sure of the temperament of your dog. If she is liable to nip at you, do not use this approach, Martin warns.

THE SIT: USING A LEASH

In some ways, I agree with Ian Dunbar that a leash can unintentionally become a "crutch" that is hard to give up if you establish it as the basis for your relationship with your dog. After all, I grew up with the free-roaming packs of dogs on my grandfather's farm and didn't know the purpose of a leash for a dog during most of my early childhood. My long-term goal is always for you to have the ultimate bond with your dog, and that includes enjoying an off-leash relationship wherever it's safe and legal.

However, we do live in a leash-oriented society, and having a leash and collar on your dog allows you a certain amount of control that many people feel they need in the early days of training. Personally, I do not mind any type of collar, provided it is used correctly and without harshness. What works best for me is a simple leather show leash attached to a collar, or even what I call my thirty-five-cent leash—just a rope or nylon with a loose loop on the end. Martin Deeley prefers a rope slip leash or a slip chain.

Walk slowly with your dog and choreograph your movements so that she comes to a stop and stands along your left side.

With the leash in your right hand, gradually apply an upward pressure by lifting the leash, creating an upward pull. Don't jerk the leash! Just lift upward with a gentle constant pressure. The moment her butt goes to the floor, the upward pressure is released and the leash goes slack.

Some dogs sit automatically in response to this pressure. If your dog does not, put your left hand on her back just behind the shoulders and slide it slowly down to her butt area. Now, with your middle finger and thumb straddling the spine, palm on her back, exert a little downward pressure. Again—don't push! Just apply pressure down and slightly backward. Be firm but gentle. Through this action, you are lifting the head with the leash. "Make sure you have the leash the right length and are not overreaching yourself," says Martin.

The moment your dog puts her rear to the floor, loosen the leash, releasing the upward pull. Repeat your praise and rewards. Once your dog is going into a sit the moment she feels the leash being lifted, add the command "sit" just before you begin to lift the leash.

Gradually, your dog will learn "sit" and know that a slight lift of the

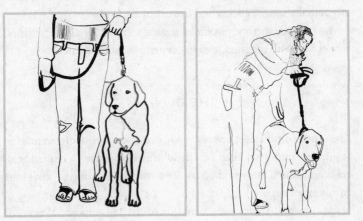

leash means "sit." The command prompts the behavior, and soon she will also begin to learn that the change in weight of the clips fastening the leash to the collar means a "sit" is coming. She will begin to read the subtle leash signals coming from you, just as a horse does with the reins used by a rider. This kind of micro-control can make communicating with your dog during your walks much easier.

THE SIT: USING THE CLICKER

Kirk Turner continues the saga of Sparky the miniature dachshund that he successfully taught to come using a clicker and a piece of Duck Jerky. Since Sparky now associates the click with a forthcoming piece of jerky, teaching the sit command comes naturally. "Now, when I call Sparky, he comes running and sits waiting for his click and treat. I just wait until he offers the sit behavior. As I see him sitting, I bring in the word *sit*. Very quickly, it becomes a conditioned response. I just walk around avoiding him, and he makes sure he gets in front of me, and I will say, 'Sit,' and I wait until his hind end hits the floor, and that's when I click and give the little guy a treat. Again, I will only occasionally actually use the clicker and treat, moving to only praise."

Like all the methods outlined in this section, the clicker method works best with repeated sessions, repetition, and patience.

THE DOWN

The down command is a really useful exercise for your dog to master. It puts her into what I call a calm-submissive posture, where she can relax and watch the world go by. It's a way to get a dog to "chill out" in any situation.

My pit bull Daddy was a master of the self-imposed down—it

wasn't anything that I taught him. When he was with me and we were in a waiting mode, he'd lie down flat on the ground next to me—front legs splayed forward, rear legs to the back. Of course, as he got older he got into this position a lot more often, just because he tired more easily. Daddy raised my now two-and-a-half-year-old pit bull Junior, who picked up the position by copying Daddy. Imitation is one of the most important ways dogs learn. Today Junior plops down next to me in the same position that Daddy used to assume. Junior is so in tune with me that he automatically understands when we are in waiting mode, just by sensing my energy. He learned from Daddy, "When Cesar is in this state, this is when we rest." Of course, Junior is an adolescent and usually prefers a little more action, but teaching patience to a dog is a mental exercise for them too. The patience that Junior learned by watching Daddy—and that I am still teaching him to practice every day of his life—has helped me to create a new generation of mellow, obedient pit bulls as role models.

For the most part, I have found that lying down is not the most natural behavior for dogs to do on command, since they usually

Daddy in the "splay" position

assume that position only when they are tired, not when they are alert. It doesn't always make sense right away when a human asks them to do it. This was the hardest position for Junior to get into in his first session with Ian Dunbar. When I teach this behavior, as I did with Angel the miniature schnauzer in *How to Raise the Perfect Dog,* I like to give myself a lot of time, and I try not to expect too much right away.

For Martin Deeley, who trains both companion and hunting dogs, being able to get a reliable "down" command is important when he needs his dogs to be in waiting mode. He says of the down: "I see this as being a three-stage exercise. The first part is to teach the dog the command so he understands what it means; the second part is to have him do it without a food reward; and the last stage is to ask him to stay there until released from this position."

"Food is the obvious way with most dogs that are food-oriented," says Martin. "However, even with food, I prefer to have an older dog on a leash so that he cannot just ignore me and walk away—plus it indicates a little control to the dog. He should know what the leash means by now, and he should know the 'sit' command. With puppies that are more likely to want to be with you and when you can be in an enclosed area, you can do the 'sit,' 'down,' and 'stand' with food without the leash. Puppies are usually a lot easier than an older dog that has not learned these commands yet."

Ian Dunbar, on the other hand, never trains the down with a leash. He teaches it off-leash, with the sit and stand command in rapid sequence, as we saw in Chapter 6. Using a food lure, then quickly phasing it out, is what works best for him.

"Physical prompting with hands or leash is very slow because the dog pays selective attention to the physical contact and thus simply doesn't hear the verbal instructions. Also, hands-on and leash prompts are very difficult to phase out to get off-leash control," Ian argues. "Clicker training is also slow, since only one behavior is taught at a time. However, lure/reward training with food or toys is lightning fast, and it's much easier to phase out the lures and the rewards, so that playing the game becomes the reward. And so why not teach a bunch of commands at once? When I start off with a puppy/dog, I generally teach eight behaviors at once: come here, sit, lie down, sit up, stand, down from the stand, stand up from the down, and roll over."

As for me, I like to use training tables to teach dogs specific behaviors, because it gives them a limited area to work in—they can't "cheat" by walking away, it keeps them focused on me without any distractions, and it allows me to be at their eye level without hurting my back or my knees. Remember, dogs don't just read our body postures—they read our eyes, our facial expressions, and even our micro-expressions, so being able to search our faces for feedback is an important way dogs figure out whether or not they're doing what we want.

I've found tables to be great tools for teaching many things, but especially the down, because I can easily get down to the dog's eye level in the beginning. Mark Harden uses tables to teach his acting dogs the army crawl, which is a "modified" version of the down. A table is also

Cesar trains Angel.

a sort of middle ground between leash-based and off-leash training. The table itself is a leash, but there is no need for physical interaction with the dog, who is figuring out the behavior for herself.

Of course, it's up to you to choose the method that works best for both you and your dog.

To begin, have a little finger-size treat in your hand. Let your dog smell it so that she knows it is there and then ask her to sit. With your fingers holding the food just in front of her nose, slowly drop your fingers down in front of her chest to between her front feet. Allow her nose and head to follow your fingers down.

When her nose is close to the floor and your fingers are resting on the floor, slowly bring them forward away from your dog so that her front legs begin to walk gradually forward. Do this until she is in a down position, then praise her and give her the treat. If she gets up before going down, try again and move your hand more slowly. Do not give her the treat if she gets up. Remember Mark Harden's rule— reward the behavior you want, not an unfinished attempt at the behavior. Her whole body must be on the floor.

Martin Deeley offers a great trick that can help if you are working on a floor. "Sit on the floor and have one of your legs crooked with

the knee in the air. Then you lure her into the down by guiding her under your legs and she sees the knee as something to put her head under."

Remember what happened when I visited Ian Dunbar? Junior moved like molasses when food was used as a lure to teach him the down, but he hit the floor like a wrestler when Ian substituted the ball as a lure. If what you're using to get your dog's attention doesn't turn her on, keep trying until you find the right reward. For some dogs, just the challenge itself—or your happy, positive energy—is reward enough. Most puppies, however, respond well to small treats.

There are other actions that can help you achieve success and move toward the second stage of the command training. One way is to rest your free hand on the dog's shoulder blades and exert a light downward pressure. With your fingertips between her shoulder blades, rocking gradually and lightly pushing down can help her get the idea if she is slow to catch. Once she is down, you can use this hand also to hold her there lightly for a few seconds. Reward or praise her when she does it.

If you like to work with a leash, you can place both fingers in between your dog's shoulder blades and the leash, then use a very light

downward motion on the leash to communicate the direction you want the dog to go.

It's important that the tug be light and subtle—it is directional only, not coercive. The goal at this stage is for the dog to follow the treat. Too much pressure and she will resist it and forget the treat. By using your hands and leash in this way, you are gently reinforcing the command, and eventually you'll be able to prompt the movement without food.

When your dog is doing a reliable down on command, the next step is to phase out the treats. Start with intermittent reinforcement—ask for two or three repetitions before she gets her reward. Then, saying the down command before she begins, use just the lightest leash tug or the finger pressure to guide her into position.

"One way I have been successful with dogs that are not interested in food," Martin Deeley suggests, "is to put the leash under your foot so it runs in the gap between sole and heel. Then, as you pull upwards or walk while standing on the leash, moving closer to the dog's collar in small stages, gradually the dog learns the most comfortable posi-

tion is on the ground. And don't forget that you can also use a different reward, such as a tennis ball, just like you would a treat."

As I've said before, for me it's ideal when the dog finds the position on her own and then I reward it. But people like Hollywood animal trainers do not always have the time to wait for a dog to figure out "down" on their own, in which case a light pressure or leash tug will do the trick.

Either way, your dog isn't going to learn anything if it's not interesting or pleasant for her to do so. If you and your dog are in sync, communicate well, and understand the nuances of one another's body language, you'll know right away if your dog finds something fun and is motivated or if she's unhappy and is only doing the behavior to get you off her back. Always check your own energy. Do you feel confident and at ease with what you are doing? Or are you forcing it? Are you getting annoyed at your dog because she is taking a long time to figure this out or find the position that's comfortable for her body? If this is the case, look for a command that your dog can do perfectly—it may be the simple "sit"—and always end the session on a high note.

Then regroup, take a break, and try again later. Training should be fun, not frustrating, for both dog and human in order for it to work.

The third stage of this command is for your dog to learn how to go down on command alone and to stay there. Don't move to this stage until you are absolutely sure your dog knows that the command "down"—or whatever signal, verbal or physical, you are using—means to lie down. Martin Deeley often does this with a leash, and Ian Dunbar always works without one, but the universal similarity between both off- and on-leash methods is consistent follow-through. Also, don't put a clock on your dog if learning "down" is slow going for her at first—every trainer I've spoken to says this is a behavior any dog can master, so be as patient as necessary.

"With your dog in the sit position in front of you," says Martin, "ask her to 'down,' and with your hand that held the food or pulled the leash to the floor, mime the physical motion of this action in front of her. Your hand moves from your waist and pushes down almost to the floor. Exaggerate the movement at first."

Remember, your dog is always trying to read your body language. Watch her reaction, and the moment she makes the decision to begin going down, praise her calmly and smile so that you do not interrupt her thought process—don't forget that overexcitement can completely distract a dog from the lesson. Then calmly praise her again when she is down. Repeat the gesture with the body language and combining it with the command; then, if you want to use words alone, gradually phase out the body language.

"If she does not go down," Martin suggests, "use your fingers on her back or the gentle leash movement down to follow through and ensure that she does. Once she is down, put your foot or hand [if you are kneeling] on the leash so she cannot get up and then sit down and spend some time with her. If she attempts to get up, just stay there and let her readjust her position so her down feels comfortable."

THE DOWN: USE BEDTIME TO CAPTURE THE BEHAVIOR

Another way to reinforce the "down" command is to capture the behavior at bedtime. Take your dog to her bed or to the place in which she most often lies down at the end of the day. Tell her, "Bed," or "Place," or use whatever word or sound or gesture you want her to associate with lying quietly at rest. Then wait until she is beginning to lie down and use the command for "down" when she does. Repeat this a few times, and in a short time she will learn to go to her bed and lie down at your request.

Down is not a very exciting movement, but if you make it fun and put some excitement in your voice as your dog is moving, and follow up with a reward such as a ball or treat, then the game does become fun, and your dog will often go down quicker and more happily.

THE DOWN: TEACHING DOWN WITH A CLICKER

When teaching the down with a clicker as an aid, Kirk Turner stresses that, as with any other method, you've got to have patience to get the behavior you want from your dog. "I just wait. And wait some more. Eventually Sparky is going to lie down. All dogs do. They know how. Sparky wants my attention, but I am not looking at him or talking. Sparky is getting bored now. So he just lies down and . . . *Click! Treat! Ignore.* Pretty soon he is lying down all over the place where he knows I will see him. Now is the time to bring in the word *down* as I can predict he will do it anyway. Within a few minutes, I can say the word, and he will do the behavior three times for every one time he gets a click and a treat."

THE STAY

The joint headquarters of my *Dog Whisperer* production company, MPH Entertainment, and my own business, Cesar Millan Inc., is a dog-friendly office. Any dog that is balanced, sociable, and well behaved is welcome, as long as the owner registers his or her dog and agrees to pay a $25 cleaning fee if there is an "accident." As a result, our workplace is a joyous, dog-filled environment with anywhere from six to a dozen pets on the property at any one time.

All of these mellow, laid-back dogs in the office have been raised using the "Cesar's Way" formula of exercise, discipline, and then affection, which means that high-energy lunchtime pack walks are common and afternoon ball-playing sessions in the parking lot or the back hallway help drain the dogs' pent-up energies and keep them relaxed, calm, and submissive during the workday. Many of the dogs in the office have workplace canine "best friends" with whom they are allowed to visit and play, as long as things don't get too intense. The dogs in the office listen to their humans and follow their leads as to how to behave.

Many employees who used to leave their dogs at home in previous jobs have noticed a world of improvement in their pet's overall behavior at home and at work, since coming to the office every day fulfills their need to be part of a pack. I'm a big champion of dog-friendly offices for a number of reasons. Not only is it better for the dogs, but it's better for work productivity and the stress levels of the humans who work there. If you are a boss and you are reading this, I urge you to think about implementing this policy at your workplace. You will be amazed by how much having dogs in the office lightens everybody's mood and creates a more upbeat, relaxed environment.

Something I've noticed, however, is that whenever one of our employees gets up and walks across the expansive office to do something on the other side, his dog almost always follows him. This is totally natural and one sign of a good leader-follower relationship, but if the employee is going to a busy meeting in the conference room or a screening in a small editing bay, he doesn't always want his dog with him. Some of our workers have baby gates on their office doors, and those who are out in the bullpen cubicles bring in zip-up tents or use leashes to keep their dogs in place. But there is another way to be able to leave a location and keep your dog in place, and that is by mastering the "stay" command. A dog that understands the concept of "stay" will be able to remain in the place you left her, even if you go out of sight.

Martin Deeley explains how he accomplishes the "stay" command using a leash. "When you have trained your dog to sit or down and stay there, stand in front of her, repeat the command, and when she has complied, take a very small step backwards—sometimes even just a fraction of a step. It should be enough to make a small movement away, but not enough to have your dog want to get up and follow you. With many dogs, this step is the cue that prompts them to follow you. If this happens, guide your dog back to the position she was in and begin again.

"To keep her in a sit-and-stay, which I teach first before down-and-stay, lift the leash lightly to gently hold her there, arm slightly outstretched over her head holding the leash, and then take a very small step back.

"Remember, do not try to back away too far to begin with; start with a small amount at a time and gradually build up to increased distances. Always return to your dog at this stage from any distance and give her gentle praise—enough to show you are pleased with her, but not so much that it triggers excitement that inspires her to move. Never call her up to you, or she will begin to anticipate the call-up and move when you do not wish her to. Returning to the dog is the secret of steadiness. Little by little, over a period of time, build up the distance,

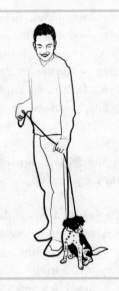

always going back to praise the dog. If your dog moves forward even the slightest amount, calmly walk back to her and take her back to the original spot, emphasizing 'sit and stay' before moving away again."

Once you have accomplished a successful sit-and-stay—first at a close distance, then from fairly far away—and you are absolutely confident that your dog understands the concept of the exercise, then you are ready to begin teaching her to come to you from the stay position. "With many a pup, the first time you do call her up, she will initially stay because she expects you to return to her," Martin Deeley warns. "If she does this, just encourage her to come and look happy as you do. The leash attached throughout the early sessions does help, even if you are not holding it, as it gives her a sense of your control. If you are using a leash, initially you can drop it to the floor as you increase the distance, and then as you and your dog gain confidence, remove it altogether." Even when you have taught this, go back to your dog on a stay far more times than you call her up.

Some dogs may develop the habit of crawling after you as you back away, especially from a down. "One way to stop this is to use a long line as a leash," Martin says. "Sit the dog in front of a solid post or tree and then run the line attached to her collar around the post, so that now when you hold the line, you stop her moving forward towards you. When she starts moving, now you can hold her in that position."

When you are able to walk a greater distance away from your dog and are confident that she will not move, you are ready to set up situations where you disappear from sight. You can do this inside your home to start, then move to a safe area outside when you feel a little more confident. Trees, walls, buildings, and hedges are good objects to move behind. Walk around a large tree at first so that you are out of sight for only a short period of time. After a while, take a little longer before reappearing from behind the tree. A hedge is a good place to hide because you can peek through it even though, in your dog's eyes, you have disappeared. At the slightest movement on the part of the dog, you can then repeat the command or sound to which you want her to respond.

A good exercise is to leave the dog in your secured and fenced yard and go indoors where you can view her from a window. An upstairs window works well because your dog's first instinct won't be to look up and thus, if she moves, your command comes as a surprise.

These exercises all reinforce the invisible link between you and your dog, so that your leadership continues no matter how far apart you two may be. In *How to Raise the Perfect Dog,* I used a variation of this exercise to help five-month-old Angel get over his mild case of separation anxiety. It's important to practice this exercise patiently and consistently, starting in small increments, whether you are using it to teach a reliable stay or just conditioning your dog to be able to stay alone without you for periods of time. It is not in a dog's nature to be separated from her pack, so you are working against instinct here. This is the time when your bond of trust and respect with your dog and your position of leadership will be put to the test.

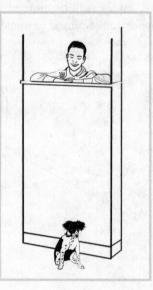

THE STAY: TEACHING CLICK AND STAY

Kirk Turner uses several techniques for teaching the stay. Some are clicker-based, and others are not. The release is an important part of teaching the "stay" command with a clicker. Kirk teaches the stay while incorporating it into the down or the sit. "After the dog is sitting or down, start moving a little and use your body to block her when she starts to get up. Say the word *stay*, count to three, and click and treat. Start stretching out the time and the distance before clicking. Now is a good time to bring in a release command that you say *while* you are clicking—like 'Free' or 'Take a break.' "

THE STAY: THE STAKE STATION STAY

Another favorite method of Kirk's is one he borrowed from the late dog trainer John Fisher, founder of the United Kingdom's version of the Association of Pet Dog Trainers. "You take four stakes, and you plant them in the ground, in a square in your backyard. And you've got your leash with your dog, and you're just kind of walking around, and you happen to walk by one of these stakes. And you surreptitiously drop the lead for the leash over the stake, give a hand signal, and say, 'Stay.' I don't combine this with the sit or down—and then I kind of hurry away.

"The dog is going to run towards me and get stopped by the leash. And then I pay no attention to the dog, I won't look at her or anything. I'll go all the way back to the stake to deliver the treat right at the stake. After a dog does this a couple times, she's not going to go out to the end of the leash again. And then, within a matter of a very short period of time, she's actually staying right there at the stake.

"So I have people do it four times at station number one, four times at station number two, four at number three, and four at number four. Once they've done that for ten days, that's 160 repetitions. Then I have them remove station number one and put it someplace else. And then station number one becomes station number four, and then we start mixing it up into different patterns, different areas. Then I'll have people use the environment. Like fence posts in the neighborhood and that sort of thing. So that's a great technique. Now, the word *stay* in itself, I think, is a little superfluous. You tell a dog, 'Sit,' then she should stay there until you tell her something else."

YIN AND YANG—DON'T FORGET THE RELEASE!

Kirk Turner's last comment is an important one. As we are also reminded by Mark Harden and Joel Silverman, both animal trainers for film and television, whenever you teach a dog to do something, you need to teach her an "out" or an opposite for the behavior. If she sits or lies down, you should be able to follow up with a "stand up" or a "go to your place," or an instruction to heel and walk with you. Otherwise, you are only partly in control. Your dog will do something you ask of her, but then she'll assume it's up to her to choose what to do afterward.

Sometimes, however, you will want your dog to not wait for another command but just to relax and be free to do as she wishes—to run, sniff, relax, or just hang out with the pack! That's why it's good to teach your dog a release command—an instruction that says, "Okay, be yourself and just chill and go play."

Martin Deeley explains how easy it is to get this release command wrong. "Sometimes we actually teach what our dog takes as a release command without realizing it, and that gets us into trouble. Our dog does as we ask—sits, for example. Once she has complied, we say, 'Okay,' smile, and exhort her to move. Then on another occasion we ask our dog to sit, and a friend who is talking to us says, 'Hi, how are you?' We answer, 'Okay,' and upon hearing this our dog jumps up, only to receive a correction for doing so. Now we have a very confused dog. So be careful about the word you use, and also about being too excited or accidentally releasing your dog when you praise her. To some dogs, your happy exclamation of 'Good!' gets interpreted as a signal to go and do whatever she likes."

The word or sound or signal you choose to use to release your dog should be distinct from praise or any other command you have been using to trigger other behaviors. As Ian Dunbar points out, dogs make *associations* between behaviors and words—they don't understand their dictionary meanings! When Ian and I took our park walk with his magnificent American bulldog Dune, he used "Go play!" as a universal release. Martin Deeley suggests the words *free* or *release*—or you may choose a word or sound or even a physical gesture that has a personal meaning for you.

To teach the sound or gesture you've chosen, start by asking your dog to sit, then after a few seconds say your release command. Encourage her to come out of the sit by putting a little more excitement in your voice, clapping your hands, or, if you are using a leash, giving an encouraging little tug. You may walk aimlessly around or jog with her or play a little—any activity that signifies that you are not practicing discipline right now, but enjoying affection. Then stop the activity, ask her to sit, wait awhile, and again follow up with your release command followed by free playtime or unstructured walking. Once you've accomplished this routine, any of your commands will signify staying in that command behavior until you give your dog a new command or the release command to just relax.

THE STAND

Ian Dunbar uses "stand up" as an integral part of his rapid-fire lure command training. Mark Harden uses "on your feet" to signify to his acting dogs that it is time to stand in position for the next command. Any command signifying "stand" can also be useful for going to the groomer or the veterinarian.

The "stand" command can be easy to teach starting with food as a lure. With the treat held between your fingers and thumb, lure your dog first into a sit and then, by putting your hand holding the treat in front of her nose and bringing it forward slowly, encourage her to stand.

Initially give her a treat each time she stands, along with some nice calm praise. Do this a few times until you feel that your dog is getting the idea from your hand movement what is required of her.

"Once she is in the stand position," says Martin Deeley, "allow her to lick and nibble at the treat, holding her in the stand position for a longer period of time. To help guide her, a light leash may be useful to provide the necessary control."

Now, using the same movement, guide her forward into the stand—but without the treat this time. She should follow your hand, and when she does, praise her. Then have her sit and stand two or three times before giving her the treat as a reward. When she is doing this nicely, you can add a verbal command—"Stand"—as you urge her forward onto her feet with your hand movement. Praise her while you work to gradually increase the length of time she stands. Over time, with repetitions, you will be able to have your dog simply understand the verbal command and go right from sit to stand to sit without food or hand signals.

"With dogs that are not food-motivated," Martin reminds us, "you can achieve the stand using a leash. With your dog sitting, encourage her forward and into the stand with the leash and your voice. Do this with calm, gentle pressure. Praise her the moment she does stand and stop moving forward. Wait a few seconds before moving forward one or two steps, and then ask her to sit before repeating the action."

Praise her calmly, and don't move too quickly or jerk the leash—sometimes just standing can make a dog a little nervous. This isn't the time for excitement; let her feel your calm energy and confidence.

Martin also suggests an alternative way to reinforce the concept of standing using the walk and a leash. "Walking slowly," he says, "gradually reduce your speed, and when she is walking at heel, casually put your hand in front of her nose, stop walking, and use your command for 'stand.' Do it as calmly as possible so your dog does not react to your hand in front of her face as a threat."

Not every dog finds it easy to just stand and do nothing, so using the walk to practice this activity is an exercise in patience. Just stop and stand and watch the world go by with your dog. If your dog sits, move her forward a step or two until she stands and then stop again. "In time," says Martin, "she will understand the 'stand' command in the context of the walk, and you will be able to give this command without the leash."

Martin Deeley's caution about not placing your hand in a position

that is threatening to your dog reminds me of the point that I hope I have made clearly throughout this book: training is a time when your confidence in and knowledge of your dog are vital. If you have raised your dog from puppyhood or have been living with her for a long time, you should be able to put your hand anywhere on your dog without upsetting her. The two of you will have a shorthand language between you, and she will usually get the general idea of what you are communicating to her, even if she doesn't understand specific commands.

If you have just brought a new dog home from a shelter and haven't established complete trust or aren't sure of her limits, don't try any training or use any gestures that may be perceived as invading her private space. As her owner, you will need to work up to that level of complete trust, no matter what your dog's history has been—but such a relationship can sometimes take time. I believe you should know your dog—and make sure she knows you—before you attempt any style of training with her.

8

BASIC INSTINCTS

How Dogs Teach Us

Angel sniffs for cancer.

How did dog training really begin? Nobody knows for sure, of course, but in my mind's eye I see a group of ancient humans and canines, roaming the plains together thousands of years ago and working cooperatively to find food, water, and safe shelter. Some people imagine that whatever the very first dog "trainers" did back over five thousand years ago involved some kind of force, but I'm not so sure about that. I'm more aligned with the theory that some more-docile, doglike wolves ingratiated themselves with early humans, choosing us as much as we co-opted them.[1] I picture that first curious "psychologist" or behaviorist of dogs realizing that a playful puppy would do anything for a piece of food or a stick—of course there were no pet stores back then! Maybe the puppy would bring some of those things back and the human would tug on them and entertain both himself and the puppy at the same time. So there were two of a dog's biggest motivations right there on display—play drive and food drive.

And then there was prey drive. Whoever that pioneer "dog handler" may have been, I'll bet you that his first thought wasn't about all the different ways he could educate the animals. He wasn't worrying about which leash to use, which theory to follow, or which treats to offer. I'm certain he was far more focused on finding out what those amazing proto-dogs were able to teach *him*. How did they work together to lead their pack to the closest prey? How did they track, stalk, surround, and take down the prey? How did they know to go in the direction of the nearest water? How could they be so alert to dangerous predators, long before the human sentries could hear a beast or an enemy coming near?

These early dog men and women may have realized something that modern dog owners and trainers sometimes forget—almost everything we are able to "train" a dog to do really derives from that dog's natural instincts. Far beyond finding a better way to get a dog to sit or roll over or stop jumping on visitors at the door, it is my belief that the future of dog training will look more like the way this art and science might have begun—with our dogs, using their amazing inborn talents, teaching *us*.

So many of a dog's abilities are far superior to the high-tech solutions we keep dreaming up when we try to copy what a dog does naturally. Our challenge in the future will be not to teach the dogs to do what *we* want, but to learn from what *they* are already doing—and to find better ways to help them communicate their innate knowledge to us. And the beautiful thing is that our dogs *want* to work with us!

That's why it's so crucial that we honor their instincts and help our dogs to fulfill their instincts. That is the real way to a well-behaved dog.

THE HERDING INSTINCT

"Okay, so I've got my own theory on how humans and dogs actually hooked up," says champion herding dog trainer Jerome "Jerry" Stewart. "Now, this idea came from a trip I took down to the Borrego Springs in California, where I stopped on the side of the road overlooking a valley and watched a pack of coyotes trying to hit up a herd of cattle. I noticed where each coyote was positioning itself in relation to each other. And then the hunt was on. That made me think that way back when, centuries ago, men must have done the same thing, spotted this behavior and watched the natural hunting pack style and realized that they could use a dog to do work for them."

Titan, a rottweiler, at Jerome Stewart's
sheepherding facility

Jerry Stewart has been involved in the sport of herding since 1986, when he acquired his first Shetland sheepdog. Since then, he's become a fixture in the herding ring, teaching all-breed herding classes, offering clinics throughout the United States, and serving as an AKC and AHBA herding test and trial judge. He continued to speculate on how the first herding breeds may have come about. "So there's some traits the early man wouldn't want. You wouldn't want a total alpha that's gonna actually do the kill, because if you're domesticating animals, you wouldn't want the dogs eating your food. That's my theory, anyway. None of us ever can really know. But basically we all agree that herding came about from a canine's natural hunting pack style. And how man capitalized on that is anybody's guess."

There are at least twenty different breeds in the category of herding dogs, but the herding instinct still survives and bubbles up in mixed breeds and even in a few dogs that shouldn't logically have a herding background at all.[2] That is because centuries ago humans took the natural prey drive of a canine and modified it by taking away the aspect of the kill. This left them with a helpful animal with the ingrained genetic compulsion to organize herds of domesticated livestock. Many herding dogs aren't bred to guard their flocks from predators, though dogs raised with the animals they will grow up to tend protect the flock that has become their pack. "If you haven't bred against those traits, then those traits are probably still going to be there in the dog," Jerry explains. "That's why you can get a mutt that wants to do herding. Because if things have not occurred in that dog's genetics to preclude it from doing it, it's going to want to herd. Can't help it.

"Some breeds of dogs are better at it than others. And it's because they've been specifically bred for different traits that the herdsman wants, whoever the herdsman is, whatever kind of animals he's working. The traits that will vary will be the size of the dog, stubbornness of the dog, traits like heeling—that means the dog's biting the heels of the sheep or the cows—or heading—that means the dog's going to the head and stopping the animal. These are all different traits that a different stockman would need in a dog to run his operation, however he's got his operation configured and whatever type of animals he's working with. So that's why there's so many different breeds that herd—corgis, border collies, cattle dogs, Australian shepherds. It's because there are so many different ways they were used."

Where would we be without herding dogs? Could we, the human race, have come as far as we have with domesticated flocks and herds of cattle, sheep, and goats if we didn't have dogs to do that crucial work for us? With all the technology at our command, herding dogs are still a livestock manager's most useful tool. Today herding is still more art than craft, more instinct than training, even though for many dogs some human instruction is helpful in bringing out the best herder in them. "You can't teach a dog to herd that doesn't have it in him, that's for sure," says Jerry.

So what can we give back to modern-day herding dogs that even comes close to what they have given us? Of course, the best thing in the world for a herding dog is to simply give it a job and let it herd. At my new Dog Psychology Center, I am building an arena for this very purpose. Since ordinary people don't have herds of livestock anymore, there are also classes like those Jerry offers in which pet and owner can both participate in the activity that the dog was born for.

"So many dog problems happen because mankind, we have a very unnatural lifestyle now," Jerry muses. "You can't stop a herding dog from trying to do what they do, but they try it places that, as far as we're concerned, are inappropriate. The dog is heeling pets or house-guests, for example, nipping at heels. All its life, a herding dog is trying to do what every cell in its body is telling it to do, but being told 'No, that's a bad dog.' And you know, people working up regimens to get the dog trained away from doing it. They try to find all these different training techniques to get the dog to quit it. But that goes against this dog's natural instinct. He's only doing it because he has a genetic imperative to do it," Jerry explains.

"When people come to herding classes, all of a sudden the dog just stops these little traits that were bothering them. They just go away. You know, things like heeling at home with a pet can be annoying. Now the owners see *why* the dog is doing it. 'Oh, this wasn't bad behavior after all,' and all of a sudden the dog has a correct place to do it. The owners turn around and find out that this dog can actually do something that they both can participate in together. And all the tension in that dog just melts away."

So what do you do if you have a herding dog and there's no one like Jerry Stewart anywhere near where you live? They are not the perfect substitutes, but there's Flyball. There's Frisbee. There's agility. "I tell people, especially those with herding dogs or dogs with high prey drive, that these are dogs that need a job," says trainer Joel Silverman. "If you don't give them a job, if you don't train them, they're going to do their own thing. They're going to find a thing to do which you're probably not going to like. So scent work. I think agility work is awesome. If that's what your dog needs, you need to find some way to learn about that dog and what he likes to do."

HUNTING INSTINCTS

Bird dogs, tracking dogs, retrieving dogs, working terriers that go after rodents and vermin in the ground . . . for centuries all these dogs have joyfully offered up to us their extraordinary powers of scenting, stalking, digging, and retrieving—everything that goes along with the hunting instinct minus taking the kill for themselves. Once again, I wonder what we humans would have done without those amazing hunters by our sides.

"In our dogs, the nose and its scenting ability is the most important and unique sense," says Martin Deeley, who understands the power of scent in his training of retrievers and other gundogs. "It is so sensitive that we are able to employ it for so many jobs in our world.

"Initially, man utilized the dog as a hunting companion. Possibly not just to run down prey but particularly to use his nose to find prey. A dog has an inherent instinct to find prey, chase it when found, catch it, kill it, and then share it with family members. Training a dog as a hunting companion harnesses these skills, with one of the main attributes being the use of the nose in the finding of prey such as birds, rabbits, and other game. The hunter may kill the game after the find, but then the dog uses another inherent skill: that of carrying the game to the family or pack—the hunter.

"Therefore, hunting, nose work, and retrieving are all strong natural skills and attributes we can harness. With some dogs, they have been enhanced through breeding. Dogs such as spaniels, retrievers, and pointers especially have been bred for these skills through selection of the best to breed the best."

As we have seen, however, using their nose becomes a reward in itself for many kinds of dogs because they are fulfilling an intrinsic desire—the very "life rewards" that Ian Dunbar talks about. "The retrieve actually becomes the final reward for the nose work," says Martin of his hunting dogs. "The carrying of an object they enjoy is fulfillment of successful nose work.

"A working terrier loves to work—it lives for that magic moment when the scent drifts up from the hole and its genetic code explodes within, taking everything else with it like a tidal bore," writes Patrick Burns of his life's passion, working Jack Russell terriers. "A working terrier would rather work than eat, drink, or rest. The work itself is a self-validating experience for the dog; it tells him what he is, and that he is right for this world. When people ask me how I reward my dogs for going to ground and baying a critter to a stop end, I reply: '*I let them do it again.*' They love the work, and it is its own reward."[3]

But much like herding, the ability to go to ground, track, and retrieve is both partially instinct and partially trained. "The terrier has the curiosity to follow scent, but the dog often has to be trained [i.e., given a few easy experiences] to understand the *reward* of going underground," Patrick explains. "A small, dark, tight tunnel is not an obviously fun place for a dog. They have to discover the fun—the code has to explode. Once it does, the dog will repeat the experience for the thrill of it."

What can we offer these dogs in return?

First, we can honor their being by making sure we communicate with them with respect for the rule of nose-eyes-ears. We can employ their noses using scent work, as in the Dunbars' demonstration, so that their favorite sense is always engaged and fulfilled. Instead of simply trying to eradicate those instincts so they can live peacefully with us in an apartment, we can share activities with them that channel their desire to run, to track, to dig, and to retrieve. We can take responsibility for the instincts we have bred into them instead of calling them bad behavior.

THE PROTECTION INSTINCT

In the survey discussed in Chapter 2, 22 percent of our readers said that they felt it was very important for their dogs to help warn them or even protect them from dangerous situations. Most anthropologists believe that dogs' habit of barking to warn of potential dangers was one of the most important things that early man found useful about his canine companions. Historical records show that attack dogs have been used for personal protection and even in warfare for thousands of years. Legend has it that in 350 B.C., Alexander the Great's dog Peritas saved his master by attacking a charging elephant. It's clear that we humans have relied on our dogs as defenders for as long as they've been with us.

Many years ago, I did a lot of work in protection dog training. It was a hobby and, to a certain extent, a business. My journey has long since taken me past this phase of my life, but back when I was very involved in it, I saw that many trainers in this field taught their dogs to override their canine common sense while in attack mode. The key to all protection training is to teach the "off" switch first, before anything else. Most trainers focus instead on getting the dog into a frenzy and egging him on to the strike. A dog in crazed attack mode is blind and deaf and has broken the needle of the intensity meter. Once a dog has gotten past that level ten of intensity, he's not listening to anything anymore—not his instincts, not his common sense, and certainly not his handler.

Back in the early '90s, I worked with a dog named Sa, a German shepherd sent to me from the Long Beach Police Department Canine Division. This dog put three hundred stitches on one handler and one hundred on another. Each time it happened when the handler asked him to let go, the "out" command. The dog would let go and then go after the handler. I rehabilitated him, but they didn't want him back, and so I sold him to a client who wanted a protection dog. Sa was absolutely fantastic after that. He was already trained. He just didn't know how to out and be calm about it. I was able to condition him to understand that the most important part of his job was listening to when to go "on" and when to go "off"—the attack itself was secondary.

The way I saw protection dogs being trained back then was similar to the way dogs are trained for illegal and inhumane dogfights. There was a lot of sound—a lot of crazy barking—which the handlers seemed to think was proof that their dogs were "tough." There was a lot of yelling and physical prodding and swearing at the dogs by the handlers. To me, this training method drowned out the best of the dogs' natural instincts and abilities. The handlers taught their dogs using sound and sight, never engaging their noses or helping them practice their natural self-control. I was able to prove that there was a far better way.

A dog's protection instincts derive from his prey and hunting instincts. If you watch any animal hunting in the wild, the hunt is not a frenzied thing until maybe at the very last minute. The lead-up to the hunt is very calm, very disciplined. It's all about patience and waiting and organization. And it is very, very quiet.

I trained my dogs by starting with a rag attached to the end of a crop, which I would move around to stimulate the prey drive. I wanted the dogs to use their natural stalking ability and their natural common sense. Only when they were ready did I let them catch it. Other trainers would have their dogs leap in the air for the rag, which was more of an impulse.

I wanted to encourage my dogs to use self-control. To me, this is a much more natural challenge, because this is what dogs know. They're programmed to wait out their prey until it gets tired or compromised. Eventually, I transferred this kind of controlled stalking behavior to a decoy human wearing protection gear. I liked to play the decoy myself. That way, I could turn the game into play—something fun that we did together. I could be 100 percent certain that my dogs understood that I always controlled when the game began and ended, just the way Ian Dunbar practices his tug games with Dune and Hugo.

Many protection trainers teach the "aus," or "out," command by pulling or forcing a dog off a target. That is a good way to have that leftover frenzied aggression directed at yourself, and that is what happened with Sa. In teaching the "aus" command, I would allow a dog to bite my arm (wearing protection gear, of course), and then I would stop moving, sit very still, and wait. When the dog naturally let go, I would say the command. I put myself in a position where I just had to wait and let the dog have fun. When he was ready to let go, then I said, "Aus." That way, I was going with the flow. I didn't use food rewards, but I did use a lot of praise and pride. I was using the dog's natural knowledge of when to let go of its prey by just putting it on command.

These are all techniques I borrowed from traditional Schutzhund training exercises. *Schutzhund* is the German word for "protection dog," and it has evolved over hundreds of years into an exacting sport that tests and challenges the temperament and split-second obedience, or "soundness," of a dog. Many protection trainers use German words because they derive from Schutzhund. However, not all protection training is Schutzhund training. Schutzhund is a disciplined sport that does not result in a mean or defensive dog. In fact, Schutzhund-trained dogs are "just the opposite," says Diane Foster, who, along with her husband, Doug, breeds German shepherds and trains dogs in the Schutzhund tradition. "You can trust a dog that is trained for this. A Schutzhund dog will not attack anyone unless the person comes at him."

Even after successfully completing training exercises, some of the handlers I knew could not safely trust their protection dogs in public settings. These animals had been conditioned in a very unnatural way, and so they were overly keyed up to sudden sounds and movements—similar to the way Gavin the ATF dog became overly sensitive to sounds. Like Schutzhund-trained dogs, my dogs, I insisted, were safe under any conditions, with any human. After all, I raised them around my kids.

Most people are shocked to find out that I trained my late pit bull Daddy to be a top-notch protection dog. Mellow, laid-back Daddy? The best pit bull on this earth? He learned these skills alongside a pack of rottweilers that I raised him with from the time he was four months old. Yet as every *Dog Whisperer* fan knows, I could take Daddy with me anywhere in the world and completely trust him with any person or animal, in any situation. If we were doing a *Dog Whisperer* episode and another dog became aggressive toward Daddy, he would not respond in a defensive way just because he'd had protection training. His training kicked in only under two very specific circumstances: one, if I triggered it with a command; and two, if a threatening adult male human made a truly aggressive move toward one of his pack. Because I had not messed with Daddy's instincts, he knew from the deepest animal-dog part of himself the difference between a bad guy with a real serious motive to harm and someone just joking around.

I trusted Daddy's instincts 100 percent. I never spent a moment worrying about him. Daddy lived sixteen years and never once hurt or bit anyone. He preferred licking people's faces, sprawling on the ground near people's feet, and, of course, getting his stomach rubbed. But he definitely came to the rescue on more than one occasion. Former Dog Psychology Center employee Tina Madden remembers one such incident that happened back in 2007, when Daddy was thirteen years old.

"Daddy was diagnosed with cancer during the first few months that I worked for Cesar, and I drove Daddy to one of his chemotherapy appointments. I remember driving back down into the rough neighborhood of South Central one day and not really knowing the area all that well. I pulled into a drive-thru to get myself some lunch, and Daddy was sleeping on the front seat of my truck, and I had the windows down for air for him. Suddenly I caught the eye of these two guys who were definitely big trouble. And they looked right at me and made a beeline for the car really fast, and I thought, 'Oh no, why did I make eye contact? What was I thinking?' I was stuck at the drive-thru, car in front of me, car behind me. I was terrified. I knew something really awful was about to happen to me.

"I completely forgot that Daddy was sleeping right there next to me. And the guys kept coming, and one of them started to lean into the car. The next thing I knew, Daddy was awake and had jumped up and just let loose with this really scary growl. It was like I had a grown lion in the car with me. These two guys turned white and ran like nobody's business, screaming. They were gone, in six seconds or less. I gasped with relief and looked at Daddy. This was right after his chemo and everything. And then after they were gone and I rolled up the window, he just looked at me, lay down, and went back to sleep. I told Cesar about it, and he said to me, 'Make sure you thank Daddy for that.' I said, 'I've thanked him every single day since.' He really saved me from a very bad situation. I bet you those boys had soiled underwear that day. Thank God for Daddy."

Daddy's protégé, Junior, is also a pit bull, and I raised him from a puppy in much the same way that I raised Daddy. The big difference between them is that I don't want Junior to have any access to that protection dog side of himself. I live in the suburbs now and don't need a dog for protection anymore. Junior has not been trained in how to bite or how to hold on. I don't even play tug-of-war or dominance games with him. I have not tapped in to his prey instinct side or the side that wants to defend the pack. Instead, Junior is the peacemaker. He knows that his teeth are not to be used on another animal, period, unless it is an inhibited bite during play. To Junior an outstretched hand means to drop whatever he is holding and not to touch. Even a child can put her hand in Junior's food bowl while he is eating and Junior will politely back away. I want Junior to be the opposite of a pit bull: a happy-go-lucky guy who uses his instincts and energy and intensity for exercise—for lots of play, of course, but also for helping other animals become balanced, which, in a way, makes him the opposite of a pit bull.

The protection instinct in dogs is not one to mess around with, even if your dog is not the obvious breed for this purpose, like a German shepherd, rottweiler, Belgian malinois, or Doberman. The only criterion for a great protection dog is courage, and courage doesn't have a breed. Pretty much every terrier will kick your ass, since they were bred to hunt for animals that can turn on them and fight back, like rodents and vermin and even foxes. A Jack Russell terrier might have to target a mugger's feet, but he'd be right there to defend you. We've seen on *Dog Whisperer* how little Chihuahuas and Yorkies can become weapons when they're not socialized properly and instead are carried around by their owners all the time; many will attack people who reach out to pet them. Even a lower-energy bulldog like Mr. President could have become a protection dog if I hadn't raised him to respect and be submissive to all humans, though he'd get hot and tired pretty fast.

I advise people to think long and hard about whether they want their dogs to be their defenders. It is a lot of responsibility to put on any dog, especially if the training isn't done exactly right. If this is something you are serious about, you should look into Schutzhund or other disciplined training that promises not to turn your dog into a weapon without an "off" switch.

This is where dog psychology has an advantage over traditional dog training. If you are your dog's leader in all situations, you can always switch him off. Like Daddy, your dog can always have access to his own best instincts and quickly return to balance once the time to be on alert is over. The trust and respect between you and your dog—something that goes far beyond simple command training—is what gives you the ability to snap him out of an alert, excited dominant state and back to peaceful, calm submission. If you are not 100 percent comfortable in your position as your dog's pack leader, then get a good alarm system or a can of Mace and let your dog just enjoy being a dog.

DOGS AS HEALERS

For many years, people have been collecting anecdotal evidence about dogs' ability to detect physical instabilities in people and predict epileptic seizures, heart attacks, strokes, and diabetic comas—all manner of disorders with onsets that are still largely a mystery to modern medicine. I believe the real future of dog training will be in teaching ourselves to understand these important communications dogs are sending us about our health.

In most of these areas, the science isn't in yet as to how dogs sense what they do about our physical condition, and humans still have very few ideas about how to train or make use of this innate ability in dogs. But at the Pine Street Clinic in San Anselmo, California, the proof is in the puppy—and, more important, in the statistics.

A Visit to the Pine Street Clinic

The streets of picture-perfect San Anselmo, California, are lined with funky boutiques, antique stores, and colorful Victorian homes from the Gold Rush era. At the end of one of these streets is a small, pink, adobe-style storefront with an awning that reads PINE STREET CLINIC. Inside, an old-fashioned raised pharmacy counter spans a cozy room carpeted with Oriental rugs and framed by book-lined walls. It's a casual, healing environment—there's even an aviary filled with quietly chirping finches.

When I first entered this peaceful sanctuary with miniature schnauzer Angel trotting brightly by my side, I immediately felt at home. I am a great supporter of many alternative medicine practices, and for thirty years the Pine Street Clinic has specialized in integrating Western therapies, drugs, and supplements with time-tested Eastern herbs, acupuncture, and philosophy.

But Pine Street is more than just a clinic. It's the home of a foundation that for the past nine years has been conducting a series of amazing clinical trials that prove dogs can detect lung, breast, pancreatic, and ovarian cancer from human breath samples. I had come here to see the world-famous cancer-sniffing dogs in action and

The Pine Street Clinic

to see if little Angel could learn how to perform this fantastic feat himself.

For hundreds of years, a certain story has emerged among people in every culture and from every walk of life: people report that their dog started acting strangely shortly before they were diagnosed with cancer or another illness. Often the dog seemed to hone right in on the part of the body where the disease was taking hold. We had a case just like that in season four of *Dog Whisperer*. The Make a Wish Foundation contacted us for help in fulfilling the dream of Michelle Crowley, a cancer survivor whose rottweiler, Major, had actually discovered her disease. Scientists began to take such reports seriously only a decade or so ago, when they theorized that dogs can smell even the tiniest molecular changes in our bodies.[4]

"It started with a group out of the University of Florida at Tallahassee in the early '90s," says Michael Broffman, director of the Pine Street Foundation. "Some researchers there, plus a local dermatologist, got together with a terrific dog trainer, and they actually demonstrated that the dogs, successfully, with a high degree of accuracy, could really differentiate between a melanoma lesion and a non-melanoma lesion on a variety of people. They published the study, and based on that we decided to launch our own program. At the same time, the British were working on a program with dogs, looking at prostate cancer, so we decided in the mid-'90s to start looking at lung cancer and breast cancer."

Cancer cells, even in the disease's earliest stages, excrete a specific waste product that researchers predicted would show up in human breath. The Pine Street folks decided to see whether dogs could reliably detect the presence of cancer at stages I, II, III, or IV in breath samples. In 2003, the clinic started its lung and breast cancer trials with two dogs—two beige-colored standard poodles adopted from a top breeder, chosen specifically for their scent-oriented behavior. "The two dogs we selected seemed to be the ones that were exploring the world with their noses immediately," says Broffman. Shortly after that, the Pine Street Foundation hired its first head trainer, Kirk Turner.

Turner chose a poodle puppy named Shing Ling, two Portuguese water dog puppies, and an adult Labrador retriever to join the study. "With the other dogs in the program who were already adult dogs, we were really looking for dogs that were work-motivated, because the research involved three or four hours a day, several days a week, for several months," Broffman explains. "So we needed a dog that was interested in working, happy to work, had some motivation, wouldn't get bored, and would stay with it for that duration." Surprisingly, the obvious candidates for scent work, like beagles and bloodhounds, were rejected because they didn't have the stamina, focus, and work ethic of the poodles, Portuguese water dogs, and Labradors.

Unique Motivators

As we've seen throughout this book, no training can succeed without an understanding of what motivates each specific dog. "We found three different motivations," says Broffman. "Play and food are both obvious for the Labs and the Portuguese water dogs. For the poodles, it was sort of fascinating because, on the one hand, they were very easy to train, with very high work motivation, but their reward was more our acknowledgment that they got it correct, as opposed to play or food."

The poodles enjoyed doing their jobs, and everybody on the research team was impressed by their work ethic. But Michael Broffman and his team soon learned that poodles are, to put it in human terms, "perfectionists." "We had mixed up our samples between which ones were the cancer samples and which ones were the control. And so, as the dog was going through the training on a given day, the dog kept on identifying a sample as being cancer, and we kept on saying, 'No.' This went on for a couple of hours until we realized that the dog was right, and we had actually made a mistake. And the poodle basically just quit working for a few weeks based on that. You know, a Lab would've been upset an hour or two and then just got back at it, but the poodles tend to carry these things a little bit farther."

In other words, don't try to mess with a poodle's instincts!

As the trials progressed and the dogs became more and more adept at picking out the cancer samples from the controls, the poodles' simple need for acknowledgment and recognition of a job well done actually caused some problems outside the laboratory setting. "We'd be on the street on a day off, and suddenly the dogs would identify a complete stranger, just someone minding their own business." Michael Broffman still shakes his head in amazement as he recounts this story. "And it would create a lot of awkward moments to have to walk up to a complete stranger and say, 'Excuse me, but our dogs were telling us that you have lung cancer. And they could be wrong, but they're over ninety percent accurate in this lab study we're doing. We feel obligated to tell you maybe you should see your doctor.' And it took us a number of months to figure out how to get the poodles to stop working outside of the very specific research setting."

At least two of the strangers whom the Pine Street poodles had pinpointed on the street called the organization later to report that, yes, the poodles had been correct—they had been diagnosed with cancer. Both of them were very thankful to have had the canine early warning.

Not only did the dogs perform exceptionally well in these studies, but they did so consistently over a four-month period of 12,295 separate scent trials—each one documented on videotape. "What is important about this study," the Pine Street Foundation's Web site reports, "is that (1) ordinary dogs, with no prior scent discrimination training, could be rapidly trained to identify lung and breast cancer patients by smelling samples of their breath, when compared to blank unused sample tubes; (2) dogs could accurately and reliably distinguish breath samples of lung and breast cancer patients from those of healthy controls; and (3) the dog's diagnostic performance was not affected by disease stage of cancer patients, age, smoking, or most recently eaten meal among either cancer patients or controls."[5]

The first peer-reviewed paper published by the Pine Street Foundation came out in the journal *Integrative Cancer Therapies* in 2006. In a study of eighty-six people—fifty-five with lung cancer and thirty-one with breast cancer—five professionally trained scent dogs accurately distinguished between breath samples from diseased patients and those from eighty-three healthy controls. The dogs' ability to correctly identify or rule out lung and breast cancer, at both early and late stages, was around 90 percent.[6]

The success of this study earned the foundation another grant to begin its current study, which is testing dogs' ability to detect ovarian cancer from breath samples. Ovarian cancer has a high fatality rate because its sufferers often don't show any symptoms until very late in the progression of the disease. Canine scent work promises a method for early detection with the potential of saving millions of women's lives.

Kirk Turner was in charge of selecting the dogs for this next phase of the project. Some of the dogs auditioned for the role were retired guide dogs. "We probably went through forty dogs to come up with the five that ended up continuing in December," says Kirk. "They can't live in a house where anybody smokes because that'll ruin the scenting ability of any dog in six weeks. And they had to be happy, bright dogs without any kind of emotional problems, and also not too spoiled by the owners."

An Amazing Demonstration

The day Angel and I went to the Pine Street Clinic, the two Michaels— Broffman and McCulloch—and trainer Kirk Turner arranged a full demonstration of what their cancer dogs could do. Kirk has been training dogs for this special task for over seven years, and he can now do it in a very short period of time. "Two and a half weeks," Kirk told me. "That's what it takes for me to train a cancer dog. Five runs, and then they get taken out and walked. And then it's the next dog's turn. They usually do this between two and three times a day, which means the dogs do no more than fifteen runs a day. The runs usually take less than a minute."

"That's an amazing learning curve," I said, impressed.

"Our big research grants over the years have come from the Department of Defense," Michael Broffman added. "And this caused a big flap when we published our research a couple of years ago. Because we were able to train our dogs to do scent detection in about a third of the time that it took the Department of Defense's best dog trainer at their Alabama facility to do for the military. And it caused a lot of problems within their dog training world as to how and why we were able to train our dogs that much more efficiently and more accurately than their best guy. And I think it was largely because we were taking the position of actually nurturing and highlighting the dog's natural instincts and not trying to overlay some heavy training methodology."

"We do want them to go home and be dogs too," Kirk said. "That's why we use people's pet dogs. We don't own the dogs."

Today Kirk had brought along a very enthusiastic, muscular black Labrador named Freeman to demonstrate the process. Freeman is a retired guide dog with a great work ethic but a very high-energy personality. To keep Freeman's energy focused on the task at hand, Kirk warned me and my crew not to give the dog affection before the demonstration began. "The last time, he fell in love with a cameraman and his brain went out the window."

Kirk trains the cancer-detecting dogs using the clicker method and a hands-off approach to training. "I really didn't focus on the obedience part," he said. "When it came to indicating cancer, I used a clicker, and it worked really well. And you know, I think that's why it was so quick, because I was basically letting the dog choose for himself."

When it came time for the demonstration, the Pine Street Foundation team set up five basic storage containers, the kind that you can buy at any store, with special holes cut into the center of the lids. Into each hole went the small aerated dishes that held the breath specimen. The ovarian cancer breath specimens were collected from volunteers, who breathed into a special tube that captured, condensed, and sealed the samples for future use. The researchers collected specimens from cancer-free women to use as controls.

For each trial, the researchers put cancer-free control specimens into four of the five containers, with only one container holding the sample of cancerous breath. Kirk always stays out of the room while his team sets up the samples, because there's always the danger that, through his body language and attitude, he'll subconsciously indicate to Freeman which specimen dish holds the cancer.

Now it was time to let Freeman out of his crate. When he works with this high-energy Lab, Kirk likes to keep the leash on, for the first run at least. "I want to have the leash on just to show him what I want him to do, which is sniff the containers. He hasn't worked in several months, so it may take him a run or two to get up to speed again." Kirk led Freeman around the containers. Freeman sniffed each one and sat down next to one. Sitting down next to a sample is the signal the dog is supposed to give when it identifies cancer. Freeman's choice was not the correct one. Kirk released him, and Freeman continued to sniff. Then he sat down next to two more containers. Kirk did not acknowledge or reward him in any way. Then they went back to the starting position. It was time for the real thing.

Now Kirk let Freeman off the leash and told him, "Go to work!" This time Freeman went down the line, smelling each container until he sat down next to one. This time he sat down next to the correct container. Kirk gave a quick click on his clicker, recalling Freeman. Kirk rewarded Freeman with a treat and lots of praise.

Freeman sniffs for cancer.

*While I look on, Freeman identifies a
cancer specimen.*

Kirk and Freeman went back outside. "Another thing I like to do is to get him out here to smell something else in between," Kirk explained. This is like what happens when you shop for perfume or cologne, and the salesperson makes you smell coffee in between brands. The smells are so different that if you smell them one after the other, you can very easily tell them apart.

The team did several more runs while I watched in amazement. After each run, they'd change the lids on the containers, because Freeman's wet nose would contaminate the smell. Freeman took a minute to warm up, but before long he was detecting the cancer on his first try. Each correct detection got a click and a treat from Kirk. By the time they were done with the demonstration, Freeman was seven for eight.

As Freeman performed his work, researcher Michael McCulloch

looked on, beaming, writing down notes on a clipboard. These dogs are very good at what they do. "We actually had a case where one of our dogs detected breast cancer recurrence eighteen months before it was found in routine follow-up care," he told me. "That was in our 2006 published study. This was a person who enrolled in the study that we thought was in the control group. But twenty-four times out of twenty-five that the dogs sniffed her breath sample, they indicated, that is a cancer sample. And this is the same reaction from more than one dog. So we went to interview her and found that she had actually been in remission for breast cancer for which she had been treated some years before. About a year after the study was concluded, we learned that they had just then detected by a scan in the margin of where she had her prior surgery a tiny, tiny tumor that would have been undetectable at the time that we were doing the study. So that's how good these dogs seem to be—they may be able to provide very early detection. We're now doing a follow-up study on ovarian cancer, which is still open for recruitment, and women can join at www.pinestreetfoundation.org."

The next phase of the Pine Street Foundation's research involves comparing scent-detected cancer samples with chemically analyzed samples from the same subject. Will modern chemical analysis in a laboratory be able to come up with the same success rate as the dogs? Can science ever figure out exactly what tiny molecular changes the dogs are smelling? For right now, the only known fact is this: a dog's brain and nose are among the most sophisticated odor-detecting devices on the planet, and modern science hasn't even begun to match them yet.

Angel's New Career

I had brought miniature schnauzer Angel with me on this visit because, having raised him from a puppy for the book *How to Raise the*

Perfect Dog, I know what an incredible nose he has. Once, when he was still a young puppy, Angel found a cigarette butt that was buried under three inches of dirt. I wanted to see if Angel had what it takes to become a lifesaving, cancer-sniffing dog.

Kirk showed me the very basics of the training. Since Angel had never had any formal "training" except agility classes, Kirk had to introduce the clicker to him. Keeping him on his leash, Kirk held a treat in his hand, and when Angel came up and took the treat, Kirk gave him a click. "I just want to establish that the click noise means that the next thing that happens is he gets a treat," Kirk said. Next, Kirk established that when Angel looked him in the eyes, he would get a click and treat. Angel, always an incredibly quick learner, picked right up on both these concepts without breaking a sweat.

Kirk then brought Angel to the containers and let him smell the lids. Each time Angel put his nose to the lid and sniffed, he was rewarded with a click and a treat. "On the cancer one, I would have him sit, or down, or however he wants to do it," Kirk explained. "But the whole idea is to first smell."

Kirk pointed to the lid of the container that had the cancer sample. He then stood, and following his physical cue, Angel sat down. Again, he got a click and a treat. This was reinforced again and again until Angel would smell the lid and sit, without Kirk's physical command.

"How did he do?" I asked Kirk, eagerly.

"Angel is an excellent candidate for this kind of work because he's got a great work ethic and already knows the basics of how to communicate with a human. Yeah, Angel did great," he reassured me.

In fact, Angel was such a natural and such an apt pupil that statistician Michael McCulloch asked me if he was up for adoption! "Sorry, no, he belongs to SueAnn Fincke, the *Dog Whisperer* director," I answered.

Kirk, too, was disappointed. "It's always been my dream to teach smaller dogs," he said. "The very first melanoma cancer–detecting dog

Kirk Turner trains Angel.

A fast learner!

was a schnauzer. Miniature schnauzers would be a good choice for this kind of work because they're very, very smart. They love to learn and work. And if you teach everything as almost a game and make it really fun, especially the scenting stuff, I think this would be a very good breed. But you know, one of the advantages of teaching a bunch of small dogs is that they're more portable. You can get a bunch of them in one vehicle."

Kirk has another dream that he hopes to realize now that the Pine Street Foundation's research has quantified a formerly mysterious ability. "Our study provides compelling evidence that cancers hidden deep within the body can be detected simply by examining the odors of a person's breath. So that's one of the reasons why I wanted to start our own company. We could take on projects from other organizations involved in scent detection, but my most ambitious vision is to train doctors and dogs to work with each other and communicate with each other. Just imagine the possibility—dogs and doctors going together through villages in Third World countries, where you can't drag along expensive equipment, and doing early diagnostic work and other kinds of therapy. This is really a possibility now."

HONORING INSTINCTS IN TRAINING

In my opinion, the very best dog training lets a dog be a dog first. As dog handlers, owners, and pack leaders, we want to be in control of our dogs' instincts—for example, we definitely don't want a dog's prey instinct to kick in full force when the neighbor's beloved cat crosses our yard—but we also must make sure that we listen to and honor those instincts, especially when they have something to teach us. When we simply try to force a training method on a dog or try to make him do something that doesn't make sense to him on an instinctual level, we do him and ourselves a huge disservice. Though we may be able to teach him how to do something, at the same time we completely blind him and isolate him from his own common sense. A dog that isn't connected to his natural common sense can't relate to other dogs and can't really be balanced or fulfilled in his life. And as we've seen in case after case on the *Dog Whisperer* show, when a dog isn't fulfilled, he can't possibly be the best companion for the humans who live with him either.

When we properly instruct a dog in how to best use an instinct he was born with, he gets something very powerful from us in return—something that he cannot get in the natural world. Not only does he experience the joy of performing the activity, but he gets a kind of euphoria when his human praises and rewards him and shares in his triumph with him. This allows him to experience a feeling that he will never be able to share with another dog, which is a celebration of his personal achievement.

A dog's instincts are what first motivated humans to join forces with another species thousands of years ago. And yet instincts are often the very thing we try to suppress in our modern dogs. Some dog owners have come to believe that "dog training" is a good way to get a dog to put his instincts behind him forever.

Being in control of a dog's instincts is not the same thing as trying to eliminate them. Encouraging instinct is simply rewarding natural behavior or not extinguishing it through punishment. When we honor a dog's instincts and make them the cornerstone of our relationship, it can open up a whole new world for us.

Through centuries of breeding, humans have been learning to understand more about how dogs learn and training them to enhance their skills. By understanding and recognizing the sensitivity and ability of a dog's nose, humans have been able to teach a dog to scent so many different things, from drugs to fruit and explosives to bedbugs and, ultimately, cancer. A scent hound can track down one person out of thousands if we familiarize him with even the most minute odor that the person left behind. A search-and-rescue dog can detect where humans are buried under snow and rubble. He can scent the chemical changes in a human body that indicates a medical condition such as a seizure.

If we honor our dogs' natural abilities and train ourselves first, then we can develop with our dogs the greatest animal-human partnership ever imagined.

FOR MORE READING
AND RESEARCH

From Cesar and All the Experts

ON GENERAL DOG BEHAVIOR AND BIOLOGY

Coppinger, Raymond, and Lorna Coppinger. *Dogs.* Chicago: University of Chicago Press, 2001.

Dunbar, Ian, PhD, MRCVS. *Dog Behavior: Why Dogs Do What They Do.* Neptune, NJ: TFH Publications, 1979.

———. *An Owner's Guide to a Happy, Healthy Pet: Dog Behavior.* Hoboken, NJ: Howell Book House/Wiley Publications, 1999.

Fogle, Bruce, DVM. *The Dog's Mind.* New York: Macmillan, 1990.

Grandin, Temple, and Catherine Johnson. *Animals in Translation: Using the Mysteries of Autism to Decode Animal Behavior.* New York: Scribner, 2005.

MacDonald, D. W., and C. Sillero-Zubiri. *Biology and Conservation of Wild Canids.* New York: Oxford University Press, 2004.

Pfaffenberger, Clarence. *The New Knowledge of Dog Behavior.* New York: Howell Book House, 1963.

Scott, J. P., and J. Fuller. *Genetics and the Social Behavior of the Dog.* Chicago: University of Chicago Press, 1965.

Serpell, James, ed. *The Domestic Dog: Its Evolution, Behavior, and Interactions with People.* New York: Cambridge University Press, 1995.

Wynne, Clive D. L. *Animal Cognition: The Mental Lives of Animals.* New York: Palgrave Macmillan, 2002.

ON OPERANT CONDITIONING

Bailey, B., and M. B. Bailey. *Patient Like the Chipmunks* (video). Hot Springs, AR: Eclectic Science Productions, 1999.

Burch, Mary R., PhD, and Jon S. Bailey, PhD. *How Dogs Learn.* Hoboken, NJ: Howell Book House/Wiley Publications, 1999.

Skinner, B. F. *The Behavior of Organisms: An Experimental Analysis.* New York: Appleton-Century, 1938.

ON DOG TRAINING

Brown-Cali, Bonnie, IACP, CPDT. *Dog Dynamics* (training courses). Available at: www.dogdynamics.org.

De Groodt, Barbara. *From the Heart Behavior and Training* (courses/information). Available at: www.fromtheheart.info.

Dunbar, Ian. *How to Teach a New Dog Old Tricks.* Berkeley, CA: James & Kenneth Publishers, 1996.

———. *Before and After Getting Your Puppy.* Novato, CA: New World Library, 2004.

———. *Dog Training for Children.* Berkeley, CA: James & Kenneth Publishers, 2007.

———. *SIRIUS® Puppy Training* (DVD). Berkeley, CA: James & Kenneth Publishers, 2007.

———. *SIRIUS® Adult Dog Training* (DVD). Berkeley, CA: James & Kenneth Publishers, 2008.

Silverman, Joel. *What Color Is Your Dog?* (book, DVD). Available at: www.companionsforlife.net.

Weston, David. *Dog Training: The Gentle Modern Method.* Edmonton, Alberta: Howell Books, 1992.

ON POSITIVE REINFORCEMENT

Donaldson, Jean. *The Culture Clash: A Revolutionary New Way of Understanding the Relationship Between Humans and Domestic Dogs.* Berkeley, CA: James & Kenneth Publishers, 1996, 2005.

Pryor, Karen. *Don't Shoot the Dog! The New Art of Teaching and Training.* Surrey, U.K.: Ringpress Books, 2003.

Ramirez, Ken, ed. *Animal Training: Successful Animal Management Through Positive Reinforcement.* Chicago: Shedd Aquarium Society, 1999.

ON CLICKER TRAINING

Alexander, Melissa C. *Click for Joy!* Waltham, MA: Sunshine Books, 2003. Available at: www.clickertraining.com.

Tillman, Peggy. *Clicking with Your Dog.* Waltham, MA: Sunshine Books, 2000.

Wilkes, Gary. *Click and Treat Training* (DVD). Available at: www.clickandtreat.com.

ON BREED-RELATED TOPICS

Burch, Mary, PhD. *The Border Collie: An Owner's Guide to a Happy, Healthy Pet.* New York: Howell Book House, 1996.

Burns, Patrick. *American Working Terriers.* 2005. Available at: www.terrierman.com.

Deeley, Martin, IACP, CDT. *Working Gundogs.* Wiltshire, U.K.: Crowood Press, 1990.

WEB SITES

American Humane Association (AHA)
http://www.americanhumane.org/
http://www.americanhumane.org/humaneeducation

American Society for the Prevention of Cruelty to Animals (ASPCA)
http://www.aspca.org/
http://www.aspcabehavior.org/search.aspx?petCat=1&mode=all&sort=title&dir=ASC

Association of Pet Dog Trainers (APDT)
http://www.apdt.com/

Boone's Animals for Hollywood
http://www.boonesanimals.com/

Brain State Technologies
http://www.brainstatetech.com/

Brain Well Center
http://www.brainwellcenter.com/

Humane Society of the United States (HSUS)
http://www.humanesociety.org/
http://www.humanesociety.org/search/search.jsp?query=dog+training

International Association of Canine Professionals (IACP)
http://canineprofessionals.com/

No Animals Were Harmed (American Humane Association, Film and TV
    Unit)
http://www.americanhumane.org/protecting-animals/programs/no-animals-were
    -harmed/

Pine Street Foundation
http://pinestreetfoundation.org/

NOTES

CHAPTER 1: THOSE MAGICAL AMERICAN DOGS

1. You can find information about certification programs through the Web site of the American Society for the Prevention of Cruelty to Animals, aspca.org; see also links to the Certification Council for Professional Dog Trainers (ccpdt.org), the Association of Pet Dog Trainers (apdt.com), and the International Association of Canine Professionals (canineprofessionals.com).

CHAPTER 2: THE BASICS OF BALANCE

1. Carl Zimmer, "The Secrets Inside Your Dog's Mind," *Time,* September 21, 2009.
2. Bruce Pomeranz and Daryl Chiu, "Naloxone Blockade of Acupuncture Analgesia: Endorphin Implicated," *Life Sciences* 19, no. 11 (December 1, 1976): 1757–62.

CHAPTER 3: REWARDS, PUNISHMENT, AND EVERYTHING IN BETWEEN

1. Randall Parker, "Dogs Evolved to Read Human Cues," Future Pundit, http://www.futurepundit.com/archives/001944.html.
2. E. Bougerol, "Ten Dogs That Changed the World," CNN.com, http://www.cnn.com/2007/LIVING/wayoflife/11/01/ten.dogs/.
3. W. N. Hutchinson, *Dog Breaking: The Most Expeditious, Certain and Easy Method, Whether Great Excellence or Only Mediocrity Be Required,* 6th ed. (London: John Murray, Albemarler Street, 1876): 11 and 237.

4. Edward L. Thorndike, *Animal Intelligence: Experimental Studies* (New York: Macmillan, 1911), http://www.archive.org/details/animalintelligen00thor (retrieved June 2, 2010).

5. Mary R. Burch, PhD, and Jon S. Bailey, PhD, authors of the highly respected reference on operant conditioning *How Dogs Learn* (Howell Book House, 1999), wrote of Koehler, "We met Bill Koehler and watched him work with dogs and students in the 1980s. He appeared then to be a kind and gentle man, and he clearly loved dogs. At the time Koehler developed his procedures, he was one of the few people in the country who was known for his ability to rehabilitate tough dogs. For many dogs, Koehler was their last hope" (page 17).

6. Timeline/History adapted with permission from an original blog post by Patrick Burns. Terrierman's Daily Dose, http://www.terrierman.com/.

7. A. Arakani, S. Mathew, and D. Charney, "Neurobiology of Anxiety Disorders and Implications for Treatment," *Mount Sinai Journal of Medicine* 73, no. 7 (2006): 941–49.

8. Chart designed by Alice Clearman, PhD.

9. Deborah L. Wells and Peter G. Hepper, "Prenatal Olfactory Learning in the Domesticated Dog," *Animal Behavior* 72, no. 3 (September 2006): 681–86.

10. Patrick Burns, "Biting the Hand That Clicks Us!" *Dogs Today* (June 2010): 14, available at: http://www.dogstodaymagazine.co.uk/.

11. Patrick Burns, "Calm and Assertive Clicker Training," March 1, 2010, Terrierman's Daily Dose, http://terriermandotcom.blogspot.com/2010/02/calm-and-assertive-clicker-training.html.

12. Keller Breland and Marian Breland, "The Misbehavior of Organisms," *American Psychologist* 16 (1961): 681–84, http://psychclassics.asu.edu/Breland/misbehavior.htm.

13. Temple Grandin and Catherine Johnson, *Animals in Translation: Using the Mysteries of Autism to Decode Animal Behavior* (New York: Scribner, 2005), 11.

CHAPTER 4: CESAR'S RULES FOR A TEACHABLE DOG . . .

1. Christopher Reed, "Best Friend Bests Chimp," *Harvard Magazine* 105:4 (March–April 2003).

2. Sung Lee, MD, "The Brain Well: To Lead, Be Balanced," January 9, 2010, The Brain Well, http://www.sedona.biz/brainwell-center-sedona 012910.php.

3. See the Open Paw Web site at: http://www.openpaw.org/.

4. See the Senior Dog Project Web site at: http://www.srdogs.com/index .html.

CHAPTER 5: HONOR THE ANIMAL

1. See the American Kennel Club's Web site: http://www.akc.org/breeds.

CHAPTER 7: A WORLD OF WAYS
TO BASIC OBEDIENCE

1. Daniel F. Tortora, "Safety Training: The Elimination of Avoidance-Motivated Aggression in Dogs," *Journal of Experimental Psychology: General* 112, no. 2 (June 1983): 176–214.

2. "Temple Grandin: The Woman Who Talks to Animals," *Fresh Air*, February 5, 2010, NPR, http://www.npr.org/templates/transcript/transcript .php?storyId=123383699.

3. Here are the American Humane Association's cautionary words about the choke collar:

> *Not recommended* as it has unlimited choking action when pulled, which can cause pain and injury—especially if tightening is prolonged. The potential for misuse, ineffective use, and danger to your dog outweigh the possible benefits. (Limited use of slip collars may be needed for safety reasons during defensive handling, such as in containment or control of potentially dangerous dogs in an animal shelter or animal control setting.)
>
> *Limitations:* Proper fitting and the techniques required to maximize effectiveness in the least aversive way can be difficult for the average person to master, resulting in prolonged choking, the tendency to use brute force, and frustration. Improper use can cause choking that typically does not maintain the dog's attention, change the behavior effectively, or give accurate guidance. Choke collars typically do not stop the un-

wanted behavior within a minimal number of applications, as all successful aversives do. This collar can only be worn safely during training and must be removed at all other times.

Warnings: Slip collars can cause gasping, choking, and closed airways when the leash tightens, resulting in death or serious injuries such as blindness or brain damage. The narrower the gauge and width of the collar and the higher the collar is placed on the dog's neck, the greater risk of pain and injury. If left on the dog unsupervised, there is substantial risk of death by strangulation should the collar become caught. If put on incorrectly, the collar is continuously tight.

CHAPTER 8: BASIC INSTINCTS

1. Stephen Budiansky, "The Truth About Dogs," *The Atlantic* (July 1999): 39–53, http://www.theatlantic.com/past/issues/99jul/9907dogs.htm.
2. "A World of Herding Dogs," Herding on the Web, http://www.herdingontheweb.com/dogs.htm; "AKC Breeds by Group," American Kennel Club, http://www.akc.org/breeds/herding_group.cfm.
3. Patrick Burns, "The Self-Actualized Terrier: Happy in the Field," June 3, 2009, Terrierman's Daily Dose, http://terriermandotcom.blogspot.com/2007/06/happy-in-field.html.
4. Rebecca Leung, "Can Dogs Sniff Cancer?" *60 Minutes,* January 9, 2005, http://www.cbsnews.com/stories/2005/01/06/60minutes/main665263.shtml.
5. "Diagnostic Accuracy of Canine Scent Detection of Lung and Breast Cancers in Exhaled Breath," May 17, 2009, Pine Street Foundation, http://pinestreetfoundation.org/2009/05/17/canine-scent-detection-breast-and-lung-cancer/.
6. Michael McCulloch, Tadeusz Jezierski, Michael Broffman, Alan Hubbard, Kirk Turner, and Teresa Janecki, "Diagnostic Accuracy of Canine Scent Detection in Early- and Late-Stage Lung and Breast Cancers," *Integrative Cancer Therapies* 5 (2006): 30, http://ict.sagepub.com/cgi/reprint/5/1/30.

PHOTOGRAPH CREDITS

INDEX

Note: Page references in *italics* indicate photographs.

Index

ABOUT THE AUTHORS

Founder of the Dog Psychology Center in Los Angeles, CESAR MILLAN is the #1 *New York Times* bestselling author of *Cesar's Way, Be the Pack Leader, A Member of the Family,* and *How to Raise the Perfect Dog.* He is the star of *Dog Whisperer with Cesar Millan,* National Geographic Channel's top-rated show. In addition to his educational seminars and work with unstable dogs, Cesar has founded the Millan Foundation, a nonprofit organization dedicated to helping shelters and rescue groups.

MELISSA JO PELTIER, an executive producer and writer of *Dog Whisperer with Cesar Millan,* has been honored for her film and television writing and directing with an Emmy, a Peabody, and more than fifty other awards. She lives in Nyack, New York, with her husband, writer-director John Gray, and stepdaughter, Caitlin.

www.CesarsWay.com

Also by Cesar Millan with Melissa Jo Peltier

How to Raise the Perfect Dog:
Through Puppyhood and Beyond
$15.00 paperback (Canada: $17.00)
978-0-307-46130-8

Puppyhood Deck:
50 Tips for Raising the Perfect Dog
$14.99 (Canada: $18.99)
978-0-307-46348-7

A Member of the Family:
The Ultimate Guide to Living with
a Happy, Healthy Dog
$15.00 paperback (Canada: $18.95)
978-0-307-40903-4

Be the Pack Leader:
Use Cesar's Way to Transform Your
Dog . . . and Your Life
$14.00 paperback (Canada: $17.00)
978-0-307-38167-5

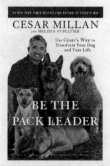

Cesar's Way Deck:
50 Tips for Training and
Understanding Your Dog
$14.95 (Canada: $16.95)
978-0-307-39632-7

Cesar's Way Journal:
A Resource and Record Book for
Dog Owners
$15.95 (Canada: $18.95)
978-0-307-39631-0

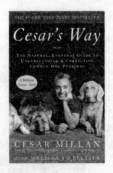

Cesar's Way:
The Natural, Everyday Guide to
Understanding and Correcting
Common Dog Problems
$13.95 paperback (Canada: $16.95)
978-0-307-33797-9

Available wherever books are sold.